New SAT® READING:
Vice and Virtue
in the Exploration of Democracy

✔

ADVANCED

PRACTICE
SERIES

◇ For the Redesigned 2016 SAT

◇ 50 High-Complexity Passages

◇ Essential Historical Context

ies
TEST
PREP

Authors
Khalid Khashoggi, CEO IES
Arianna Astuni, President IES

Editorial
Patrick Kennedy, Executive Editor
Christopher Carbonell, Editorial Director

Design
Kay Kang, www.kaygraphic.com

Contributors
Arianna Astuni
Christopher Carbonell
Patrick Kennedy
Khalid Khashoggi
Rajvi Patel
Cassidy Yong

Published by IES Publications
www.IESpublications.com
© IES Publications, 2016

ON BEHALF OF

Integrated Educational Services, Inc.

355 Main Street

Metuchen, NJ 08840

www.ies2400.com

We would like to thank the IES Publications team as well as the teachers and students at IES2400 who have contributed to the creation of this book. We would also like to thank our Chief Marketing Officer, Sonia Choi, for her invaluable input.

The SAT® is a registered trademark of the College Board, which was not involved in the production of, and does not endorse, this product.

ISBN-10: 1535244887

ISBN-13: 978-1535244886

QUESTIONS OR COMMENTS? Visit us at ies2400.com

TABLE OF CONTENTS

Dear student,

In the past, we at Integrated Educational Services have used a hands-on approach to hone and optimize our books for classroom use. But the story of this New SAT History Documents book is somewhat different: more than any other book we have crafted, this volume began with our in-the-classroom experiences. While prepping students for the New SAT Reading section, I discovered that students at all skill levels are uniquely challenged by a single passage type. Dubbed the "Founding Documents and Great Global Conversation" passages by the College Board, these texts present students with classic speeches and documents  from the entire scope of modern history, politics, and social theory. The concepts involved are demanding, the required attention to detail is intense, and the language is at times borderline impenetrable. Even the best test-taker needs a trusted guide to this material.

This book was designed to speak to exactly such needs: with fifty Founding Documents and Great Global Conversation passages, and covering a time period reaching from the Renaissance to today, this is the most extensive and authoritative treatment of this aspect of the New SAT. For tutoring and seminars in New SAT Reading, this volume is indispensable. But if you intend to use it for individual practice, you will encounter supporting materials that are both lucid and informative. The answer explanations will show you how to use evidence efficiently, and how to eliminate the toughest false answers quickly. And for historical background, our chapter intros succinctly define major historical trends and changes—and the major historical figures behind them.

However, the value of this book does not end with the New SAT. Historical document passages and questions can also be found on the AP U.S. History and AP Language and Composition exams: students who aim to succeed in these areas would be well advised to start out, or supplement their practice, with a book such as this. These are, indeed, some of the highest-complexity passages that the New SAT offers. But you will finish the fifty passages in this book confident in your reading abilities, your knowledge of history, and your potential to master a peerlessly tough section of the New SAT.

Wishing you the greatest success in your test-taking endeavors.

-Khalid Khashoggi
CEO, IES Publications

CHAPTER 1
Age of Empires

Age of Empires
1500-1776

With the end of the Middle Ages and the beginning of the Renaissance, art, science, and worldwide exploration flourished—and in the process, many of the classics of modern political thought were born. Writers and intellectuals across Europe both sought to make sense of their own times and looked to history for rigorously logical answers. For many, political science as we know it today begins with Niccolo Machiavelli's *The Prince*, a sixteenth-century text that emphasizes efficiency and results (not divine or religious privilege) as the basis of sound governance. But Machiavelli was simultaneously a political prognosticator and a historian: later Renaissance intellectuals, such as British essayist Francis Bacon, would find their own ways of looking backwards and forwards with equal insight.

The innovations of the sixteenth- and seventeenth-century Renaissance would be followed by the social, political, and cultural theories of the eighteenth-century Enlightenment. Adam Smith laid down the fundamentals of modern trade, mass production, and market competition—the system known today as "capitalism"—in his book *The Wealth of Nations*. Meanwhile, Smith's colleague David Hume examined the essential interactions of governments and their subjects in works such as *A Treatise of Human Nature*. Both of these men followed earlier philosophers, such as John Locke, in explaining governance using rational principles. Social interactions of other sorts were subjected to some of the same critical searching: the place of women in civic and international culture, for instance, was explored by British writers such as Lady Mary Wortley Montagu and Hannah More.

Yet across the Atlantic, equally intensive ideas about government would lead to revolutionary results. The British Colonies in North America had developed a thriving merchant and business class, as exemplified by the pragmatic Benjamin Franklin—a class that rankled at British attempts to rein in its liberties. Some (such as British legislator Edmund Burke) believed that conflict could be avoided; others (such as American patriot Patrick Henry) were convinced that Britain's encroachments had made a clash inevitable. And when the American Revolution finally did erupt, it was seen not simply as a violent collision of material interests (even though numerous surviving documents, such as the letters of John and Abigail Adams, give us a detailed view of the day-to-day progress of the hostilities). Instead, this was the Colonies' chance to put the principles of liberty and reason enshrined by Locke, Smith, and Jean-Jacques Rousseau into action. The emphasis on justice through practicality that was glimpsed during the Renaissance would, perhaps, become fully visible in America.

Questions 1-10 are based on the following passage.
1.01
Adapted from *The Prince*, a sixteenth-century tract on the principles of effective government and statesmanship written by Niccolo Machiavelli.

It makes a prince hated above all things, as I have said, to be rapacious, and to be a violator of the property of his subjects, from which he must abstain. And when neither their Line property nor their honor is touched, the majority of men live
5 content, and he has only to contend with the ambition of a few, whom he can curb with ease in many ways.

It makes him contemptible to be considered fickle, frivolous, mean-spirited, irresolute, from all of which a prince should guard himself as from a rock; and he should endeavour
10 to show in his actions greatness, courage, gravity, and fortitude; and in his private dealings with his subjects let him show that his judgments are irrevocable, and maintain himself in such reputation that no one can hope either to deceive him or to get round him.

15 That prince is highly esteemed who conveys this impression of himself, and he who is highly esteemed is not easily conspired against; for, provided it is well known that he is an excellent man and revered by his people, he can only be attacked with difficulty. For this reason a prince ought to
20 have two fears, one from within, on account of his subjects, the other from without, on account of external powers. From the latter he is defended by being well armed and having good allies, and if he is well armed he will have good friends, and affairs will always remain quiet within when they are quiet
25 without, unless they should have been already disturbed by conspiracy; and even should affairs outside be disturbed, if he has carried out his preparations and has lived as I have said, as long as he does not despair, he will resist every attack, as I said Nabis the Spartan did.

30 But concerning his subjects, when affairs outside are disturbed he has only to fear that they will conspire secretly, from which a prince can easily secure himself by avoiding being hated and despised, and by keeping the people satisfied with him, which it is most necessary for him to accomplish,
35 as I said above at length. And one of the most efficacious remedies that a prince can have against conspiracies is not to be hated and despised by the people, for he who conspires against a prince always expects to please them by his removal; but when the conspirator can only look forward to offending
40 them, he will not have the courage to take such a course, for the difficulties that confront a conspirator are infinite. And as experience shows, many have been the conspiracies, but few have been successful; because he who conspires cannot act alone, nor can he take a companion except from those whom
45 he believes to be malcontents, and as soon as you have opened your mind to a malcontent you have given him the material

with which to content himself, for by denouncing you he can look for every advantage; so that, seeing the gain from this course to be assured, and seeing the other to be doubtful and
50 full of dangers, he must be a very rare friend, or a thoroughly obstinate enemy of the prince, to keep faith with you.

And, to reduce the matter into a small compass, I say that, on the side of the conspirator, there is nothing but fear, jealousy, prospect of punishment to terrify him; but on the
55 side of the prince there is the majesty of the principality, the laws, the protection of friends and the state to defend him; so that, adding to all these things the popular goodwill, it is impossible that any one should be so rash as to conspire. For whereas in general the conspirator has to fear before
60 the execution of his plot, in this case he has also to fear the sequel to the crime; because on account of it he has the people for an enemy, and thus cannot hope for any escape.

1

According to Machiavelli, rulers can best protect themselves from violence by

A) building up strong military forces.
B) being well respected by their subjects.
C) studying history and political theory.
D) monitoring and punishing possible rebels.

2

Which choice provides the best evidence for the answer to the previous question?

A) Lines 15-17 ("That prince . . . against")
B) Lines 19-21 ("For this . . . powers")
C) Lines 27-29 ("as long . . . did")
D) Lines 41-43 ("And as . . . successful")

3

Which best describes the developmental pattern of the passage?

A) A course of action is recommended and its positive consequences are outlined.
B) A set of virtues is described and a few possible drawbacks are explained.
C) A policy is proposed and a debate over its usefulness is recapitulated.
D) A historical example is introduced and a new analysis of that example is set forward.

7

CONTINUE

4

Which of the following statements, if true, would most effectively contradict the assertion in lines 35-41 ("And one . . . infinite?")

A) Conspiracies are most common in countries with strong armies.

B) The leaders of conspiracies tend to be politicians themselves.

C) Many historical conspiracies have been directed against popular leaders.

D) Most conspirators are aware that their plans run a high risk of failure.

5

One of the qualities of an exceptional ruler that Machiavelli cites is

A) innovativeness.

B) religiosity.

C) respect for tradition.

D) decisiveness.

6

As used in line 21, "external" most nearly means

A) superficial.

B) irrelevant.

C) foreign.

D) unmistakable.

7

As used in line 60, "execution" most nearly means

A) depiction.

B) implementation.

C) decapitation.

D) legalization.

8

According to the passage, one factor that undermines groups of conspirators is

A) limited financial resources.

B) weak and suspect loyalties.

C) awareness that rebellion is unjust.

D) excessive and irrational confidence.

9

Which choice provides the best evidence for the answer to the previous question?

A) Lines 30-33 ("But concerning . . . despised")

B) Lines 39-41 ("but when the . . . infinite")

C) Lines 48-51 ("so that . . . you")

D) Lines 54-56 ("on the side . . . him")

10

Throughout the passage, Machiavelli builds his argument about how to govern by presenting

A) allusions to his own era in history.

B) descriptions of predictable behaviors.

C) references to established laws.

D) differences between local and international politics.

CONTINUE

Questions 1-10 are based on the following passage.
1.02
Adapted from Francis Bacon, "Of the Vicissitude of Things" (1601).

Upon the breaking and shivering of a great state and empire, you may be sure to have wars. For great empires, while they stand, do enervate and destroy the forces of the natives
Line which they have subdued, resting upon their own protecting
5 forces; and then when they fail also, all goes to ruin, and they become a prey. So was it in the decay of the Roman empire; and likewise in the empire of Almaigne, after Charles the Great, every bird taking a feather; and were not unlike to befall to Spain, if it should break. The great accessions and unions of
10 kingdoms, do likewise stir up wars; for when a state grows to an over-power, it is like a great flood, that will be sure to overflow. As it hath been seen in the states of Rome, Turkey, Spain, and others. Look when the world hath fewest barbarous peoples, but such as commonly will not marry or generate,
15 except they know means to live (as it is almost everywhere at this day, except Tartary), there is no danger of inundations of people; but when there be great shoals of people, which go on to populate, without foreseeing means of life and sustentation, it is of necessity that once in an age or two, they discharge a
20 portion of their people upon other nations; which the ancient northern people were wont to do by lot; casting lots what part should stay at home, and what should seek their fortunes. When a warlike state grows soft and effeminate, they may be sure of a war. For commonly such states are grown rich in the time of
25 their degenerating; and so the prey inviteth, and their decay in valor, encourageth a war.
As for the weapons, it hardly falleth under rule and observation: yet we see even they, have returns and vicissitudes. For certain it is, that ordnance was known in the city of the
30 Oxidrakes in India; and was that, which the Macedonians called thunder and lightning, and magic. And it is well known that the use of ordnance, hath been in China above two thousand years. The conditions of weapons, and their improvement, are; First, the fetching afar off; for that outruns the danger; as it is seen in
35 ordnance and muskets. Secondly, the strength of the percussion; wherein likewise ordnance exceeds all arietations and ancient inventions. The third is, the commodious use of them; as that they may serve in all weathers; that the carriage may be light and manageable; and the like.
40 For the conduct of the war: at the first, men rested extremely upon number: they did put the wars likewise upon main force and valor; pointing days for pitched fields, and so trying it out upon an even match and they were more ignorant in ranging and arraying their battles. After, they grew to
45 rest upon number rather competent, than vast; they grew to advantages of place, cunning diversions, and the like: and they grew more skilful in the ordering of their battles.

In the youth of a state, arms do flourish; in the middle age of a state, learning; and then both of them together
50 for a time; in the declining age of a state, mechanical arts and merchandize. Learning hath his infancy, when it is but beginning and almost childish; then his youth, when it is luxuriant and juvenile; then his strength of years, when it is solid and reduced; and lastly, his old age, when it waxeth dry
55 and exhausted. But it is not good to look too long upon these turning wheels of vicissitude, lest we become giddy. As for the philology of them, that is but a circle of tales, and therefore not fit for this writing.

1

According to Bacon, wars can be caused by

A) the creation of a new technology.
B) either the expansion or the collapse of a nation.
C) either repressive measures or attempted reforms.
D) a needless emphasis on learning and the arts.

2

Over the course of the first three paragraphs Bacon shifts his focus from

A) whether war is advisable to why war is common.
B) how armies use terrain to how armies use technology.
C) wars fought by primitive nations to wars fought by highly advanced nations.
D) why wars originate to how battles are fought.

3

According to Bacon, failing countries tend to be

A) devoted to their traditions.
B) extremely belligerent.
C) materially prosperous.
D) allied to younger nations.

4

Which choice provides the best evidence for the answer to the previous question?

A) Lines 1-2 ("Upon the breaking . . . wars")
B) Lines 29-31 ("For certain . . . magic")
C) Lines 31-32 ("And it is . . . years")
D) Lines 48-51 ("In the youth . . . merchandize")

CONTINUE

5

The main purpose of the third paragraph (lines 40-47) is to

A) summarize different stages of evolution in how wars have been waged.

B) urge the military strategists of Bacon's own time to improve their practices.

C) explain why China will become a more formidable military power.

D) indicate that Rome could have prevented its own collapse.

6

According to Bacon, a major change in how wars were fought involved a shift from

A) field warfare to siege warfare.

B) limited participation to national involvement.

C) brute force to clever strategy.

D) the use of citizen soldiers to the use of mercenaries.

7

As used in line 36, "exceeds" most nearly means

A) is more powerful than.

B) is more famous than.

C) is more costly than.

D) is less regulated than.

8

Which action, on the basis of the passage, would be characteristic of a great military power?

A) Sending political dissidents into exile

B) Forming alliances and reducing its military commitments

C) Accepting numerous short-term defeats to achieve larger goals

D) Conquering and controlling indigenous populations

9

Which choice provides the best evidence for the answer to the previous question?

A) Lines 2-5 ("For great . . . forces")

B) Lines 17-20 ("but when . . . nations")

C) Lines 44-45 ("After . . . vast")

D) Lines 55-56 ("But it . . . giddy")

10

As used in line 58, "fit" most nearly means

A) attractive.

B) appropriate.

C) energetic.

D) competent.

CONTINUE

Questions 1-10 are based on the following passage.
1.03
Adapted from John Locke, "Of the Beginning of Political Societies," a chapter of Locke's *Second Treatise of Government* (1690).

Men being, as has been said, by nature, all free, equal, and independent, no one can be put out of this estate, and subjected to the political power of another, without his own consent. The
Line only way whereby any one divests himself of his natural liberty,
5 and puts on the bonds of civil society, is by agreeing with other men to join and unite into a community for their comfortable, safe, and peaceable living one amongst another, in a secure enjoyment of their properties, and a greater security against any, that are not of it. This any number of men may do, because it
10 injures not the freedom of the rest; they are left as they were in the liberty of the state of nature. When any number of men have so consented to make one community or government, they are thereby presently incorporated, and make one body politic, wherein the majority have a right to act and conclude the rest.
15   For when any number of men have, by the consent of every individual, made a community, they have thereby made that community one body, with a power to act as one body, which is only by the will and determination of the majority: for that which acts any community, being only the consent of
20 the individuals of it, and it being necessary to that which is one body to move one way; it is necessary the body should move that way whither the greater force carries it, which is the consent of the majority: or else it is impossible it should act or continue one body, one community, which the consent of every
25 individual that united into it, agreed that it should; and so every one is bound by that consent to be concluded by the majority. And therefore we see, that in assemblies, empowered to act by positive laws, where no number is set by that positive law which empowers them, the act of the majority passes for the act
30 of the whole, and of course determines, as having, by the law of nature and reason, the power of the whole.
And thus every man, by consenting with others to make one body politic under one government, puts himself under an obligation, to every one of that society, to submit to the
35 determination of the majority, and to be concluded by it; or else this original compact, whereby he with others incorporates into one society, would signify nothing, and be no compact, if he be left free, and under no other ties than he was in before in the state of nature. For what appearance would there be of any
40 compact? what new engagement if he were no farther tied by any decrees of the society, than he himself thought fit, and did actually consent to? This would be still as great a liberty, as he himself had before his compact, or any one else in the state of nature hath, who may submit himself, and consent to any acts
45 of it if he thinks fit.
For if the consent of the majority shall not, in reason, be

received as the act of the whole, and conclude every individual; nothing but the consent of every individual can make any thing to be the act of the whole: but such a consent is next to
50 impossible ever to be had, if we consider the infirmities of health, and avocations of business, which in a number, though much less than that of a commonwealth, will necessarily keep many away from the public assembly. To which if we add the variety of opinions, and contrariety of interests, which
55 unavoidably happen in all collections of men, the coming into society upon such terms would be only like Cato's coming into the theatre, only to go out again. Such a constitution as this would make the mighty Leviathan of a shorter duration, than the feeblest creatures, and not let it outlast the day it was
60 born in: which cannot be supposed, till we can think, that rational creatures should desire and constitute societies only to be dissolved: for where the majority cannot conclude the rest, there they cannot act as one body, and consequently will be immediately dissolved again.

1

As used in line 22, "greater" most nearly means

A) more noble.

B) more oppressive.

C) more famous.

D) more abundant.

2

Locke's main purpose in writing this passage is to

A) outline the motives and structure behind a functioning civil society.

B) describe the ideal society and show how social disputes can be eliminated.

C) present a broad political theory in response to recent events.

D) argue that governments based on popular rule are more stable than authoritarian governments.

CONTINUE

3

Which of the following is a major feature of the type of "community" (line 16) that Locke analyzes?

A) Members of the community discard property rights and work together for common defense.

B) Members of the community must arrive at unanimous decisions in order to take action.

C) Members of the majority will naturally attempt to form alliances with members of smaller communities.

D) Members of the minority consent to popular decisions that may not reflect their beliefs.

4

Which choice provides the best evidence for the answer to the previous question?

A) Lines 3-7 ("The only . . . another")

B) Lines 15-17 ("For when . . . as one body")

C) Lines 32-35 ("And thus . . . by it")

D) Lines 42-45 ("This would be . . . thinks fit")

5

As explained in the passage, the state of nature does not involve

A) awareness of political principles.

B) any appreciable education or culture.

C) the possession of private property.

D) clear obligations to other people.

6

Which of the following assumptions about the formation of a government is present in this passage?

A) The majority of people in any consolidated government will tend to make decisions that are morally just.

B) The people who make up any government may not at any time reinterpret that government's founding principles.

C) Those who wish to remain outside a government will not be harmed by the creation of that government.

D) Those who initially remain outside a government will eventually decide that they are better off supporting that government.

Basically Blind guess

7

Which choice provides the best evidence for the answer to the previous question?

A) Lines 9-11 ("This any . . . nature")

B) Lines 21-23 ("it is necessary . . . majority")

C) Lines 39-42 ("For what . . . consent to?")

D) Lines 62-64 ("for where . . . again")

used blind guess

8

Locke uses the term "mighty Leviathan" (line 58) to describe

A) a citizen who has escaped the state of nature.

B) a nation that faces a special set of circumstances.

C) a political arrangement that cannot exist in reality.

D) a leader whose actions should serve as a cautionary tale.

9

As used in line 38, "free" most nearly means

A) with generosity.

B) with autonomy.

C) with forgiveness.

D) with honesty.

10

In the final paragraph, Locke suggests that consent of the majority is

A) a practical necessity, because more elaborate attempts to consider public opinion would lead to chaos.

B) a necessary evil, because this mode of government tends to undermine the pursuit of learning.

C) a fanciful construct, because most countries have adopted political systems based on the authority of a single leader.

D) an undeniable asset, because no individual would willingly re-enter the state of nature.

CONTINUE

Questions 1-10 are based on the following passage.
1.04
Adapted from Adam Smith, *The Wealth of Nations* (1776). In the reading that follows, Smith considers the role of open and competitive trade in society: throughout his book, Smith compares a freely-operating and largely self-regulating commercial system (known today as "capitalism") with older economic practices.

The increase and riches of commercial and manufacturing towns contributed to the improvement and cultivation of the countries to which they belonged, in three different ways:

Line First, by affording a great and ready market for the
5 rude produce of the country, they gave encouragement to its cultivation and further improvement. This benefit was not even confined to the countries in which they were situated, but extended more or less to all those with which they had any dealings. To all of them they afforded a market for
10 some part either of their rude or manufactured produce, and, consequently, gave some encouragement to the industry and improvement of all. Their own country, however, on account of its neighbourhood, necessarily derived the greatest benefit from this market. Its rude produce being charged with less
15 carriage, the traders could pay the growers a better price for it, and yet afford it as cheap to the consumers as that of more distant countries.

Secondly, the wealth acquired by the inhabitants of cities was frequently employed in purchasing such lands as
20 were to be sold, of which a great part would frequently be uncultivated. Merchants are commonly ambitious of becoming country gentlemen, and, when they do, they are generally the best of all improvers. A merchant is accustomed to employ his money chiefly in profitable projects; whereas a mere country
25 gentleman is accustomed to employ it chiefly in expense. The one often sees his money go from him, and return to him again with a profit; the other, when once he parts with it, very seldom expects to see any more of it. Those different habits naturally affect their temper and disposition in every sort of business.
30 The merchant is commonly a bold, a country gentleman a timid undertaker. The one is not afraid to lay out at once a large capital upon the improvement of his land, when he has a probable prospect of raising the value of it in proportion to the expense; the other, if he has any capital, which is not
35 always the case, seldom ventures to employ it in this manner. If he improves at all, it is commonly not with a capital, but with what he can save out or his annual revenue. Whoever has had the fortune to live in a mercantile town, situated in an unimproved country, must have frequently observed how much
40 more spirited the operations of merchants were in this way, than those of mere country gentlemen. The habits, besides, of order, economy, and attention, to which mercantile business naturally forms a merchant, render him much fitter to execute,

with profit and success, any project of improvement.
45 Thirdly, and lastly, commerce and manufactures gradually introduced order and good government, and with them the liberty and security of individuals, among the inhabitants of the country, who had before lived almost in a continual state of war with their neighbours, and of servile
50 dependency upon their superiors. This, though it has been the least observed, is by far the most important of all their effects. Mr Hume is the only writer who, so far as I know, has hitherto taken notice of it.

In a country which has neither foreign commerce nor
55 any of the finer manufactures, a great proprietor, having nothing for which he can exchange the greater part of the produce of his lands which is over and above the maintenance of the cultivators, consumes the whole in rustic hospitality at home. If this surplus produce is sufficient to
60 maintain a hundred or a thousand men, he can make use of it in no other way than by maintaining a hundred or a thousand men. He is at all times, therefore, surrounded with a multitude of retainers and dependants, who, having no equivalent to give in return for their maintenance, but being
65 fed entirely by his bounty, must obey him, for the same reason that soldiers must obey the prince who pays them. . . . It seems to be common in all nations to whom commerce and manufactures are little known. I have seen, says Doctor Pocock, an Arabian chief dine in the streets of a town where
70 he had come to sell his cattle, and invite all passengers, even common beggars, to sit down with him and partake of his banquet.

1

Which of the following best describes the developmental pattern of the passage?

A) A discussion of a few distinct yet related premises

B) A series of recommendations for more effective governance

C) An explanation of a controversy that Smith hopes to resolve

D) An economic treatise informed by Smith's travels

2

Which of the following does Smith believe about the connection between commerce and government?

A) It is a fact of life that members of the aristocracy refuse to accept.

B) It is a consequential though not widely considered area of inquiry.

C) A good government will intervene in the economy.

D) A good government will not be impacted by changes in the economy.

CONTINUE

3

Which choice provides the best evidence for the answer to the previous question?

A) Lines 14-17 ("Its rude . . . countries")

B) Lines 37-41 ("Whoever has had . . . gentlemen")

C) Lines 50-53 ("This, though . . . of it")

D) Lines 62-66 ("He is at . . . pays them")

4

As used in line 19, "employed in" most nearly means

A) kept interested by.

B) hired for.

C) preoccupied with.

D) utilized for.

5

In lines 10 and 14, Smith's use of the word "rude" is intended primarily to

A) criticize older and outdated economic ideas.

B) criticize cities that preferred agriculture to trade.

C) distinguish between two different types of goods.

D) distinguish between two different levels of technological advancement.

6

According to Smith, compared to country gentlemen merchants are more willing to

A) make considerable investments.

B) assist their neighbors.

C) travel abroad.

D) better themselves through education.

7

As used in line 42, "economy" most nearly means

A) resourcefulness.

B) stinginess.

C) income.

D) brevity.

8

One of the major advantages of a commercial and trading town is that it

A) enables people to access new forms of luxury and entertainment.

B) has helped merchants to grow in political power.

C) has caused democratic institutions to become more popular.

D) does not merely improve the economic life of the nation where it is located.

9

Which choice provides the best evidence for the answer to the previous question?

A) Lines 1-3 ("The increase . . . ways")

B) Lines 6-9 ("This benefit . . . dealings")

C) Lines 23-25 ("A merchant . . . expense")

D) Lines 45-48 ("Thirdly, and . . . the country")

10

As described in the passage, the "mere country gentleman" (lines 24-25) and the "great proprietor" (line 55) are similar in that both

A) are more concerned with their reputations than with earnings and profit.

B) consume resources instead of finding new endeavors and investments.

C) cultivate large and diverse social circles.

D) only visit commercial towns a few times a year.

CONTINUE

Questions 1-10 are based on the following passage.
1.05
Adapted from the essay "On True Happiness," which appeared in *The Memoirs of Benjamin Franklin*.

The desire of happiness in general is so natural to us, that all the world are in pursuit of it; all have this one end in view, though they take such different methods to attain it, and are so
Line much divided in their notions of it.

5   Evil, as evil, can never be chosen; and, though evil is often the effect of our own choice, yet we never desire it, but under the appearance of an imaginary good.

Many things we indulge ourselves in may be considered by us as evils, and yet be desirable; but then they are only
10 considered as evils in their effects and consequences, not as evils at present, and attended with immediate misery.

Reason represents things to us not only as they are at present, but as they are in their whole nature and tendency; passion only regards them in the former light. When this
15 governs us, we are regardless of the future, and are only affected with the present. It is impossible ever to enjoy ourselves rightly, if our conduct be not such as to preserve the harmony and order of our faculties, and the original frame and constitution of our minds; all true happiness, as all that is truly
20 beautiful, can only result from order.

While there is a conflict between the two principles of passion and reason, we must be miserable in proportion to the struggle; and when the victory is gained, and reason so far subdued as seldom to trouble us with its remonstrances, the
25 happiness we have then is not the happiness of our rational nature, but the happiness only of the inferior and sensual part of us, and, consequently, a very low and imperfect happiness to what the other would have afforded us.

If we reflect upon any one passion and disposition of
30 mind, abstract from virtue, we shall soon see the disconnexion between that and true, solid happiness. It is of the very essence, for instance, of envy to be uneasy and disquieted. Pride meets with provocations and disturbances upon almost every occasion. Covetousness is ever attended with solicitude and
35 anxiety. Ambition has its disappointments to sour us, but never the good fortune to satisfy us; its appetite grows the keener by indulgence, and all we can gratify it with at present serves but the more to inflame its insatiable desires.

The passions, by being too much conversant with
40 earthly objects, can never fix in us a proper composure and acquiescence of mind. Nothing but an indifference to the things of this world, an entire submission to the will of Providence here, and a well-grounded expectation of happiness hereafter, can give us a true, satisfactory enjoyment of ourselves. Virtue
45 is the best guard against the many unavoidable evils incident to us; nothing better alleviates the weight of the afflictions, or gives a truer relish of the blessings, of human life.

What is without us has not the least connexion with happiness, only so far as the preservation of our lives and
50 health depends upon it. Health of body, though so far necessary that we cannot be perfectly happy without it, is not sufficient to make us happy of itself. Happiness springs immediately from the mind; health is but to be considered as a condition or circumstance, without which this happiness cannot be tasted
55 pure and unabated.

Virtue is the best preservation of health, as it prescribes temperance, and such a regulation of our passions as is most conducive to the well-being of the animal economy; so that it is, at the same time, the only true happiness of the mind, and
60 the best means of preserving the health of the body.

If our desires are to the things of this world, they are never to be satisfied. If our great view is upon those of the next, the expectation of them is an infinitely higher satisfaction than the enjoyment of those of the present.

65   There is no happiness, then, but in a virtuous and self-approving conduct. Unless our actions will bear the test of our sober judgments and reflections upon them, they are not the actions, and, consequently, not the happiness, of a rational being.

1

In the first paragraph, Franklin describes a situation that is
A) paradoxical.
B) absurd.
C) tragic.
D) misunderstood.

2

Franklin draws a contrast between good and evil by indicating that
A) evil things are commonplace, while good things are difficult to obtain.
B) evil things are only harmful based on circumstances, while good things are always objectively good.
C) evil things are not knowingly chosen, while people consciously seek goodness.
D) evil is associated with passion, while goodness is the result of education.

CONTINUE

3

Which choice provides the best evidence for the answer to the previous question?

A) Lines 5-7 ("Evil . . . good")

B) Lines 9-11 ("they . . . misery")

C) Lines 12-14 ("Reason . . . light")

D) Lines 21-23 ("While there . . . struggle")

4

As used in line 7, "imaginary" most nearly means

A) visionary.

B) creative.

C) illusory.

D) immature.

5

Franklin would most likely agree with which of the following statements about health?

A) Health is not the root of happiness, but facilitates the enjoyment of happiness.

B) Health has been subjected to scientific study and can be regulated with increased precision.

C) Health motivates individuals who would naturally choose evil to choose good instead.

D) Health produces a form of happiness that is totally unrelated to the happiness produced by the intellect.

6

Which choice provides the best evidence for the answer to the previous question?

A) Lines 16-20 ("It is impossible . . . order")

B) Lines 50-52 ("Health of . . . itself")

C) Lines 52-55 ("Happiness . . . unabated")

D) Lines 56-58 ("Virtue is . . . economy")

7

True happiness, according to Franklin, is the product of

A) prosperity and generosity.

B) health and passion.

C) intellect and ambition.

D) morality and logic.

8

As used in line 52, "immediately" most nearly means

A) promptly.

B) directly.

C) rapidly.

D) candidly.

9

In lines 61-64 ("If our . . . present"), Franklin presents

A) a set of conditions.

B) an impossible goal.

C) a surprising digression.

D) a personal narrative.

10

Franklin mentions "Pride" (line 32), "Covetousness" (line 34), and "Ambition" (line 35) as examples of qualities that

A) should be rigorously avoided, but are seldom found together in a single person.

B) are detrimental to true happiness, but can still confer clear social benefits.

C) may appear to be conducive to happiness, but are in fact present sources of unease.

D) have often been understood as similar, but are in fact completely distinct from one another.

16

CONTINUE

Questions 1-10 are based on the following passage.
1.06
Adapted from *A Treatise of Human Nature* (1738) by David Hume.

Nothing is more certain, than that men are, in a great measure, governed by self-interest, and that even when they extend their concern beyond themselves, it is not to any
Line great distance; nor is it usual for them, in common life, to
5 look farther than their nearest friends and acquaintance. It is no less certain, that it is impossible for men to consult, their interest in so effectual a manner, as by an universal and inflexible observance of the rules of justice, by which alone they can preserve society, and keep themselves from falling
10 into that wretched and savage condition, which is commonly represented as the state of nature. And as this interest, which all men have in the upholding of society, and the observation of the rules of justice, is great, so is it palpable and evident, even to the most rude and uncultivated of human race; and it
15 is almost impossible for any one, who has had experience of society, to be mistaken in this particular. Since, therefore, men are so sincerely attached to their interest, and their interest is so much concerned in the observance of justice, and this interest is so certain and avowed, it may be asked how any
20 disorder can ever arise in society, and what principle there is in human nature so powerful as to overcome so strong a passion, or so violent as to obscure so clear a knowledge?

It has been observed, in treating of the passions, that men are mightily governed by the imagination, and proportion their
25 affections more to the light, under which any object appears to them, than to its real and intrinsic value. What strikes upon them with a strong and lively idea commonly prevails above what lies in a more obscure light; and it must be a great superiority of value, that is able to compensate this advantage.
30 Now as every thing, that is contiguous to us, either in space or time, strikes upon us with such an idea, it has a proportional effect on the will and passions, and commonly operates with more force than any object, that lies in a more distant and obscure light. Though we may be fully convinced, that the
35 latter object excels the former, we are not able to regulate our actions by this judgment; but yield to the solicitations of our passions, which always plead in favour of whatever is near and contiguous.

This is the reason why men so often act in contradiction
40 to their known interest; and in particular why they prefer any trivial advantage, that is present, to the maintenance of order in society, which so much depends on the observance of justice. The consequences of every breach of equity seem to lie very remote, and are not able to counter-balance any
45 immediate advantage, that may be reaped from it. They are, however, never the less real for being remote; and as all men are, in some degree, subject to the same weakness,

it necessarily happens, that the violations of equity must become very frequent in society, and the commerce of men,
50 by that means, be rendered very dangerous and uncertain. You have the same propension, that I have, in favour of what is contiguous above what is remote. You are, therefore, naturally carried to commit acts of injustice as well as me. Your example both pushes me forward in this way by
55 imitation, and also affords me a new reason for any breach of equity, by showing me, that I should be the cully of my integrity, if I alone should impose on myself a severe restraint amidst the licentiousness of others.

This quality, therefore, of human nature, not only is
60 very dangerous to society, but also seems, on a cursory view, to be incapable of any remedy. The remedy can only come from the consent of men; and if men be incapable of themselves to prefer remote to contiguous, they will never consent to any thing, which would oblige them to such a
65 choice, and contradict, in so sensible a manner, their natural principles and propensities. Whoever chooses the means, chooses also the end; and if it be impossible for us to prefer what is remote, it is equally impossible for us to submit to any necessity, which would oblige us to such a method of
70 acting.

1

As used in line 27, "lively" most nearly means
A) humorous.
B) sociable.
C) chaotic.
D) vivid.

2

According to Hume, people are most strongly affected by things that are
A) closely and clearly related to them.
B) interesting yet distant from them.
C) new and unusual.
D) sanctioned by tradition.

3

Which choice provides the best evidence for the answer to the previous question?
A) Lines 19-22 ("it may be . . . knowledge?")
B) Lines 30-34 ("Now as every . . . light")
C) Lines 43-45 ("The consequences . . . from it")
D) Lines 66-70 ("Whoever chooses . . . acting")

CONTINUE

4

Hume employs a question in lines 16-22 in order to

A) call attention to a puzzling phenomenon that is later explained.

B) suggest that earlier commentators on human nature have been mistaken.

C) encourage policymakers to re-examine their assumptions.

D) indicate that injustice is impossible to oppose.

5

In presenting his ideas on society, Hume uses language that

A) is notable for its use of anecdotes from everyday life.

B) indicates the need for specific social and political reforms.

C) is meant to impress the reader with its use of imagery.

D) relates his specific ideas to both the reader and himself.

6

As used in line 43, "breach" most nearly means

A) uprising.

B) gulf.

C) violation.

D) division.

7

According to Hume, which of the following explains why people follow established social rules?

A) Patriotic beliefs and sentiments

B) Disdain for less advanced civilizations

C) Generosity towards others

D) Fear of widespread chaos

8

Which choice provides the best evidence for the answer to the previous question?

A) Lines 5-11 ("It is no . . . nature")

B) Lines 23-26 ("It has been . . . value")

C) Lines 54-56 ("Your example . . . equity")

D) Lines 59-61 ("This quality . . . any remedy")

9

The "quality" that Hume mentions in line 59 is best defined as the tendency of people to

A) prefer democratic government to non-representative government.

B) prioritize immediate self-interest over broad collective interests.

C) vainly pursue material wealth.

D) rebel against established authorities.

10

Hume's purpose in writing this passage is to explain a phenomenon that

A) determines how effectively society functions.

B) will be eliminated through self-discipline.

C) has led to political and cultural revolutions.

D) is prevalent mainly in primitive societies.

CONTINUE

Questions 1-10 are based on the following passages.
1.07
Passage 1 is adapted from the "Preface" to the *Letters of Lady Mary Wortley Montagu* (1725), most likely written by Montagu herself; Passage 2 is adapted from *Essays for Young Ladies* (compiled in 1777) by Hannah More.

Passage 1

I confess, I am malicious enough to desire, that the world should see to how much better purpose the LADIES travel than their LORDS; and that, whilst it is surfeited with
Line Male travels, all in the same tone, and stuffed with the same
5 trifles; a lady has the skill to strike out a new path, and to embellish a worn-out subject with variety of fresh and elegant entertainment. For, besides the vivacity and spirit which enliven every part, and that inimitable beauty which spreads through the whole; besides the purity of the style, for which it
10 may justly, be accounted the standard of the English tongue; the reader will find a more true and accurate account of the customs and manners of the several nations with whom this lady conversed, than he can in any other author. But, as her ladyship's penetration discovers the inmost follies of the heart,
15 so the candour of her temper passed over them with an air of pity, rather than reproach; treating with the politeness of a court, and the gentleness of a lady, what the severity of her judgment could not but condemn.

In short, let her own sex at least, do her justice; lay
20 aside diabolical Envy, and its brother Malice . . . with all their accursed company, sly whispering, cruel back-biting, spiteful detraction, and the rest of that hideous crew, which, I hope, are very falsely said to attend the Tea-table, being more apt to think, they frequent those public places, where
25 virtuous women never come. Let the men malign one another, if they think fit, and strive to pull down merit, when they cannot equal it. Let us be better natured, than to give way to any unkind or disrespectful thought of so bright an ornament of our sex, merely because she has better sense; for
30 I doubt not but our hearts will tell us, that this is the real and unpardonable offence, whatever may be pretended. Let us be better Christians, than to look upon her with an evil eye, only because the giver of all good gifts has entrusted and adorned her with the most excellent talents. Rather let us freely own the
35 superiority, of this sublime genius, as I do, in the sincerity of my soul; pleased that a woman triumphs, and proud to follow in her train.

Passage 2

It appears then, that notwithstanding the great and real improvements, which have been made in the affair of
40 female education, and notwithstanding the more enlarged and generous views of it, which prevail in the present day,

that there is still a very material defect, which it is not, in general, enough the object of attention to remove. This defect seems to consist in this, that too little regard is paid
45 to the dispositions of the mind, that the indications of the temper are not properly cherished, nor the affections of the heart sufficiently regulated.

In the first education of girls, as far as the customs which fashion establishes are right, they should undoubtedly
50 be followed. Let the exterior be made a considerable object of attention, but let it not be the principal, let it not be the only one.—Let the graces be industriously cultivated, but let them not be cultivated at the expense of the virtues.—Let the arms, the head, the whole person be carefully polished, but
55 let not the heart be the only portion of the human anatomy, which shall be totally overlooked.

The neglect of this cultivation seems to proceed as much from a bad taste, as from a false principle. The generality of people form their judgment of education by
60 slight and sudden appearances, which is certainly a wrong way of determining. Music, dancing, and languages, gratify those who teach them, by perceptible and almost immediate effects; and when there happens to be no imbecillity in the pupil, nor deficiency in the matter, every superficial observer
65 can, in some measure, judge of the progress.—The effects of most of these accomplishments address themselves to the senses; and there are more who can see and hear, than there are who can judge and reflect.

1

In Passage 1, Montagu establishes a contrast between

A) travel within England and travel abroad.

B) religious ideals and artistic appreciation.

C) aristocratic travelers and less wealthy travelers.

D) typical male and female temperaments.

2

The second paragraph of Passage 1 (lines 19-37) resembles the second paragraph of Passage 2 (lines 48-56) in that both paragraphs use

A) references to religion that elevate and dignify a specific course of studies.

B) impassioned rhetoric that underscores the differences between men and women.

C) extended analogies to express the hope that conditions for women will improve.

D) similar sentence structures to make recommendations about female conduct.

CONTINUE ➡

3

As used in line 29, "ornament of" most nearly means

A) excess of.

B) luxury of.

C) reward for.

D) credit to.

4

Montagu in Passage 1 argues that women should not

A) voice unconventional opinions.

B) envy other women.

C) resent talented men.

D) become comfortable with domestic life.

5

Which choice provides the best evidence for the answer to the previous question?

A) Lines 5-7 ("a lady . . . entertainment")

B) Lines 13-16 ("But, as . . . reproach")

C) Lines 25-27 ("Let men malign . . . equal it")

D) Lines 31-34 ("Let us be . . . talents")

6

A major difference between Passage 1 and Passage 2 is that Passage 2

A) argues that pleasant appearances are more important than high principles.

B) presents anecdotes about women's education.

C) argues that women do not need to travel.

D) does not at any point address the issue of travel.

7

In Passage 2, More suggests that the flaws in female education can be linked to

A) a belief that morality cannot be taught.

B) an emphasis on immoral pursuits.

C) a problematic system of priorities.

D) a poor understanding of how people think.

8

Which choice provides the best evidence for the answer to the previous question?

A) Lines 43-46 ("This defect . . . cherished")

B) Lines 48-50 ("In the first . . . followed")

C) Lines 58-60 ("The generality . . . appearances")

D) Lines 61-63 ("Music, dancing . . . effects")

9

As used in line 59, "generality" most nearly means

A) theorization.

B) vagary.

C) multitude.

D) extension.

10

Which statement best describes the contrast between how the two passages depict women?

A) As politically empowered in Passage 1; as intelligent but widely oppressed in Passage 2.

B) As willing to venture beyond their communities in Passage 1; as enthusiastic about established customs in Passage 2.

C) As incisive observers in Passage 1; as requiring considerable refinement in Passage 2.

D) As uncomfortable with their virtues in Passage 1; as intellectually and spiritually vibrant in Passage 2.

CONTINUE

Questions 1-10 are based on the following passages.

1.08

Passage 1 is adapted from "Colonies and the British Constitution," a speech delivered in 1775 by British politician Edmund Burke; Passage 2 is adapted from "Liberty or Death!" by American politician Patrick Henry, a speech that was also delivered in 1775.

Passage 1

My hold of the colonies is in the close affection which grows from common names, from kindred blood, from similar privileges, and equal protection. These are ties, which, though
Line light as air, are as strong as links of iron. Let the colonies
5 always keep the idea of their civil rights associated with your government;—they will cling and grapple to you; and no force under heaven will be of power to tear them from their allegiance. But let it be once understood that your government may be one thing, and their privileges another; that these two
10 things may exist without any mutual relation; the cement is gone; the cohesion is loosened; and everything hastens to decay and dissolution. As long as you have the wisdom to keep the sovereign authority of this country as the sanctuary of liberty, the sacred temple consecrated to our common
15 faith, wherever the chosen race and sons of England worship freedom, they will turn their faces towards you. The more they multiply, the more friends you will have; the more ardently they love liberty, the more perfect will be their obedience. Slavery they can have anywhere. It is a weed that grows in
20 every soil. They may have it from Spain, they may have it from Prussia. But, until you become lost to all feeling of your true interest and your natural dignity, freedom they can have from none but you. This is the commodity of price, of which you have the monopoly. This is the true act of navigation,
25 which binds to you the commerce of the colonies, and through them secures to you the wealth of the world. Deny them this participation of freedom, and you break that sole bond, which originally made, and must still preserve, the unity of the empire. Do not entertain so weak an imagination, as that your
30 registers and your bonds, your affidavits and your sufferances, your cockets and your clearances, are what form the great securities of your commerce. Do not dream that your letters of office, and your instructions, and your suspending clauses, are the things that hold together the great contexture of this
35 mysterious whole. These things do not make your government. Dead instruments, passive tools as they are, it is the spirit of the English communion that gives all their life and efficacy to them. It is the spirit of the English constitution, which, infused through the mighty mass, pervades, feeds, unites, invigorates,
40 vivifies every part of the empire, even down to the minutest member.

Passage 2

They tell us, sir, that we are weak; unable to cope with so formidable an adversary. But when shall we be stronger? Will it be the next week, or the next year? Will it be when
45 we are totally disarmed, and when a British guard shall be stationed in every house? Shall we gather strength by irresolution and inaction? Shall we acquire the means of effectual resistance, by lying supinely on our backs, and hugging the delusive phantom of hope, until our enemies
50 shall have bound us hand and foot? Sir, we are not weak if we make a proper use of those means which the God of nature hath placed in our power. Three millions of people, armed in the holy cause of liberty, and in such a country as that which we possess, are invincible by any force which our
55 enemy can send against us. Besides, sir, we shall not fight our battles alone. There is a just God who presides over the destinies of nations; and who will raise up friends to fight our battles for us. The battle, sir, is not to the strong alone; it is to the vigilant, the active, the brave. Besides, sir, we
60 have no election. If we were base enough to desire it, it is now too late to retire from the contest. There is no retreat but in submission and slavery! Our chains are forged! Their clanking may be heard on the plains of Boston! The war is inevitable and let it come! I repeat it, sir, let it come.
65 It is in vain, sir, to extenuate the matter. Gentlemen may cry, Peace, Peace but there is no peace. The war is actually begun! The next gale that sweeps from the north will bring to our ears the clash of resounding arms! Our brethren are already in the field! Why stand we here idle? What is it that
70 gentlemen wish? What would they have? Is life so dear, or peace so sweet, as to be purchased at the price of chains and slavery? Forbid it, Almighty God! I know not what course others may take; but as for me, give me liberty or give me death!

One of the main assumptions behind Burke's argument in Passage 1 is that

A) the colonists are well aware of the oppressive conditions in other countries.

B) shared values can ensure obedience more effectively than specific policies.

C) the colonies would have weak economies without British support.

D) current laws should be abolished in order to prevent rebellion.

CONTINUE

2

Which choice provides the best evidence for the answer to the previous question?

A) Lines 1-3 ("My hold . . . protection")

B) Lines 16-18 ("The more they . . . obedience")

C) Lines 19-21 ("Slavery they . . . Prussia")

D) Lines 35-38 ("These things . . . them")

3

In Passage 1, Burke explains the nature and value of liberty by presenting

A) personal reminiscences.

B) a sequence of analogies.

C) a new theory of politics.

D) a synopsis of British history.

4

As used in line 36, "passive" most nearly means

A) deferential.

B) tactful.

C) relatively unimportant.

D) fundamentally peaceful.

5

As used in line 61, "retire from" most nearly means

A) settle down after.

B) renounce the society of.

C) decline to participate in.

D) leave the employment of.

6

Unlike Burke in Passage 1, Henry in Passage 2 argues that liberty is

A) a virtue that unites the British and the colonists.

B) a principle that the British have fully compromised.

C) a quality that can only be found in a few countries.

D) a value that the colonists associate primarily with religion.

7

In Passage 2, Henry seeks to move his listeners to action by claiming that

A) their countrymen have already taken initiative and may be in peril.

B) the colonies can raise a greater number of soldiers than the British can.

C) British policies are reducing the colonies to poverty.

D) polite debate has never solved a tense political dispute.

8

Which choice provides the best evidence for the answer to the previous question?

A) Lines 44-47 ("Will it be the . . . inaction?")

B) Lines 52-55 ("Three millions . . . against us")

C) Lines 65-66 ("Gentlemen may . . . peace")

D) Lines 67-69 ("The next . . . idle?")

9

Which choice best describes the relationship between the two passages in their depiction of Britain and the Colonies?

A) Passage 1 praises the values of the British; Passage 2 shows why the colonists have rejected these values.

B) Passage 1 points out the futility of rebellion; Passage 2 indicates that rebellion can be pragmatic and beneficial.

C) Passage 1 criticizes past British policies; Passage 2 expresses hope that the British will renounce their current approach.

D) Passage 1 explains how conflict can be avoided; Passage 2 asserts that conflict has become impossible to avoid.

10

Henry in Passage 2 would most likely characterize Burke in Passage 1 as

A) one of the "enemies" (line 49).

B) one of the "vigilant" (line 59).

C) one of the "Gentlemen" (line 65).

D) one of the "brethren" (line 68).

22

CONTINUE

Questions 1-10 are based on the following passages.

1.09

These readings are taken from the correspondence of John and Abigail Adams. Passage 1 is from a letter by John Adams dated September 29, 1774, while Passage 2 is from one of Abigail Adams's letters, dated October 16, 1774. Both discuss the increasing hostility between the American colonies and Great Britain. At the time of writing, Adams was meeting with other American politicians to determine a course of action for the colonies.

Passage 1

Sitting down to write you is a scene almost too tender for the state of my nerves.

It calls up to my view the anxious, distressed state you
Line must be in, amidst the confusion and dangers which surround
5 you. I long to return and administer all the consolation in my power, but when I shall have accomplished all the business I have to do here, I know not, and if it should be necessary to stay here till Christmas, or longer, in order to effect our purposes, I am determined patiently to wait.
10 Patience, forbearance, long-suffering, are the lessons taught here for our province, and, at the same time, absolute and open resistance to the new Government. I wish I could convince gentlemen of the danger or impracticability, of this as fully as I believe it myself. The art and address of ambassadors
15 from a dozen belligerent powers of Europe; nay, of a conclave of cardinals at the election of a Pope; or of the princes in Germany at the choice of an Emperor, would not exceed the specimens we have seen; yet the Congress all profess the same political principles. They all profess to consider our province
20 as suffering in the common cause, and indeed they seem to feel for us as if for themselves. We have had as great questions to discuss as ever engaged the attention of men, and an infinite multitude of them.

Passage 2

My much loved friend—I dare not express to you, at
25 three hundred miles' distance, how ardently I long for your return. I have some very miserly wishes, and cannot consent to your spending one hour in town, till, at least, I have had you twelve. The idea plays about my heart, unnerves my hand, whilst I write; awakens all the tender sentiments that years
30 have increased and matured, and which, when with me, every day was dispensing to you. The whole collected stock of ten weeks' absence knows not how to brook any longer restraint, but will break forth and flow through my pen. May the like sensations enter thy breast, and (spite of all the weighty cares
35 of state) mingle themselves with those I wish to communicate; for, in giving them utterance, I have felt more sincere pleasure than I have known since the 10th of August. Many have been

the anxious hours I have spent since that day; the threatening aspect of our public affairs, the complicated distress of this
40 province, the arduous and perplexed business in which you are engaged, have all conspired to agitate my bosom with fears and apprehensions to which I have heretofore been a stranger; and, far from thinking the scene closed, it looks as though the curtain was but just drawn, and only the first
45 scene of the infernal plot disclosed. And whether the end will be tragical, Heaven alone knows. You cannot be, I know, nor do I wish to see you, an inactive spectator; but if the sword be drawn, I bid adieu to all domestic felicity, and look forward to that country where there are neither wars nor
50 rumors of war, in a firm belief, that through the mercy of its King we shall both rejoice there together.

I greatly fear that the arm of treachery and violence is lifted over us, as a scourge and heavy punishment from Heaven for our numerous offenses, and for the
55 misimprovement of our great advantages. If we expect to inherit the blessings of our fathers, we should return a little more to their primitive simplicity of manners, and not sink into inglorious ease. We have too many high-sounding words, and too few actions that correspond with them. I have
60 spent one Sabbath in town since you left. I saw no difference in respect to ornament, etc.; but in the country you must look for that virtue, of which you find but small glimmerings in the metropolis. Indeed, they have not the advantages, nor the resolution, to encourage our own manufactories, which
65 people in the country have. To the mercantile part, it is considered as throwing away their own bread; but they must retrench their expenses, and be content with a small share of gain, for they will find but few who will wear their livery. As for me, I will seek wool and flax, and work willingly with
70 my hands; and indeed there is occasion for all our industry and economy.

1

Both John Adams in Passage 1 and Abigail Adams in Passage 2 desire to

A) see each other once again.
B) make peace with Britain.
C) debate political problems.
D) contribute goods to the defense of the colonies.

CONTINUE

2

The two passages differ in that Passage 1

A) celebrates the accomplishments of specific politicians, while Passage 2 criticizes those same politicians.

B) argues that the Colonies should rebel, while Passage 2 argues that such rebellion is doomed to fail.

C) calls attention to intellectual discourse, while Passage 2 argues that practical measures are needed.

D) envisions a quick and easy resolution, while Passage 2 laments the possibility of new troubles.

3

As used in line 6, "power" most nearly means

A) government.

B) ability.

C) dominance.

D) divinity.

4

In Passage 1, the "Congress" is described in a general tone of

A) ambivalence.

B) amusement.

C) annoyance.

D) admiration.

5

As used in line 29, "tender" most nearly means

A) affectionate.

B) awkward.

C) young.

D) vulnerable.

6

Which choice provides the best evidence that John Adams in Passage 1 "cannot be" an "inactive spectator" (lines 46-47), as described by Abigail in Passage 2?

A) Lines 1-2 ("Sitting down . . . nerves")

B) Lines 5-7 ("I long . . . know not")

C) Lines 10-12 ("Patience . . . Government")

D) Lines 19-21 ("They all . . . themselves")

7

The third paragraph of Passage 1 (lines 10-23) indicates that John Adams

A) is beginning to doubt his earlier beliefs.

B) is uninterested in further discussion of politics.

C) is determined to take a more belligerent stance against Great Britain.

D) is not in complete agreement with his allies.

8

It can be inferred from Passage 2 that residents of the "country" (line 65) are superior to residents of the city in terms of

A) individual health.

B) moral values.

C) education.

D) sociability.

9

According to Passage 2, one problem with the Colonies' present situation is that too many of the colonists

A) have turned against established religion.

B) are being led by emotion rather than by reason.

C) prefer expressing ideals to taking action.

D) have participated in risky business ventures.

10

Which choice provides the best evidence for the answer to the previous question?

A) Lines 31-33 ("The whole . . . my pen")

B) Lines 52-55 ("I greatly . . . advantages")

C) Lines 58-59 ("We have . . . them")

D) Lines 65-68 ("To the mercantile . . . gain")

24

CONTINUE

Questions 1-10 are based on the following passages.

1.10

The first of these readings is an excerpt from *The Social Contract* (1762) by Jean-Jacques Rousseau, while the second consists of excerpts from the Declaration of Independence of the United States.

Passage 1

    If we ask in what precisely consists the greatest good of all, which should be the end of every system of legislation, we shall find it reduce itself to two main objects, liberty and
Line equality—liberty, because all particular dependence means
5 so much force taken from the body of the State, and equality, because liberty cannot exist without it.

    I have already defined civil liberty; by equality, we should understand, not that the degrees of power and riches are to be absolutely identical for everybody; but that power shall never
10 be great enough for violence, and shall always be exercised by virtue of rank and law; and that, in respect of riches, no citizen shall ever be wealthy enough to buy another, and none poor enough to be forced to sell himself: which implies, on the part of the great, moderation in goods and position, and, on the side
15 of the common sort, moderation in avarice and covetousness.

    Such equality, we are told, is an unpractical ideal that cannot actually exist. But if its abuse is inevitable, does it follow that we should not at least make regulations concerning it? It is precisely because the force of circumstances tends
20 continually to destroy equality that the force of legislation should always tend to its maintenance.

    But these general objects of every good legislative system need modifying in every country in accordance with the local situation and the temper of the inhabitants; and these
25 circumstances should determine, in each case, the particular system of institutions which is best, not perhaps in itself, but for the State for which it is destined.

Passage 2

    When in the Course of human events, it becomes necessary for one people to dissolve the political bands which
30 have connected them with another, and to assume, among the Powers of the earth, the separate and equal station to which the Laws of Nature and of Nature's God entitle them, a decent respect to the opinions of mankind requires that they should declare the causes which impel them to the separation.
35   We hold these truths to be self-evident, that all men are created equal, that they are endowed by their Creator with certain unalienable Rights, that among these are Life, Liberty, and the pursuit of Happiness.—That to secure these rights, Governments are instituted among Men, deriving
40 their just powers from the consent of the governed,—That whenever any Form of Government becomes destructive of these ends, it is the Right of the People to alter or to abolish

it, and to institute new Government, laying its foundation on such principles and organizing its powers in such form,
45 as to them shall seem most likely to effect their Safety and Happiness. Prudence, indeed, will dictate that Governments long established should not be changed for light and transient causes; and accordingly all experience hath shown, that mankind are more disposed to suffer, while evils are
50 sufferable, than to right themselves by abolishing the forms to which they are accustomed. But when a long train of abuses and usurpations, pursuing invariably the same Object evinces a design to reduce them under absolute Despotism, it is their right, it is their duty, to throw off such Government,
55 and to provide new Guards for their future security.—Such has been the patient sufferance of these Colonies; and such is now the necessity which constrains them to alter their former Systems of Government. . .

    We, therefore, the Representatives of the United States
60 of America, in General Congress, Assembled, appealing to the Supreme Judge of the world for the rectitude of our intentions, do, in the Name, and by the Authority of the good People of these Colonies, solemnly publish and declare, That these United Colonies are, and of Right ought to be
65 Free and Independent States; that they are Absolved from all Allegiance to the British Crown, and that all political connection between them and the State of Great Britain, is and ought to be totally dissolved; and that as Free and Independent States, they have full Power to levy War,
70 conclude Peace, contract Alliances, establish Commerce, and to do all other Acts and Things which Independent States may of right do. And for the support of this Declaration, with a firm reliance on the Protection of Divine Providence, we mutually pledge to each other our Lives, our Fortunes and
75 our sacred Honor.

1

As used in line 2, "end" most nearly means

A) demise.

B) objective.

C) finale.

D) division.

2

On the basis of Passage 1, Rousseau would most likely define "equality" as

A) a theory of harmony that is irrelevant to reality.

B) a quality interchangeable with liberty.

C) even redistribution of wealth.

D) a spirit of temperance and tolerance.

CONTINUE

3

Which choice provides the best evidence for the answer to the previous question?

A) Lines 1-4 ("If we ask . . . equality")

B) Lines 7-9 ("by equality . . . everybody")

C) Lines 13-15 ("on the part . . . covetousness")

D) Lines 17-19 ("But if its . . . it?")

4

In the final paragraph of Passage 2, the authors specify

A) the military strategy that will be used to resist Britain.

B) the many capabilities of their newly-formed country.

C) the measures that will be used to publicize their decision.

D) the allied nations that will assist and defend America.

5

As used in line 47, "light" most nearly means

A) nimble.

B) pale.

C) easygoing.

D) insignificant.

6

An important difference between the two passages is that Passage 1 focuses on

A) how government generally should protect individual subjects, while Passage 2 focuses on a single government that has wronged its subjects.

B) the economic causes of injustice, while Passage 2 lists specific military policies that have perpetuated injustice.

C) how a government can encourage greater participation among its subjects, while Passage 2 explains how efforts of this sort can backfire.

D) how ideas about equality and liberty originated, while Passage 2 argues that these early ideas must be discarded.

7

The main purpose of Passage 2 is to

A) inspire the colonists by pointing out their military advantages.

B) renounce the political ideas popular in Europe.

C) show how religion and government are related.

D) explain and justify a decisive course of action.

8

Which choice best describes the relationship between the two passages?

A) Passage 2 outlines a course of action based on principles addressed in Passage 1.

B) Passage 2 predicts the worldwide acceptance of the ideals endorsed in Passage 1.

C) Passage 2 explains a drawback to the measures advocated in Passage 1.

D) Passage 2 directly celebrates the author of Passage 1.

9

Which choice provides the best evidence that the authors of Passage 2 adhere to the principles presented in the final paragraph (lines 22-27) of Passage 1?

A) Lines 32-34 ("a decent . . . separation")

B) Lines 35-36 ("We hold . . . equal")

C) Lines 48-51 ("all experience . . . accustomed")

D) Lines 55-58 ("Such has . . . Government")

10

According to both Passage 1 and Passage 2, the central purpose of government is to

A) offer a forum for debate.

B) maintain a strong army.

C) protect the rights and welfare of citizens.

D) ensure that business is fair and prosperous.

Answer Key on Next Page

Answer Key: CHAPTER ONE

SAT

1.01	1.02	1.03	1.04	1.05
1. B	1. B	1. D	1. A	1. A
2. A	2. D	2. A	2. B	2. C
3. A	3. C	3. D	3. C	3. A
4. C	4. D	4. C	4. D	4. C
5. D	5. A	5. D	5. C	5. A
6. C	6. C	6. C	6. A	6. C
7. B	7. A	7. A	7. A	7. D
8. B	8. D	8. B	8. D	8. B
9. C	9. A	9. B	9. B	9. A
10. B	10. B	10. A	10. B	10. C

1.06	1.07	1.08	1.09	1.10
1. D	1. D	1. B	1. A	1. B
2. A	2. D	2. D	2. C	2. D
3. B	3. D	3. B	3. B	3. C
4. A	4. B	4. C	4. D	4. B
5. D	5. D	5. C	5. A	5. D
6. C	6. D	6. B	6. B	6. A
7. D	7. C	7. A	7. D	7. D
8. A	8. A	8. D	8. B	8. A
9. B	9. C	9. D	9. C	9. D
10. A	10. C	10. C	10. C	10. C

Answer Explanations

Chapter 01 | Age of Empires

1.01 | Niccolo Machiavelli

1) CORRECT ANSWER: B
In lines 16-17, Machiavelli explains that an effective prince will ward off opposition and secure a strong position by gaining public respect: "he who is highly esteemed is not easily conspired against". The same idea is addressed at length in the fourth and fifth paragraphs. This information supports B. A, C, and D may all be true according to other political documents, but must be eliminated because they are not EXPLICITLY raised by Machiavelli as the most effective means of protection. In fact, a ruler who has strong military forces or knowledge of political history and theory may, logically, still not be an effective ruler if he is not widely respected for these powers.

2) CORRECT ANSWER: A
See above for the explanation of the correct answer. B describes two forces that a ruler or a prince should fear, C compares Machiavelli's ideal ruler to an earlier ruler, and D notes that conspiracies have been generally unsuccessful. Be cautious of C and D: their positive tones may seem appropriate, but they describe OUTCOMES of effective rule, now CAUSES of security as demanded by the previous question.

3) CORRECT ANSWER: A
Early in the passage, Machiavelli defines poor leadership qualities and recommends instead that a leader "should endeavour to show in his actions greatness, courage, gravity, and fortitude" (lines 9-11). These qualities will make a prince popular and serve as security "against conspiracies" (line 36), since the populace will side with the prince and against any conspirators. This information supports A and eliminates B and C, which wrongly assume that Machiavelli is negative towards or skeptical of the advice he gives earlier. (In fact, his main negative tone is applied to conspirators.) D is a distortion of how the text actually functions: Machiavelli uses a few historical examples to support his ideas (as in line 29), but never considers a single historical example in depth.

4) CORRECT ANSWER: C
In these lines, Machiavelli argues that a prince should not be "hated and despised by the people" (line 37): people who are loyal to such a prince will not be pleased by his removal, making conspirators unpopular and the difficulties confronting conspirators "infinite" (line 41). However, these ideas would be contradicted by the prevalence of historical conspiracies against popular leaders (an unlikely phenomenon under Machiavelli's logic, since it would be unwise to remove a popular ruler). C is the best answer. A (armies), B (politicians), and D (chances of failure) do not directly confront the issue of POPULARITY that is central to Machiavelli's analysis, and must be eliminated as off-topic.

5) CORRECT ANSWER: D

In the second paragraph, Machiavelli argues that a poor leader is "irresolute" (line 8) and that an effective leader makes judgments that "are irrevocable" (line 12). Thus, a strong leader is firm and decisive, so that D is the best answer. A, B, and C all raise qualities that, though potentially valuable, are not EXPLICITLY raised by Machiavelli and do not entirely fit the logic of his argument. A leader with original ideas or strong cultural principles, for instance, may still be indecisive when it comes to making the political decisions that are the focus of this passage.

6) CORRECT ANSWER: C

The word "external" refers to the "powers" (line 21) that may pose a threat to a prince: the threat posed by such external forces is thus contrasted with the problems that could be presented by the prince's own subjects. The "powers" would thus be forces from outside the prince's own country, or "foreign" nations. C is an effective choice. A and B would serve to criticize the powers (not to contrast them with domestic forces) and D introduces the issue of interpretation (whether the powers can be mistaken) NOT the most relevant issue of how the powers are situated.

7) CORRECT ANSWER: B

The word "execution" refers to how a "plot" (line 60) by a conspirator would be carried out or "implemented", so that B is the best answer. C is an overly literal meaning that refers to the act of beheading, while A and D are both irrelevant to the direct context: a conspirator would not want a plot "depicted" (since the plot is meant to be enacted but kept secret) and could not have it legalized (since the plot will instead LEAD to new legal measures once it is over).

8) CORRECT ANSWER: B

In lines 48-51, Machiavelli depicts the perspective of a conspirator and notes that only "a very rare friend, or a thoroughly obstinate enemy of the prince" can be trusted against a popular prince. This information supports B and eliminates D, since confidence might actually strengthen the normally weak ties among conspirators. A and C both raise possibilities never explicitly considered in the passage and must be eliminated.

9) CORRECT ANSWER: C

See above for the explanation of the correct answer. A explains how a prince may avoid conspiracies, B indicates that conspirators who face many difficulties may be dissuaded from rebellion against a prince, and D indicates that a popular prince will be at an enormous advantage against conspirators. Although these choices all take a generally negative stance towards conspirators, no choice except C directly aligns with a specific reason offered in the previous question.

10) CORRECT ANSWER: B

One of Machiavelli's main tactics is to describe how large groups, such as princes and subjects, will fare under specific circumstances. A prince who is popular, for instance, can "only be attacked with difficulty" (lines 18-19), while subjects will only ever "conspire secretly" (line 31) against a popular prince during a state of peace. This information supports B and eliminates D, since Machiavelli's primary focus is on national politics (not small local issues or large international disputes). Both A and C must be eliminated because no time-specific events or laws are named: Machiavelli's focus, throughout, is on broad prescriptions for political behavior.

1.02 | Francis Bacon

1) CORRECT ANSWER: B
In the first paragraph, Bacon links the outbreak of wars to both "the breaking and shivering of a great state" (line 1) and "The great accessions and unions of kingdoms" (lines 9-10). Together, this information supports B. In this passage, Bacon is concerned mainly with international affairs, not with internal laws, so that C is a poor choice. While A (technology, second paragraph) and D (learning, fourth paragraph) do refer to topics from the passage, these topics are not explicitly LINKED to the outbreak of wars: thus, these choices should be eliminated.

2) CORRECT ANSWER: D
In the first paragraph, Bacon explains why "you may be sure to have wars" (line 2) under such conditions as national collapse and population growth; the passage later shifts emphasis to "the weapons" (line 27) used in war and "the conduct of the war" (line 40). This information supports D and eliminates B, which wrongly assumes that the conduct of battle is a topic THROUGHOUT these paragraphs. A and C both distort the true function of the first paragraph: Bacon considers simply HOW war is caused (not WHETHER war is a good idea in certain cases) and groups nations together according to how they entered into war (not according to sophistication).

3) CORRECT ANSWER: C
In lines 48-51, Bacon explains that "the declining age of a state" is a period defined by "mechanical arts and merchandize". These benefits would help a declining state prosper in trade and finance, so that C is the best answer. A and D both raise topics that are not fully relevant to Bacon's analysis: traditions (only learning) and alliances (only conquest) are never discussed in the passage. B, in fact, is contradicted by line 48, which states that "arms do flourish" when a state is in its earliest stages.

4) CORRECT ANSWER: D
See above for the explanation of the correct answer. A indicates a cause of wars, B describes how certain cultures reacted to military technology, and C discusses the military technologies used by the Chinese. Do not wrongly assume that B or C describe "failing countries", since Bacon never defines the state of historical development reached by the countries in these line references.

5) CORRECT ANSWER: A
In this paragraph, Bacon explains how men at war at first "rested extremely upon number" (lines 40-41), but then shifted to strategies involving "number rather competent, than vast" (line 45). This overview of different stages makes A an appropriate answer, while other choices introduce ideas that are not directly relevant. Contemporary military strategy (B) is not considered explicitly, only the history of strategy; China (C) and Rome (D) are only raised as topics in previous paragraphs and are not directly linked to the third paragraph by Bacon.

6) CORRECT ANSWER: C
As explained in the third paragraph, early wars relied on "main force and valor" (line 42), while later wars involved "cunning diversions" (line 46) that could prove more effective

than displays of might. This information supports C. The only other major shift in warfare that Bacon cites is the development of artillery (lines 27-39): although they may seem like relevant topics, siege warfare (A) and the civic status of military forces (B, D) are never directly mentioned, so that the other answers should be eliminated as ultimately irrelevant.

7) CORRECT ANSWER: A
The word "exceeds" is used to explain how "ordnance" (line 36) exhibits stronger percussion than "ancient inventions" (lines 36-37). Because Bacon is comparing the power of a superior and an inferior military weapon, A is the best answer. B is off-topic (since the EFFECTIVENESS of ordnance, not its REPUTATION, is the required context), while C and D both introduce inappropriate negatives.

8) CORRECT ANSWER: D
In lines 2-4, Bacon explains that great empires "destroy the forces of the natives which they have subdued", so that D is a highly effective answer. A is a distortion of information in lines 17-20: the nations described send people generally, not political troublemakers or "dissidents", to new areas. B and C both make great empires seem much less aggressive than they are in Bacon's depiction, and for this reason must be eliminated.

9) CORRECT ANSWER: A
See above for the explanation of the correct answer. B indicates that overpopulation will cause people from a great nation to seek out other areas, C indicates that skill became more important than army size in military campaigns, and D offers a piece of practical advice to the reader. Only B discusses the topic of great nations, but does not align with an answer to the previous question: be especially cautious of wrongly pairing B with Question 8 A.

10) CORRECT ANSWER: B
The word "fit" is used to describe a "circle of tales" (line 57) that Bacon has declined to include in his writing: if he is not including this information, he would not find it "appropriate". B is the best answer, while A, C, and D all describe personal qualities or human virtues, not the status of information that should or should not be included.

1.03 | John Locke

1) CORRECT ANSWER: D
The word "greater" is used to describe a particular "force" (line 22), the "consent of the majority" (line 23). Because this force is based on a majority, it will be predominant or more abundant than the force displayed by the minority: D is the best answer. Note that Locke is only describing the magnitude of the force (not praising or criticizing it) at this point: thus, eliminate A and C as too positive and B as too negative for the context.

2) CORRECT ANSWER: A
In this passage, Locke explains how people may "join and unite into a community for their comfortable, safe, and peaceable living" (lines 6-7): such cooperation is based on the "will and determination of the majority" (line 18) and the consent of the rest of the people to the majority's decisions. A is thus the best answer, while B wrongly describes the society that Locke envisions as "ideal": if it were, the minority and the majority would agree in ALL regards, a possibility that Locke does not present. C ("recent

events") and D ("authoritarian governments") both refer to topics not discussed anywhere at length in the passage, and must be eliminated.

3) CORRECT ANSWER: D
In lines 32-35, Locke explains that the society he envisions involves the agreement of "every man" to accept the "determination of the majority": it is possible that some of these men do not agree with the majority, yet they must all accept the majority decisions for the sake of keeping society functioning. D is thus the best answer: the same information can be used to contradict B, which assumes TOTAL agreement among the members of society. A (complete absence of "property rights") and C ("smaller communities") refer to topics that are never discussed at length, and that would at best be secondary to the agreement with the majority that is fundamental to Locke's model of government.

4) CORRECT ANSWER: C
See above for the explanation of the correct answer. A indicates that communities are formed to ensure comfort and peace, B explains that communities are based on consent, and D highlights the liberty that individuals have to leave social contracts behind. A and B are rightly positive, but do not describe the decision-making process that is articulated in Question 3 D, while D does not align with an answer to the previous question (but may wrongly be taken as evidence for Question 3 C).

5) CORRECT ANSWER: D
Early in the passage, Locke calls attention to the "liberty of the state of nature" (line 11); later, the lack of "ties" (line 38) involved in the state of nature is contrasted with the obligations involved in social cooperation. This information supports D. A, B, and C describe things that are difficult to maintain in the insecure state of nature, but not IMPOSSIBLE. In fact, someone with no appreciable ties could know about politics and culture from past learning, and could own property in isolation.

6) CORRECT ANSWER: C
In lines 9-11, Locke argues that forming a government "injures not" the people who decline to participate, and who will naturally remain "in the liberty of the state of nature". This information supports C and contradicts D: although Locke speaks positively of government, he does not argue that it is inevitable or even necessary that people outside a government eventually join. A warps the focus of Locke's ideas (since he generally supports majority rule WITHOUT actually considering specific majority decisions), while B distorts Locke's belief that people can easily leave a government (and raises the different, rather unrelated idea that a government can be modified from within).

7) CORRECT ANSWER: A
See above for the explanation of the correct answer. B voices Locke's belief that the will of the majority will be adopted, C indicates that social compacts are based on individual consent, and D indicates that a government that does not follow the will of the majority will become unstable. Do not wrongly take B as justification for Question 6 A or C as a justification for Question 6 D.

8) CORRECT ANSWER: B
The term "mighty Leviathan" refers in context to the discussion of how a "society" (line 56) is created: in particular, Locke explains that a state of excessive disagreement, "Such

a constitution" (line 57), might lead to arrangements that are of short duration. The Leviathan that is thus fated to have a short existence is a troubled society: B is thus the best choice. A and D both wrongly refer to individuals (and may result from misreading the reference to Cato in line 56), while C involves a faulty assumption: the state of the "mighty Leviathan" is problematic, but is part of Locke's theory of how humans in fact act and, thus, is not ever defined as impossible.

9) CORRECT ANSWER: B
The word "free" describes a person who has "no other ties than he was in before in the state of nature" (lines 38-39), which is a state of freedom from social obligations. Autonomy or freedom from dependence on other people is appropriate. Choose B and eliminate A, C, and D, which are all rightly positive but would only be appropriate in a discussion of virtues or qualities. Here, Locke is simply discussing whether or not one is obligated to other people.

10) CORRECT ANSWER: A
In the final paragraph, Locke calls attention to the destabilizing effects of "variety of opinions, and contrariety of interests" (line 54); if such numerous differences were to be respected over the simple will of the majority, society could not "act as one body" (line 63) and would be "immediately dissolved again" (line 64). This information supports A as the best answer, while irrelevant topics are introduced in B ("pursuit of learning") and C ("authority of a single leader"). D is contradicted by Locke's argument elsewhere in the passage that individuals may choose to re-enter the state of nature even if a government has been formed.

1.04 | Adam Smith

1) CORRECT ANSWER: A
In the passage, Smith describes how commercial and manufacturing towns enriched their home countries "in three different ways" (line 3)": by creating an enlarged market, by promoting effective land ownership, and by promoting effective government. This information supports A. While B wrongly assumes that this positive passage is prescriptive, not HISTORICAL, C involves a faulty negative ("controversy") that is unrelated to Smith's discussion of benefits. D wrongly assumes that the information in the passage is taken from Smith's travels, when in fact no autobiographical source for his facts is provided.

2) CORRECT ANSWER: B
In lines 50-53, Smith calls attention to "by far the most important" of the effects of commercial towns, their positive influence on government: this positive effect, however, is "the least observed" and has only been discussed at length by a single commentator, Mr Hume. B is thus the best answer. A is problematic because Smith is interested only in the relationship between the aristocracy and commerce (not between the aristocracy and government), while C and D also misstate the logic of the passage: commerce can lead to good government, but how a government will address commerce itself is not one of Smith's considerations.

3) CORRECT ANSWER: C
See above for the explanation of the correct answer. A describes the benefits that a trading center can bring to a country, B praises merchants at the expense of country

gentlemen, and D notes that surplus produce in the absence of trade can only be lavished on dependents and acquaintances. None of these aligns with an answer to the previous question, though make sure not to take the critical stance towards aristocrats in B or D as a justification for Question 2 A.

4) CORRECT ANSWER: D
The phrase "employed in" refers to the "wealth" (line 18) of the inhabitants of cities, which could be put toward or utilized in making purchases. D is thus correct in context, while A and C both refer to reactions that PEOPLE would have and B is illogical in context. People or services can be "hired", but wealth itself cannot.

5) CORRECT ANSWER: C
In line 10, rude produce is contrasted with manufactured produce; then, in line 14, it is explained that rude produce is cheap to transport relative to other types of goods. These usages support C and can be used to quickly eliminate A and B, since these answers (which assume that Smith is being critical) are too negative in context. (The rude produce, after all, is cheap and useful.) D is problematic because the SAME society creates rude and manufactured produce: the real contrast is not a matter of technological advancement, but of how much technology has been APPLIED to the produce.

6) CORRECT ANSWER: A
In lines 30-31, Smith contrasts the typically "bold" merchant with the "timid" country gentleman: the basis for this comparison is that a merchant is "not afraid to lay out at once a large capital upon the improvement of his land" (lines 31-32) while a country gentleman is unwilling to make investments. This information best supports A. The investments mentioned are meant to specifically benefit the merchant investor, not neighbors (who are never mentioned, eliminating B). And while C and D may be appear to be true in completely different contexts, travel and education are not major concerns of Smith's analysis of economics: thus, eliminate both of these answers.

7) CORRECT ANSWER: A
The word "economy" is meant to describe a habit that, like "order" and "attention" (line 42), is positive. A, resourcefulness (or good sense when using resources) is an effective choice, while B is a negative that should quickly be eliminated. C and D do not describe personality traits and should be eliminated for this reason.

8) CORRECT ANSWER: D
In lines 6-9, Smith explains that the good effects of commercial towns "were not even confined to the countries in which they were situated", but spread "to all those with which they had any dealings". This idea that commercial towns benefit multiple countries justifies D. A is in fact contradicted by the passage, since Smith argues that commerce leads to investment (and, naturally, diverts money from luxury and entertainment). B and C distort arguments made in lines 45-53: Smith does note that commercial towns improve government, but does not attribute the improvement to either the political role of merchants or democratic institutions.

9) CORRECT ANSWER: B
See above for the explanation of the correct answer. A indicates that commercial towns have conferred great benefits (but not exactly what the benefits are), C indicates that merchants are more likely than country gentlemen to use their resources in gain-oriented

projects, and D indicates that commercial towns improve the state of government (but do so mainly by ensuring peace and stability). Do not wrongly take C as a justification for Question 8 B, which also mentions merchants in a positive light.

10) CORRECT ANSWER: B
While the country gentleman consumes his money in "expense" (line 25) rather than investment, the great proprietor consumes his resources "in rustic hospitality at home" (lines 58-59). This information supports B, while A wrongly combines the issue of earnings with the issue of reputation (which is not a major concern for the country gentleman). The size of social circles is only mentioned in relation to the great proprietor (eliminating C), while the great proprietor is depicted as a resident of a country WITHOUT meaningful commerce (eliminating D).

1.05 | Benjamin Franklin

1) CORRECT ANSWER: A
In the first paragraph, Franklin presents an unusual contrast that reveals a truth about human nature: "all the world" (line 2) pursues happiness, yet people take "such different methods to attain it" (line 3) despite their unanimity concerning the goal. This state of revealing contrast (or paradox) makes A an effective answer. Even though Franklin presents an unusual situation, he is not clearly negative about the activities or the people he describes: for this reason, the strong negatives in B, C, and D should be quickly eliminated.

2) CORRECT ANSWER: C
In lines 5-7, Franklin explains that evil in its own right "can never be chosen": instead, evil often appears to those who choose it in the guise of "an imaginary good". Even people who ultimately choose evil believe that they are pursuing goodness, so that C is the best answer. In describing good and evil, Franklin is preoccupied with questions of desirability, not questions of how prevalent good and evil are (eliminating A), and argues that evil things are DECEPTIVELY good, not that they can be good DEPENDING on circumstances (eliminating B). D is a trap answer: while passion and reason are indeed analyzed around line 21, the idea of education is not in fact linked to Franklin's analysis of good and evil.

3) CORRECT ANSWER: A
See above for the explanation of the correct answer. B indicates that people find evil things desirable even when the evil effects are known, C indicates that reason offers a larger scope for understanding than passion, and D indicates that conflict between reason and passion can be a source of misery. Be especially careful not to take B as evidence for Question 2 B, or to take C or D as evidence for Question 2 D.

4) CORRECT ANSWER: C
The word "imaginary" refers to a chosen "good" (line 7) that is in fact an evil: thus, the good is unreliable or illusory, so that C is the best answer. Both A and B apply inappropriate positives to the "good", which Franklin is criticizing, while D would best refer to an individual's growth and is thus out of context.

5) CORRECT ANSWER: A
In lines 52-55, Franklin notes that happiness (unlike bodily health) "springs from the

mind". However, health is still important, because it is a condition without which happiness "cannot be tasted pure and unabated". This information supports A and can be used to eliminate D, since bodily health and intellectual happiness are in fact strongly related. Although Franklin advocates health, he never discusses health in light of scientific study (eliminating B) or indicates that it is a highly direct way of preventing evil (since people must in fact intellectually choose to reject evil, eliminating C).

6) CORRECT ANSWER: C
See above for the explanation of the correct answer. A indicates that true happiness is linked to order and logic, B indicates that health alone cannot provide happiness, and D establishes a link between virtue and health. Be especially cautious of wrongly taking B as a justification for Question 5 D, or D as a justification for Question 5 C.

7) CORRECT ANSWER: D
In lines 12-38, Franklin establishes the link between happiness and particular qualities: true happiness "can only result from order" (line 20) as established by the intellect, and cannot be taken as "abstract [separate] from virtue" (line 30). This information makes D the best answer and eliminates B, since Franklin notes that passion is a quality that can compromise happiness (at least when virtue is not present). A and C both wrongly emphasize material possessions: throughout this passage, Franklin links true happiness to proper conduct, not to any form of wealth or recognition.

8) CORRECT ANSWER: B
The word "immediately" refers to how happiness is produced by "the mind" (line 53): Franklin has established that happiness and reason are closely linked and contrasts the direct role of the mind with the supporting role of "health" (line 53) in ensuring happiness. This information supports B, since there is a close or direct link. A and C refer to speeds or actions, not to the nature of a relationship, while D means "honestly" or "bluntly" and would best refer to a person or a statement.

9) CORRECT ANSWER: A
In these lines, Franklin observes that people who desire material things have desires that are "never to be satisfied" (lines 61-62): he contrasts this approach with how people who focus on things of the next world can expect "an infinitely higher satisfaction" (line 63). Because Franklin is describing how two groups act under different conditions, A is the best answer. This paragraph is closely related to the rest of Franklin's discussion of virtue and happiness (eliminating C) and never presents specific events from Franklin's own life (eliminating D). B is a trap answer: the goals in this paragraph are not in fact impossible, since the first group may in fact successfully obtain material things (but still feel empty) and the second group may reasonably look forward (in Franklin's view) to happiness in the next world.

10) CORRECT ANSWER: C
In this discussion, Franklin reflects on different passions "of mind" (lines 29-30) and argues that they are disconnected from "true, solid happiness" (line 31): the three qualities named are examples that illustrate Franklin's general point. C is thus the best answer, while the thoroughly negative tone applied to the three qualities should be used to eliminate B. A and D both misdirect Franklin's analysis: he is interested in how the three qualities relate to his ideas about happiness, NOT in the relationships that may or may not exist among the three qualities.

1.06 | David Hume

1) CORRECT ANSWER: D
The word "lively" refers to an idea that is also "strong" (line 27), and that is contrasted with what occurs in "a more obscure light" (line 28): such an idea would be clear or vivid, so that D is the best answer. A and B both refer to mood or personality (not to degree of prominence), while C is an inappropriate negative.

2) CORRECT ANSWER: A
In lines 30-34, Hume argues that "every thing, that is contiguous [directly near] to us" affects us more strongly than "any object, that lies in a more distant and obscure light". Thus, the things that are near to people and are readily discerned most strongly affect people: A is the best answer, while the same information can be used to eliminate B. C and D both mention things that COULD be far away from people, such as unusual foreign sights or traditional customs that are not observed on a regular basis, and that in any case are not Hume's primary concerns. These answers should thus be eliminated.

3) CORRECT ANSWER: B
See above for the explanation of the correct answer. A offers a question about how social disorder arises, C notes that the results of injustice may not be apparent, and D indicates the difficulty involved in choosing items that are not remote. These are supporting points related to Hume's discussion of the things that affect people, but do not DEFINE the kind of things that affect people as required by the answer to the previous question.

4) CORRECT ANSWER: A
In the course of this question, Hume notes that people are attracted to justice, but then goes on to ask why (despite this preference) disorder arises in society. He thus calls attention to a contradiction between preferences and results that is unusual or puzzling, but then goes on to explain that "favour of whatever is near" (line 37) causes people to go against seemingly distant yet just results. This information supports A and can be used to eliminate B and C, since Hume is investigating a broad problem of human nature, not pinpointing "commentators" or "policymakers". D is contradicted by the passage: people can oppose injustice by prioritizing long-term results over immediately pleasing yet problematic actions, even though doing so is difficult.

5) CORRECT ANSWER: D
Throughout the passage, Hume speaks in general terms about how human nature functions: his language uses both collective pronouns ("we", lines 34-38) and references to the reader and to himself ("you" and "I", lines 51-58). These techniques support D, while A and B assume specifics (anecdote and reforms, respectively) that are nowhere introduced into Hume's general discussion of how people act. C misstates the intent of the passage: Hume does not use any especially prominent images or metaphors, and in any case aims to argue the ACCURACY of a viewpoint, not to IMPRESS his readers.

6) CORRECT ANSWER: C
The word "breach" refers to an act involving "equity" (line 43) that seems remote: Hume has argued that people are relatively uninterested in faraway problems, so the breach would be a violation of a positive state of "equity". C is thus the best answer: A refers to a rebellion and may seem to fit the broad political context of the passage (but does NOT fit the sentence), while B and D are overly literal meanings, since a "breach" can also

signify a PHYSICAL gulf or division in other situations.

7) CORRECT ANSWER: D
In lines 5-11, Hume argues that adherence to the "rules of justice" is meant to keep men from falling into a "wretched and savage condition": thus, people fear the negative consequences of living without such rules, as indicated by D. Note that Hume presents fear of a negative, NOT belief in a positive, as a reason for following rules: A and C, which both assume positives, should thus be eliminated. B introduces a topic (comparisons of civilizations) that does not appear directly in the passage, and must be eliminated on this account.

8) CORRECT ANSWER: A
See above for the explanation of the correct answer. B explains how people perceive the world around them, C indicates that people can influence one another to commit acts of injustice, and D indicates that people are strongly inclined to commit unjust acts based on what is nearby. Though all important points in Hume's general argument, none of these choices addresses the topic of RULES as demanded by the previous question.

9) CORRECT ANSWER: B
Earlier, Hume has noted that people prefer "what is contiguous over what is remote" (line 52) and that they do not hesitate to act in problematic ways on account of this: the quality that the question pinpoints is a principle of "human nature" (line 59) that causes people to act against the interests of society, and is in fact the problematic practice of preferring what is near over what is distant. B is thus the best answer. While A, C, and D all describe negatives, the topics in these answers (government structure, wealth, and rebellion, respectively) are not Hume's direct concerns at this point of the argument. These choices should, consequently, be eliminated.

10) CORRECT ANSWER: A
In the passage, Hume argues that people are strongly invested "in the upholding of society" (line 12), but that people can act contrary to "the maintenance of order in society" (lines 41-42) by preferring what is near and problematic. This information supports A, while C ("revolutions") and D ("primitive societies") raise topics that are of little or no direct interest to Hume. B overstates Hume's case: while self-discipline can be used to combat injustice, Hume never argues that injustices and social discord will DEFINITELY be eliminated.

1.07 | Mary Wortley Montagu and Hannah More

1) CORRECT ANSWER: D
In lines 4-7, Montagu establishes a clear difference between men's predictable travels and women's engaging travels; then, in lines 25-29, she establishes a difference between male discord and female supportiveness. This information supports D, while A and C rightly raise the topic of travel but avoid the male-versus-female distinction that is the core of the passage, instead presenting false topics in location and finances. B is actually contradicted by Montagu's arguments: among the "gifts" (line 33) given by God may be artistic appreciation, so that this answer does not in fact describe a contrast.

2) CORRECT ANSWER: D
Both of the paragraphs designated use sentence structures beginning with "Let" (lines

25-34 and lines 50-56) to deliver advice to women: while Passage 1 indicates that women should "be better natured" (line 27) than men, Passage 2 urges women to cultivate a pleasing "exterior" (line 50) and clear "graces" (line 52). This information supports D, while only Passage 1 clearly references religion (eliminating A) and creates a contrast with men (eliminating B). C calls attention to the theme of improvement, but wrongly indicates that the authors use EXTENDED analogies, when the most they use are groups of DIFFERENT analogies to make their points.

3) CORRECT ANSWER: D
The phrase "ornament of" is meant as a positive reference to a woman who exhibits "the better sense" (line 29) than one of her companions. D, "credit to", indicates a person who does honor or credit to a group (such as women) and is thus the best answer. A is problematic because it is negative, while B and C both refer to items or gain, not to the qualities of praiseworthy individuals.

4) CORRECT ANSWER: B
In lines 31-34, Montagu urges women ("us") not to cast "an evil eye" on a woman who has been given "the most excellent talents". She is thus urging women not to show envy for other women, making B an effective answer but also making C problematic, because Montagu only advises women on how to react to talented women. A and D are both contradicted by ideas in the first paragraph: because women are urged to be original and adventurous in their travel accounts, they may in fact depart from conventional opinions or domestic life in the process.

5) CORRECT ANSWER: D
See above for the explanation of the correct answer. A notes that women can offer original accounts of travel, B indicates that a woman will pity flaws rather than condemn them, and C indicates how men may interact with one another. Do not wrongly take C as evidence for Question 4 C, since the line reference only considers how men react to other men.

6) CORRECT ANSWER: D
While Passage 1 discusses the issue of travel in its first paragraph (lines 1-18), Passage 2 is concerned with the topic of "female education" (line 40). Although such education may in fact include travel in other contexts, the author of Passage 2 never considers this as a direct possibility, so that D is the best answer and C must be eliminated. (Because the topic of travel is not raised, the Passage 2 cannot logically present an argument about travel.) A is contradicted by the idea that graces should not be cultivated "at the expense of virtues" (line 53), while B is contradicted by the fact that the author's direct experiences of education are never presented in narrative form, or even clearly explained, in Passage 2.

7) CORRECT ANSWER: C
In lines 43-46, More argues that education for girls neglects "the dispositions of the mind"; later, she suggests that this neglect results from focus on "the exterior" (line 50) in education for girls. This information supports C and eliminates the overly negative B, since exterior concerns are criticized as less important, not as fundamentally immoral. A and D both warp More's argument: it is possible to teach morality and understand how people think (as More's analysis itself shows), but educators have wrongly emphasized the wrong issues in women's education despite this understanding.

8) CORRECT ANSWER: A

See above for the explanation of the correct answer. B indicates that correct customs should not be disregarded, C notes that people base their opinions of good education on appearances, and D indicates that certain pursuits are considered pleasing. While C and D highlight how people RESPOND to female education, these mostly informative answers do not pinpoint FLAWS as demanded by the previous question.

9) CORRECT ANSWER: C

The word "generality" refers to a group of "people" (line 59): in context, More is describing how most people acquire their ideas about female education. C, which specifies a large group, is thus the best answer. A and B both refer to thoughts or perceptions (not to NUMBER), while D would indicate, in context, that the generality is part of a larger or dominant group. This is not the case, since the "generality" IS the primary social group that More is analyzing.

10) CORRECT ANSWER: C

While Passage 1 indicates that women can depict their travels with "vivacity and spirit" (line 7), Passage 2 argues that "there is still a very material defect" (line 42) in women's education, since such education neglects "the dispositions of the mind" (line 45) and other moral and intellectual virtues. C is thus the best answer, while A overstates the problems described in Passage 2 and D attributes a much too positive tone to Passage 2. Trap answer B distorts the actual argument of Passage 2: according to this reading, those who OBSERVE women are enthusiastic about the established custom of cultivating women's external graces. How women themselves feel about this emphasis is not considered at length.

1.08 | Edmund Burke and Patrick Henry

1) CORRECT ANSWER: B

In lines 35-38, Burke explains that authoritative measures are "Dead instruments" on their own, but that "the spirit of the English communion" will move the Colonies to accept British authority. This information supports B and eliminates D, since Burke in fact argues that a spirit of mutual respect may make CURRENT laws effective. Keep in mind that the passage is concerned mainly with the political ties between Britain and the Colonies: A (other countries) and C (economies) introduce issues that are largely irrelevant to this topic.

2) CORRECT ANSWER: D

See above for the explanation of the correct answer. A notes the strong ties that Burke feels to the Colonies, B indicates that the prosperity and growth of the Colonies are tied to British prosperity, and C indicates that oppressive conditions are present in a few different countries. While A and B do not note the interplay of policy and values (and thus cannot justify Question 1 B), C should not wrongly be taken as support for Question 1 A. Burke himself is aware of oppressive conditions in other countries: whether or not the Colonists are is never addressed.

3) CORRECT ANSWER: B

Early in the passage, Burke explains privileges and protections as ties that "though light as air, are as strong as links of iron" (lines 3-4). He later describes liberty as a "sacred temple" (line 14) and slavery as a "weed" (line 19). This emphasis on comparisons and analogies makes B an effective answer. Note that the passage is argumentative and explanatory, not narrative, and thus does not feature personal stories (A) or an overview of history (D). C is a distortion of Burke's actual intentions: he is presenting broad ideas about politics, but whether these ideas are themselves NEW or are simply being applied to a new situation is a question that he never raises.

4) CORRECT ANSWER: C
The word "passive" refers to the "tools" (line 36) or measures of the British government, which are "Dead instruments" (line 36) unless they are given "life and efficacy" (line 37) by civic loyalty. The tools are thus mostly ineffectual or relatively unimportant on their own. C is an appropriate negative, while A ("deferential" or submissive) refers to a temperament and B and D are inappropriate positives.

5) CORRECT ANSWER: C
The phrase "retire from" is used in the context of a "contest" (line 61) that presents "no election [choice]" (line 60) and no possibility of honorable retreat: it is thus impossible to walk away from or decline to participate in the contest without dishonor or disadvantage. C is the best answer, while A, B, and D are all more literal meanings of retirement that would describe the situations of individuals, not the action of a nation that cannot avoid a conflict.

6) CORRECT ANSWER: B
While Burke argues that British policy can constitute a "sanctuary of liberty" (lines 13-14), Henry argues that British policy represents "chains and slavery" (lines 71-72), making liberty and death the only remaining alternatives for the Colonists. This information supports B and can be used to eliminate A (which contradicts Henry's antagonistic tone). C raises a topic (other countries) that is only found in Passage 1, while D mistakes the perspective of Henry (who frequently mentions God in his writing) for the perspective of the Colonists (whose thoughts on religion are never directly recorded).

7) CORRECT ANSWER: A
In lines 67-69, Henry calls up the idea of a distant "clash of resounding arms", mentions that his brethren are "already on the field", and notes that his listeners are "idle". Together, this information supports A, while other answers distort some of Henry's actual arguments. He records the American population (line 52) but not the British (eliminating B), explains the injustice of British policies but not their economic effects (eliminating C), and argues that policy debate cannot resolve the conflict with Britain (not that policy debate has NEVER resolved a conflict, eliminating D).

8) CORRECT ANSWER: D
See above for the explanation of the correct answer. A indicates that urgent action against the British is necessary, B indicates that the Americans will benefit from their large population and just cause, and C indicates that attempts to make peace between Britain and the Colonies are futile. Be careful not to mistake B as evidence for Question 7 B or C as evidence for Question 7 D.

9) CORRECT ANSWER: D
In Passage 1, Burke advises the British to "Let the colonies always keep the idea of their

civil rights associated with your government" (lines 4-6): in this way, hostility between Britain and the Colonies can be avoided. In contrast, Henry in Passage 2 explains that "it is now too late" (lines 60-61) to avoid hostilities and that "The War is actually begun! (lines 66-67). This information most clearly supports D and can be used to eliminate C, since Passage 2 argues that further negotiations about the British "approach" are futile. A is problematic because Passage 2 describes a rejection of British GOVERNMENT, not a rejection of British VALUES. (In fact, Passage 2 argues in favor of liberty, which Passage 1 describes as a British value.) B is problematic because Passage 1 argues against oppressive government, NOT against rebellion.

10) CORRECT ANSWER: C
In Passage 1, Burke argues that the British still have the opportunity to offer the Colonists "participation of freedom" (line 27) and to secure peaceful cooperation. Like Burke, the "Gentlemen" believe that peace is a possibility, so that C is the best answer. While Burke speaks in favor of working with the Colonists (eliminating A as too negative), he would not agree with Henry's divisive approach or take part in wartime hostilities, eliminating B and D.

1.09 | John Adams and Abigail Adams

1) CORRECT ANSWER: A
In Passage 1, John Adams notes that he longs "to return and administer all the consolation in my power" (lines 5-6); for her part, Abigail Adams in Passage 2 tells her husband that "ardently I long for your return" (lines 25-26). This information supports A, while C only refers to Passage 1, D only refers to Passage 2, and B refers to neither passage. Passage 1 describes a deliberative body, not hoped-for peace with Britain, while Passage 2 expresses acceptance of a state of hostilities.

2) CORRECT ANSWER: C
While Passage 1 describes an assembly that has "great questions to discuss" (lines 21-22), Passage 2 criticizes "high-sounding words" (lines 58-59) and instead advocates gathering wool and flax, and other instances of practical "industry and economy" (lines 70-71). This information supports C and eliminates A (since Passage 1 praises a discussion as important, but never highlights specific "accomplishments"). Both B and D assume that Passage 1 (which describes an inconclusive debate) presents much stronger conclusions than it does, and assume that Passage 2 (which ends by endorsing action to make a cause successful) is more negative than it is.

3) CORRECT ANSWER: B
The word "power" is used in the context of Adams's hope to bring "consolation" (line 5) to his wife: he hopes that he will be able to influence her positively, making B the best answer. C is wrongly negative in context (because it would indicate that Adams is overbearing and would "dominate" his wife), while A and D both refer to social issues that are not relevant to the simple act of bringing another person comfort.

4) CORRECT ANSWER: D
Adams notes that the Congress exhibits the "art and address of ambassadors" (line 14) and that the participants "have had as great questions to discuss as ever engaged the attention of men" (lines 21-22). Because the Congress involves skilled speakers

who address meaningful issues, D is the best answer. A (indicating uncertainty) and B (indicating mild humor or belittlement) would be negative in context, while C is a strong negative that should be readily eliminated.

5) CORRECT ANSWER: A
The word "tender" refers to the "sentiments" (line 29) that have "increased and matured" (line 30) in the course of the fulfilling relationship between John and Abigail Adams. A is thus the best answer: B and D are both negative, while C ("young") is contradicted by the idea that the sentiments have "matured".

6) CORRECT ANSWER: B
The appropriate line reference should indicate that John Adams is actively involved in a political pursuit: in lines 5-7, he explains that he is immersed in "all the business" of political deliberation. B is thus the best answer. A describes John Adams's emotions (not his active involvement), C explains an approach (but does not explain how Adams is taking an ACTIVE part in it), and D mainly refers to individuals other than Adams.

7) CORRECT ANSWER: D
In this paragraph, Adams explains that he wants to convince his allies of the "danger or impracticability" (line 13) of strong resistance, but has not yet succeeded in doing so. This indication of conflict supports D. A and B both wrongly assume that Adams is not committed to his beliefs or his work (when in fact he is staying to participate in an intense debate), while C is contradicted by the evidence, since Adams in fact wants others to take a LESS belligerent stance.

8) CORRECT ANSWER: B
The reference to "people in the country" in line 65 follows a comparison between people in the country and people in the city: people in the country possess a "virtue, of which you find but small glimmerings in the metropolis" (lines 62-63) and are superior in "resolution" (line 65). B is thus the best answer, while Passage 2 notes that there is "no difference" (line 60) noticeable other than this matter of values and temperament. A, C, and D must thus all be eliminated as introducing factors unrelated to Adams's discussion of better virtues and business ambition in the country.

9) CORRECT ANSWER: C
In lines 58-59, Adams argues that there are "too many high-sounding words, and too few actions" in the colonists' approach to the conflict. This information supports C and can be used to eliminate D, since even a risky business venture would be an example of "action". Note that high-sounding speech could, logically, express religious or rational principles: A and B thus wrongly praise factors that could be bound up with the mere "words" that Adams criticizes.

10) CORRECT ANSWER: C
See above for the explanation of the correct answer. A indicates that Adams feels a strong need to express herself, B expresses her belief that the colonists (perhaps) are being punished for not using their advantages well, and D indicates that merchants are profit-oriented yet may be alienated on account of their actions. Only B describes the colonists as a general group, yet this answer does not align with an answer to the previous question. (Question 9 A, for instance, indicates that colonists are turning against God, while B indicates that God may be turning against the colonists.)

1.10 | Jean-Jacques Rousseau and the Declaration of Independence

1) CORRECT ANSWER: B
The word "end" occurs in the context of Rousseau's examination of "the greatest good of all" (lines 1-2) and of how government may achieve "two main objects" (line 3) or goals. An "end" is thus a desired outcome, or an "objective". B is an effective choice, while A and D introduce negative tones and C refers to a stage in a NARRATIVE or work of ART, not to the OUTCOME of a process.

2) CORRECT ANSWER: D
In lines 13-15, Rousseau provides one of the final elements of his understanding of "equality" (line 7): for him, equality entails different forms of "moderation" adopted by powerful citizens and the populace at large. This information supports D, while the fact that Rousseau does not advocate for changing either social group in structure (only changing their attitudes for the better) can be used to eliminate C. A reflects a viewpoint introduced in lines 16-21, but not a viewpoint attributed to Rousseau; B is inaccurate because, even after explaining "civil liberty" (line 7), Rousseau explains equality at length, thus indicating that the two qualities are not interchangeable.

3) CORRECT ANSWER: C
See above for the explanation of the correct answer. A indicates that liberty and equality are similarly desirable (NOT identical), B indicates what equality does not involve (but not what it DOES involve), and D offers a rhetorical question about the need to maintain equality. Do not wrongly align A with Question 2 B or B with Question 2 C.

4) CORRECT ANSWER: B
In the final paragraph of Passage 2, the authors indicate that their country can wage war, enter into alliances, conduct commerce, and "do all other Acts and Things which Independent States may of right do" (lines 68-72). This information supports B: although war and alliances are mentioned, it is not explained HOW these things will take shape, only that the United States CAN wage war and create alliances. Eliminate A and D as out of scope, and eliminate C as a distortion of the authors' actual writing strategies: the Declaration of Independence ITSELF publicizes a decision, and does not offer any further strategies for doing so.

5) CORRECT ANSWER: D
The word "light" is paired with the word "transient [not lasting long]" (line 48), and is used to create a contrast with the advised action of "Governments long established" (lines 46-47). Something "light" would thus be fleeting or minor in this context: D is an appropriate choice, while A and C are positives and B wrongly describes a physical quality, not a degree of importance or unimportance.

6) CORRECT ANSWER: A
While Passage 1 indicates that "liberty cannot exist without" (line 6) an effective state and that "regulations concerning" (line 18) equality can be made, Passage 2 reacts to a "long train of abuses and usurpations" (lines 51-52) that have made a break with British rule and the formation of a new country necessary. A is the best answer: B is problematic

because Passage 2 does not explain what exactly the abuses have been (only that they are severe), C is problematic because democratic participation is praised in Passage 2, and D is problematic because Passage 1 defines liberty and equality but does not explain how these ideas originated. (Passage 2 also endorses some of these ideas, and argues instead that a particular government must be discarded.)

7) CORRECT ANSWER: D

The authors of Passage 2 cite "the Right of the People to alter or to abolish" (line 42) a problematic government, and explain in the final paragraph that, based on this principle, they have broken with Britain and created a group of "Free and Independent States" (line 65). This information supports D and can be used to eliminate C, which neglects the practical measures emphasized in Passage 2. A is incorrect because military advantages (as opposed to a nation's military abilities) are never described; B is incorrect because the authors of Passage 2 are renouncing European or British rule (but may be basing some of their arguments on ideas popular elsewhere in Europe).

8) CORRECT ANSWER: A

The author of Passage 1 emphasizes the qualities of liberty and equality, and notes that government may be modified "in accordance with the local situation and temper of the inhabitants" (lines 23-24). For their part, the authors of Passage 2 cite the principles of equality (line 36) and liberty (line 38) and argue that it is "the Right of the People" (line 42) to eliminate a problematic government and create a new one: these principles are used to justify a break with the British government. A is thus the best answer, while C wrongly places the passages in disagreement. B is out of scope, since Passage 2 only argues that a SINGLE country should act on the principles outlined in Passage 1, while D is inaccurate, since Rousseau is never directly mentioned in Passage 2.

9) CORRECT ANSWER: D

The final paragraph of Passage 1 presents the idea that a governmental system may "need modifying in every country" (line 23) in response to specific events: in lines 55-58, the authors of Passage 2 note that problems have constrained the Colonies "to alter their former systems of government". D is thus the best answer. A notes that a rebelling state should declare its grievances (but does not justify rebellion itself), B endorses principles such as equality (which are discussed ELSEWHERE in Passage 1), and C simply indicates that people will accept tolerable evils or wrongs.

10) CORRECT ANSWER: C

In Passage 1, Rousseau declares that the "end [objective] of every system of legislation" (line 2) is to protect liberty and equality; similarly, the authors of Passage 2 argue that "Governments are instituted among Men" (line 39) to make rights such as life, liberty, and the pursuit of happiness possible. This information supports C. Public debates are not analyzed in either passage (although the ideas in Passage 2 may be the PRODUCT of a debate, eliminating A), military affairs are only considered in Passage 2 (eliminating B), and economic justice is only considered in Passage 1 (eliminating D).

CHAPTER 2
Emerging Democracy

Emerging Democracy
1776-1914

The end of the American Revolution did not necessarily spell the end of worldwide empires. However, it did herald in a democratic experiment of a type the world had never seen—and occasioned new examinations of age-old issues among European and American intellectuals. Anna Laetitia Barbauld revisited the premises behind just and unified government, Mary Wollstonecraft spoke vigorously for women and their intellectual powers, and Thomas Paine and Benjamin Franklin thought anew about the roots (and results) of free speech. The late eighteenth century world of these writers was a world of turmoil: France was swept up in a revolution of its own, and a shifting geopolitical order would lead to both the War of 1812 and the Napoleonic Campaigns.

Still, the early 19th century was a time of expansion and, in many ways, promise for the United States. George Washington had set precedents for limited yet firm leadership, and his successors, including Thomas Jefferson, championed the country's westward movement. Even commentators who could be critical of the United States, such as Alexis de Tocqueville, found the government of the young country in many ways stable. Yet others would not be so forgiving. A strong nonconformist streak motivated Henry David Thoreau, for instance, to protest America's expansionist policies and seek refuge from society in the relative solitude of nature. More tragically, debates over slavery continued to convulse the nation: abolitionists such as Frederick Douglass denounced the inhumanity of the entire slave system, while legislators such as Stephen Douglas and Abraham Lincoln sparred over what kind of future slavery would have in America—if any. Escalating differences between the industrialized North and the slave-bound South culminated in the Civil War: Lincoln, as president, would need to reconcile moral rectitude with high-stakes geopolitics of a kind the country had never seen.

In the aftermath of the war, a humbled South and an invigorated North faced a new round of social shifts. The mid to late nineteenth century witnessed new waves of European immigration, along with the importation of new ideas from Europe: Karl Marx's communism, though it did not shape actual international affairs until the twentieth century, was largely formulated during this time. With the rise of cities came the rise of mass industry, as celebrated by magnates such as John D. Rockefeller, and of catastrophic poverty, as documented by journalists such as Jacob Riis. Indeed, this was an era of paradox. Although slavery had been abolished, African-American intellectuals such as W.E.B. Du Bois could still point to the realities of displacement and discrimination that African Americans faced. And although women such as Clara Barton could found and lead international charities, women were still expected to be socially docile and were still denied basic voting rights: feminists such as Susan B. Anthony and Charlotte Perkins Gilman never lost sight of these hard truths.

For some, the beginning of the twentieth century was a moment of triumph: America had come into its own as a world power and its past leaders—Washington, Jefferson, Lincoln—had become almost legendary. For others, the new era was a time of frustratingly little opportunity—or at least a reminder of the work towards a better society that remained to be done.

Questions 1-10 are based on the following passage.
2.01
Adapted from Anna Laetitia Barbauld, "Sins of the Government, Sins of the Nation" (1793).

Societies being composed of individuals, the faults of Societies proceed from the Same bad passions, the Same pride, Selfishness and thirst of gain, by which individuals are led to
Line transgress the rules of duty; they require therefore the Same
5 curb to restrain them, and hence the necessity of a national religion. You will probably assert, that most nations have one; but, by a national religion, I do not mean the burning a few wretches twice or thrice in a year in honour of God, nor yet the exacting Subscription to Some obscure tenets, believed by
10 few, and understood by none; nor yet the investing a certain order of men dressed in a particular habit, with civil privileges and Secular emolument; by national religion I understand, the extending to those affairs in which we act in common and as a body, that regard to religion, by which, when we act Singly,
15 we all profess to be guided. Nothing seems more obvious; and yet there are men who appear not insensible to the rules of morality as they respect individuals, and who unaccountably disclaim them with respect to nations. They will not cheat their opposite neighbor, but they will take a pride in over-reaching
20 a neighboring State; they would Scorn to foment dissentions in the family of an acquaintance, but they will do So by a community without Scruple; they would not join with a gang of house-breakers to plunder a private dwelling, but they have no principle which prevents them from joining with a confederacy
25 of princes to plunder a province. As private individuals, they think it right to pass by little injuries, but as a people they think they cannot carry too high a principle of proud defiance and Sanguinary revenge.

This Sufficiently Shows, that whatever rule they may
30 acknowledge for their private conduct, they have nothing that can be properly called national religion; and indeed, it is very much to be Suspected, that their religion in the former case, is very much assisted by the contemplation of those pains and penalties which Society has provided against the crimes of
35 individuals. But the united will of a whole people cannot make wrong right, or Sanction one act of rapacity, injustice, or breach of faith. The first principle, therefore, we must lay down, is, that we are to Submit our public conduct to the Same rules by which we are to regulate our private actions: A nation that does this, is,
40 as a nation, religious; a nation that does it not, though it Should fast, and pray, and wear Sackcloth, and pay tithes, and build churches, is, as a nation, profligate and unprincipled.

The vices of nations may be divided into those which relate to their own internal proceedings, or to their relations with
45 other States. With regard to the first, the causes for humiliation are various. Many nations are guilty of the crime of permitting oppressive laws and bad governments to remain amongst them,
by which the poor are crushed, and the lives of the innocent are laid at the mercy of wicked and arbitrary men. This is a
50 national Sin of the deepest dye, as it involves in it most others. It is painful to reflect how many atrocious governments there are in the world; and how little even they who enjoy good ones, Seem to understand their true nature. We are apt to Speak of the happiness of living under a mild government, as if it were
55 like the happiness of living under an indulgent climate; and when we thank God for it, we rank it with the blessings of the air and of the Soil; whereas we ought to thank God for the wisdom and virtue of living under a good government; for a good government is the first of national duties. It is indeed a
60 happiness, and one which demands our most grateful thanks, to be born under one which Spares us the trouble and hazard of changing it; but a people born under a good government, will probably not die under one, if they conceive of it as of an indolent and passive happiness, to be left for its preservation, to
65 fortunate conjunctures, and the floating and variable chances of incalculable events—our Second duty is to keep it good.

1

According to Barbauld, "national religion" is

A) a rarity even among civilized and prosperous countries.
B) a code of behavior that makes the observation of more traditional religious practices unnecessary.
C) an extension of the morality practiced by individuals to public affairs.
D) incompatible with popular ideas about international politics.

2

Which choice provides the best evidence for the answer to the previous question?

A) Line 6 (You will . . . have one")
B) Lines 7-12 ("by a national . . . emolument")
C) Lines 12-15 ("by national . . . guided")
D) Lines 43-45 ("The vices . . . States")

3

As used in line 13, "affairs" most nearly means

A) intrigues.
B) situations.
C) political negotiations.
D) business transactions.

CONTINUE

4

The irony that Barbauld describes in lines 18-25 ("They will not . . . province") is that

A) people who cause public discord often claim to be the most patriotic of all.

B) people who are averse to harming individuals are not averse to harming large groups of people.

C) participation in government can lead to disrespect for individual property rights.

D) people are often most agitated by relatively minor injuries.

5

Barbauld states that people are strongly persuaded against committing social wrongs by

A) fear of punishment.

B) religious rituals.

C) the good deeds of the people around them.

D) the example set by the government.

6

Which choice provides the best evidence for the answer to the previous question?

A) Lines 31-35 ("and indeed . . . individuals")

B) Lines 39-42 ("A nation . . . unprincipled")

C) Lines 53-55 ("We are apt . . . climate")

D) Lines 59-62 ("It is indeed . . . changing it")

7

Barbauld states that it is the duty of individuals to

A) report cases even of minor wrongdoing to the authorities.

B) actively ensure that their government remains just.

C) interact with government officials on a daily basis.

D) abandon religious rituals that no longer serve any clear purpose.

8

As used in line 54, "mild" most nearly means

A) subtle.

B) unremarkable.

C) non-oppressive.

D) affectionate.

9

Barbauld characterizes the happiness offered by a "good government" (line 58) as

A) absolute.

B) precarious.

C) undefinable.

D) unappreciated.

10

Throughout the passage, Barbauld develops her argument by presenting

A) a series of distinctions.

B) recommendations for specific reforms.

C) historical anecdotes.

D) criticisms of her own government.

CONTINUE

Questions 1-10 are based on the following passages.

2.02

Passage 1 is taken from "On Freedom of Speech and the Press," an essay that appeared in *The Memoirs of Benjamin Franklin*; Passage 2 is taken from "Liberty of the Press" by Thomas Paine.

Passage 1

Freedom of speech is a principal pillar of a free government: when this support is taken away, the constitution of a free society is dissolved, and tyranny is erected on its
Line ruins. Republics and limited monarchies derive their strength
5 and vigour from a popular examination into the actions of the magistrates; this privilege, in all ages, has been, and always will be, abused. The best of men could not escape the censure and envy of the times they lived in. Yet this evil is not so great as it may appear at first sight. A magistrate who sincerely aims at
10 the good of society will always have the inclinations of a great majority on his side, and an impartial posterity will not fail to render him justice.

Those abuses of the freedom of speech are the exercises of liberty. They ought to be repressed; but to whom dare we
15 commit the care of doing it? An evil magistrate, intrusted with power to punish for words, would be armed with a weapon the most destructive and terrible. Under pretence of pruning off the exuberant branches, he would be apt to destroy the tree.

It is certain that he who robs another of his moral
20 reputation, more richly merits a gibbet than if he had plundered him of his purse on the highway. Augustus Cæsar, under the specious pretext of preserving the character of the Romans from defamation, introduced the law whereby libelling was involved in the penalties of treason against the state. This law established
25 his tyranny; and for one mischief which it prevented, ten thousand evils, horrible and afflicting, sprung up in its place. Thenceforward every person's life and fortune depended on the vile breath of informers. The construction of words being arbitrary, and left to the decision of the judges, no man could
30 write or open his mouth without being in danger of forfeiting his head.

Passage 2

The writer of this remembers a remark made to him by Mr. Jefferson concerning the English newspapers, which at that time, 1787, while Mr. Jefferson was Minister at Paris,
35 were most vulgarly abusive. The remark applies with equal force to the Federal papers of America. The remark was, that "the licentiousness of the press produces the same effect as the restraint of the press was intended to do, if the restraint was to prevent things being told, and the licentiousness of the press
40 prevents things being believed when they are told." We have in this state an evidence of the truth of this remark. The number of Federal papers in the city and state of New York are more

than five to one to the number of Republican papers, yet the majority of the elections go always against the Federal papers;
45 which is demonstrative evidence that the licentiousness of those papers is destitute of credit.

Whoever has made observation on the characters of nations will find it generally true that the manners of a nation, or of a party, can be better ascertained from the character of
50 its press than from any other public circumstance. If its press is licentious, its manners are not good. Nobody believes a common liar, or a common defamer.

Nothing is more common with printers, especially of newspapers, than the continual cry of the Liberty of the Press,
55 as if because they are printers they are to have more privileges than other people.

1

What is a primary difference between the two passages?

A) Passage 1 considers evidence taken primarily from the author's own life in politics, while Passage 2 considers evidence taken primarily from history.

B) Passage 1 considers freedom of the press a mostly advantageous practice, while Passage 2 considers freedom of the press a practice with no real benefits.

C) Passage 1 considers freedom of speech as it relates to foreign affairs, while Passage 2 considers freedom of speech as it relates to domestic politics.

D) Passage 1 considers the legal and judicial aspects of freedom of speech, while Passage 2 considers how the popular press makes use of this freedom.

2

As used in line 2, "constitution" most nearly means

A) foundation.

B) legislation.

C) formation.

D) anatomy.

51

CONTINUE

3

The author of Passage 1 would most likely respond to the remarks in lines 37-38 of Passage 2 ("the licentiousness . . . to do") by arguing that

A) freedom of the expression cannot do any harm to a truly virtuous individual.

B) freedom of expression will be abused less often as democratic principles become more popular.

C) limiting free expression is a strategy that has disastrous effects on education and the arts.

D) limiting free expression can have more destructive consequences than freedom of the press.

4

Which choice provides the best evidence for the answer to the previous question?

A) Lines 1-2 ("Freedom of . . . government")

B) Lines 4-7 ("Republics . . . abused")

C) Lines 13-14 ("Those . . . repressed")

D) Lines 23-26 ("libelling was . . . place")

5

The author of Passage 1 uses the comparison in lines 19-21 ("It is . . . highway") to convey

A) the fragility of the right to freedom of speech.

B) the immorality of misusing freedom of speech.

C) the mentality of an unfair magistrate.

D) the illogicality of the measures instituted by Augustus Caesar.

6

The author of Passage 2 argues which of the following points about the "Federal papers" (line 36)?

A) They follow tactics that are neither ethical nor particularly effective.

B) They were at one point supportive of measures that would strategically limit freedom of speech.

C) They are a root cause of America's sharply diminishing reputation abroad.

D) They have until only recently been outnumbered by the Republican papers.

7

Which choice provides the best evidence for the answer to the previous question?

A) Lines 37-39 ("the licentiousness . . . told")

B) Lines 41-43 ("The number . . . papers")

C) Lines 43-46 ("the majority . . . credit")

D) Lines 47-50 ("Whoever . . . circumstance")

8

Both Passage 1 and Passage 2 articulate the idea that

A) Americans have used free speech more rationally than people from other cultures have.

B) efforts to restrict free speech can make a society paranoid and insecure.

C) free speech is a foundational right that makes all other rights possible.

D) national identity is strongly defined by how a nation utilizes free speech.

9

As used in line 49, "character" most nearly means

A) traits.

B) personality.

C) individuality.

D) integrity.

10

The final paragraph of Passage 2 (lines 53-56) mainly serves to

A) characterize members of the press as more corrupt than members of other professions.

B) suggest that the public has helped printers to claim bizarre and extravagant privileges.

C) highlight a recent and specific abuse of freedom of speech.

D) comment on how the press uses the ideal of freedom of speech to justify libel.

CONTINUE

Questions 1-10 are based on the following passage.
2.03
Adapted from Mary Wollstonecraft, *A Vindication of the Rights of Woman* (1792).

Women are every where in this deplorable state; for, in order to preserve their innocence, as ignorance is courteously termed, truth is hidden from them, and they are made to assume
Line an artificial character before their faculties have acquired any
5 strength. Taught from their infancy, that beauty is woman's sceptre, the mind shapes itself to the body, and, roaming round its gilt cage, only seeks to adorn its prison. Men have various employments and pursuits which engage their attention, and give a character to the opening mind; but women, confined to
10 one, and having their thoughts constantly directed to the most insignificant part of themselves, seldom extend their views beyond the triumph of the hour. But was their understanding once emancipated from the slavery to which the pride and sensuality of man and their short sighted desire, like that of
15 dominion in tyrants, of present sway, has subjected them, we should probably read of their weaknesses with surprise. I must be allowed to pursue the argument a little farther.

Perhaps, if the existence of an evil being was allowed, who, in the allegorical language of scripture, went about
20 seeking whom he should devour, he could not more effectually degrade the human character than by giving a man absolute power.

This argument branches into various ramifications. Birth, riches, and every intrinsic advantage that exalt a man above
25 his fellows, without any mental exertion, sink him in reality below them. In proportion to his weakness, he is played upon by designing men, till the bloated monster has lost all traces of humanity. And that tribes of men, like flocks of sheep, should quietly follow such a leader, is a solecism that only a desire of
30 present enjoyment and narrowness of understanding can solve. Educated in slavish dependence, and enervated by luxury and sloth, where shall we find men who will stand forth to assert the rights of man; or claim the privilege of moral beings, who should have but one road to excellence? Slavery to monarchs
35 and ministers, which the world will be long in freeing itself from, and whose deadly grasp stops the progress of the human mind, is not yet abolished.

Let not men then in the pride of power, use the same arguments that tyrannic kings and venal ministers have used,
40 and fallaciously assert, that woman ought to be subjected because she has always been so. But, when man, governed by reasonable laws, enjoys his natural freedom, let him despise woman, if she do not share it with him; and, till that glorious period arrives, in descanting on the folly of the sex, let him not
45 overlook his own.

Women, it is true, obtaining power by unjust means, by practising or fostering vice, evidently lose the rank which

reason would assign them, and they become either abject slaves or capricious tyrants. They lose all simplicity, all dignity of
50 mind, in acquiring power, and act as men are observed to act when they have been exalted by the same means.

It is time to effect a revolution in female manners, time to restore to them their lost dignity, and make them, as a part of the human species, labour by reforming themselves to reform
55 the world.

1

The passage focuses primarily on the

A) economic difficulties and social oppression that women have faced.
B) various theories on the nature of power and validity of these ideologies.
C) efforts of women to be seen as equals and to achieve as much power as men.
D) effects of the restriction and possession of power on men and women.

2

Which of the following best describes the function of the first sentence of the passage?

A) It prepares for the central thesis by mentioning a common struggle of both genders.
B) It provides a specific example of a phenomenon which the author will later argue against.
C) It introduces an argument for which support will be given later in the paragraph.
D) It acknowledges a potential counterargument and discusses the flaw of that argument.

3

Wollstonecraft makes what distinction between men and women?

A) Men are given absolute power in areas outside the home, while women are given power in domestic spheres.
B) Men are given the opportunity to pursue various careers and walks of life, while women are only assigned one role.
C) Men are accustomed to freedom and take advantage of their privilege, while women are unsure of what to do with their power.
D) Men allow themselves to become mindless followers of tyrants and monarchs, while women challenge those in positions of power.

CONTINUE

4

Which choice provides the best evidence for the answer to the previous question?

A) Lines 7-10 ("Men . . . one")

B) Lines 12-15 ("But . . . them")

C) Lines 31-34 ("Educated . . . excellence?")

D) Lines 34-37 ("Slavery . . . abolished")

5

The passage indicates that men born into privilege can be all of the following EXCEPT:

A) greedy and power-hungry opportunists.

B) tyrannical and abusive of their power.

C) leaders whom other men follow blindly.

D) lazy and materialistic followers.

6

As used in line 30, "solve" most nearly means

A) correct.

B) change.

C) explain.

D) settle.

7

The sentence that begins in line 38 ("Let not . . . ") marks a shift from

A) a discursive musing to a direct argument.

B) a discussion of a problem to a proposed solution.

C) a historical perspective to a contemporary one.

D) a skeptical stance to a more optimistic one.

8

As used in line 53, "lost" most nearly means

A) baffled.

B) compromised.

C) wandering.

D) irretrievable.

9

Wollstonecraft states that in order to gain their rights, women must

A) improve their own characters so that they do not become corrupted by power.

B) demand that men use their education and privilege to expose discrimination.

C) assert their own power by demanding legislation giving women and men equal rights.

D) allow themselves to gain power through dishonest or immoral ways.

10

Which choice provides the best evidence for the answer to the previous question?

A) Lines 18-22 ("Perhaps . . . power")

B) Lines 46-48 ("Women . . . them")

C) Lines 49-51 ("They . . . means")

D) Lines 53-55 ("make . . . world")

CONTINUE

Questions 1-10 are based on the following passage.
2.04
Adapted from the First Inaugural Address (1801)
delivered by Thomas Jefferson.

A rising nation, spread over a wide and fruitful land,
traversing all the seas with the rich productions of their
industry, engaged in commerce with nations who feel power
and forget right, advancing rapidly to destinies beyond the
5 reach of mortal eye—when I contemplate these transcendent
objects, and see the honor, the happiness, and the hopes of this
beloved country committed to the issue and the auspices of
this day, I shrink from the contemplation, and humble myself
before the magnitude of the undertaking. Utterly, indeed,
10 should I despair did not the presence of many whom I here
see remind me that in the other high authorities provided by
our Constitution I shall find resources of wisdom, of virtue,
and of zeal on which to rely under all difficulties. To you,
then, gentlemen, who are charged with the sovereign functions
15 of legislation, and to those associated with you, I look with
encouragement for that guidance and support which may
enable us to steer with safety the vessel in which we are all
embarked amidst the conflicting elements of a troubled world.
During the contest of opinion through which we have
20 passed the animation of discussions and of exertions has
sometimes worn an aspect which might impose on strangers
unused to think freely and to speak and to write what they
think; but this being now decided by the voice of the nation,
announced according to the rules of the Constitution, all will,
25 of course, arrange themselves under the will of the law, and
unite in common efforts for the common good. All, too, will
bear in mind this sacred principle, that though the will of
the majority is in all cases to prevail, that will to be rightful
must be reasonable; that the minority possess their equal
30 rights, which equal law must protect, and to violate would be
oppression. Let us, then, fellow-citizens, unite with one heart
and one mind. Let us restore to social intercourse that harmony
and affection without which liberty and even life itself are but
dreary things. And let us reflect that, having banished from our
35 land that religious intolerance under which mankind so long
bled and suffered, we have yet gained little if we countenance
a political intolerance as despotic, as wicked, and capable
of as bitter and bloody persecutions. During the throes and
convulsions of the ancient world, during the agonizing spasms
40 of infuriated man, seeking through blood and slaughter his
long-lost liberty, it was not wonderful that the agitation of the
billows should reach even this distant and peaceful shore; that
this should be more felt and feared by some and less by others,
and should divide opinions as to measures of safety. But every
45 difference of opinion is not a difference of principle. We have
called by different names brethren of the same principle. We
are all Republicans, we are all Federalists.

If there be any among us who would wish to dissolve
this Union or to change its republican form, let them
50 stand undisturbed as monuments of the safety with which
error of opinion may be tolerated where reason is left free
to combat it. I know, indeed, that some honest men fear
that a republican government can not be strong, that this
Government is not strong enough; but would the honest
55 patriot, in the full tide of successful experiment, abandon
a government which has so far kept us free and firm on
the theoretic and visionary fear that this Government,
the world's best hope, may by possibility want energy to
preserve itself? I trust not. I believe this, on the contrary,
60 the strongest Government on earth. I believe it the only one
where every man, at the call of the law, would fly to the
standard of the law, and would meet invasions of the public
order as his own personal concern. Sometimes it is said that
man can not be trusted with the government of himself. Can
65 he, then, be trusted with the government of others? Or have
we found angels in the forms of kings to govern him? Let
history answer this question.

1

Over the course of the first paragraph, Jefferson shifts
from

A) recapitulating America's history to listing the policies
that will shape its future.
B) addressing the populace at large to praising a small
group of privileged citizens.
C) pessimistically describing America's present to
optimistically envisioning its later progress.
D) celebrating America's prospects to explaining how
the country will address its challenges.

2

The stance that Jefferson takes in the passage is best
described as that of

A) an engaged American promoting cooperation.
B) an idealistic leader proposing major reforms.
C) a disillusioned scholar reflecting on the past.
D) a pragmatic politician seeking to glorify his
accomplishments.

CONTINUE

3

Which choice provides the best evidence for the answer to the previous question?

A) Lines 5-8 ("I contemplate . . . this day")

B) Lines 9-13 ("Utterly, indeed . . . difficulties")

C) Lines 19-23 ("During the . . . think")

D) Lines 31-34 ("Let us, then . . . things")

4

It can be inferred that the "contest of opinion" mentioned in line 19 is

A) an earlier phase that has given way to a more tranquil time.

B) a stage of development when America was at its most powerful.

C) a dispute that nearly destroyed the American government.

D) a condition that Jefferson hopes to re-create.

5

According to Jefferson, a republican government is especially potent because it

A) can raise a larger military than a non-republican government.

B) facilitates intellectual and spiritual growth.

C) can engage in free commerce with foreign powers.

D) fosters immense loyalty among its citizens.

6

Which choice provides the best evidence for the answer to the previous question?

A) Lines 38-42 ("During the . . . shore")

B) Lines 44-46 ("But every . . . principle")

C) Lines 52-54 ("I know, indeed . . . enough")

D) Lines 60-63 ("I believe it . . . concern")

7

As used in line 14, "charged with" most nearly means

A) accused of.

B) agitated by.

C) entrusted with.

D) billed for.

8

As used in line 50, "monuments" most nearly means

A) institutions.

B) edifices.

C) prominent specimens.

D) grand commemorations.

9

In the final paragraph, Jefferson presents a contrast between

A) democracy and dictatorship.

B) doubt and confidence.

C) spirituality and practicality.

D) publicity and privacy.

10

Which of the following does Jefferson hope will be eliminated from American social life?

A) Religious intolerance

B) Political intolerance

C) Differences of opinion

D) Excessive patriotism

56

CONTINUE

Questions 1-10 are based on the following passage.
2.05
Adapted from "Parties in the United States," a section of *Democracy in America* (1835) by Alexis de Tocqueville.

When the citizens entertain different opinions upon subjects which affect the whole country alike, such, for instance, as the principles upon which the government is to
Line be conducted, then distinctions arise which may correctly be
5 styled parties. Parties are a necessary evil in free governments; but they have not at all times the same character and the same propensities.

At certain periods a nation may be oppressed by such insupportable evils as to conceive the design of effecting a
10 total change in its political constitution; at other times the mischief lies still deeper, and the existence of society itself is endangered. Such are the times of great revolutions and of great parties. But between these epochs of misery and of confusion there are periods during which human society seems
15 to rest, and mankind to make a pause. This pause is, indeed, only apparent, for time does not stop its course for nations any more than for men; they are all advancing towards a goal with which they are unacquainted; and we only imagine them to be stationary when their progress escapes our observation, as men
20 who are going at a foot-pace seem to be standing still to those who run.

But however this may be, there are certain epochs at which the changes that take place in the social and political constitution of nations are so slow and so insensible that men
25 imagine their present condition to be a final state; and the human mind, believing itself to be firmly based upon certain foundations, does not extend its researches beyond the horizon which it descries. These are the times of small parties and of intrigue.
30 The political parties which I style great are those which cling to principles more than to their consequences; to general, and not to especial cases; to ideas, and not to men. These parties are usually distinguished by a nobler character, by more generous passions, more genuine convictions, and a more bold
35 and open conduct than the others. In them private interest, which always plays the chief part in political passions, is more studiously veiled under the pretext of the public good; and it may even be sometimes concealed from the eyes of the very persons whom it excites and impels.
40 Minor parties are, on the other hand, generally deficient in political faith. As they are not sustained or dignified by a lofty purpose, they ostensibly display the egotism of their character in their actions. They glow with a factitious zeal; their language is vehement, but their conduct is timid and irresolute.
45 The means they employ are as wretched as the end at which they aim. Hence it arises that when a calm state of things succeeds a violent revolution, the leaders of society seem

suddenly to disappear, and the powers of the human mind to lie concealed. Society is convulsed by great parties, by
50 minor ones it is agitated; it is torn by the former, by the latter it is degraded; and if these sometimes save it by a salutary perturbation, those invariably disturb it to no good end.

America has already lost the great parties which once divided the nation; and if her happiness is considerably
55 increased, her morality has suffered by their extinction. When the War of Independence was terminated, and the foundations of the new Government were to be laid down, the nation was divided between two opinions—two opinions which are as old as the world, and which are perpetually
60 to be met with under all the forms and all the names which have ever obtained in free communities—the one tending to limit, the other to extend indefinitely, the power of the people. The conflict of these two opinions never assumed that degree of violence in America which it has frequently
65 displayed elsewhere. Both parties of the Americans were, in fact, agreed upon the most essential points; and neither of them had to destroy a traditionary constitution, or to overthrow the structure of society, in order to ensure its own triumph.

1

One of Tocqueville's primary objectives in this passage is to

A) draw a clear distinction between great and minor political parties.
B) explain the principles of America's two great political parties.
C) show why great political parties are more common in America than in Europe.
D) demonstrate that minor parties must be tolerated even in the most prosperous nations.

2

As used in line 16, "course" most nearly means

A) studies.
B) area.
C) passage.
D) plan.

CONTINUE

3

Tocqueville suggests that the men who "imagine their present condition to be a final state" (line 25) are

A) mistaken.

B) agitated.

C) dishonest.

D) thoughtful.

4

It can be reasonably inferred that Tocqueville would define a minor political party as one that

A) can only result from the collapse and fragmentation of a major party.

B) is in large part the product of economic and military insecurity.

C) was created mainly to support a few specific policies and politicians.

D) can help a chaotic country to become more peaceful.

5

Which choice provides the best evidence for the answer to the previous question?

A) Lines 5-7 ("Parties are . . . propensities")

B) Lines 30-32 ("The political . . . men")

C) Lines 49-51 ("Society is . . . degraded")

D) Lines 63-65 ("The conflict . . . elsewhere")

6

Which of the following, according to the passage, was a point of difference between America's two main political parties?

A) How much political power they thought the public should wield.

B) How necessary they believed social and cultural revolution to be.

C) How willing they were to embrace minor parties.

D) How long each one lasted before radically altering its identity.

7

Which choice provides the best evidence for the answer to the previous question?

A) Lines 35-39 ("In them . . . impels")

B) Lines 53-55 ("America has . . . extinction")

C) Lines 58-63 ("the nation was . . . the people")

D) Lines 65-69 ("Both parties . . . triumph")

8

As used in line 35, "private" most nearly means

A) secret.

B) intimate.

C) unsociable.

D) individual.

9

One of the functions of the first paragraph is to

A) provide Tocqueville's definition of a political party.

B) suggest that political parties do not have any good effects.

C) present Tocqueville's system for classifying political parties.

D) imply that most political parties are easily confused.

10

Tocqueville believes that a minor political party, in contrast to a major political party, is more likely to be prominent

A) when a country is at war.

B) when a country is stable.

C) when a country is expanding.

D) when a country is in decline.

CONTINUE

Questions 1-10 are based on the following passage.
2.06
From "Abolition Fanaticism in New York," a speech delivered in 1847 by anti-slavery activist and former slave Frederick Douglass.

I am very glad to be here. I am very glad to be present at this Anniversary—glad again to mingle my voice with those with whom I have stood identified, with those with whom
Line I have labored, for the last seven years, for the purpose of
5 undoing the burdens of my brethren, and hastening the day of their emancipation.

I do not doubt but that a large portion of this audience will be disappointed, both by the manner and the matter of what I shall this day set forth. The extraordinary and unmerited
10 eulogies which have been showered upon me, here and elsewhere, have done much to create expectations which, I am well aware, I can never hope to gratify. I am here, a simple man, knowing what I have experienced in Slavery, knowing it to be a bad system, and desiring, by all Christian means, to
15 seek its overthrow. I am not here to please you with an eloquent speech, with a refined and logical address, but to speak to you the sober truths of a heart overborne with gratitude to God that we have in this land, cursed as it is with Slavery, so noble a band to second my efforts and the efforts of others in the noble
20 work of undoing the Yoke of Bondage, with which the majority of the States of this Union are now unfortunately cursed.

Since the last time I had the pleasure of mingling my voice with the voices of my friends on this platform, many interesting and even trying events have occurred to me. I have experienced,
25 within the last eighteen or twenty months, many incidents, all of which it would be interesting to communicate to you; but many of these I shall be compelled to pass over at this time, and confine my remarks to giving a general outline of the manner and spirit with which I have been hailed abroad, and welcomed
30 at the different places which I have visited during my absence of twenty months.

You are aware, doubtless, that my object in going from this country, was to get beyond the reach of the clutch of the man who claimed to own me as his property. I had written a
35 book giving a history of that portion of my life spent in the gall and bitterness and degradation of Slavery, and in which I also identified my oppressors as the perpetrators of some of the most atrocious crimes. This had deeply incensed them against me, and stirred up within them the purpose of revenge, and
40 my whereabouts being known, I believed it necessary for me, if I would preserve my liberty, to leave the shores of America, and take up my abode in some other land, at least until the excitement occasioned by the publication of my Narrative had subsided. I went to England, Monarchical England, to get rid
45 of Democratic Slavery, and I must confess that, at the very threshold, I was satisfied that I had gone to the right place.

Say what you will of England—of the degradation—of the poverty—and there is much of it there—say what you will of the oppression and suffering going on in England at this time,
50 there is Liberty there—there is Freedom there, not only for the white man, but for the black man also. The instant I stepped upon the shore, and looked into the faces of the crowd around me, I saw in every man a recognition of my manhood, and an absence, a perfect absence, of everything like that disgusting
55 hate with which we are pursued in this country. I looked around in vain to see in any man's face a token of the slightest aversion to me on account of my complexion. Even the cabmen demeaned themselves to me as they did to other men, and the very dogs and pigs of old England treated me as a man! I
60 cannot, however, my friends, dwell upon this anti-Prejudice, or rather the many illustrations of the absence of Prejudice against Color in England—but will proceed, at once, to defend the Right and Duty of invoking English aid and English sympathy for the overthrow of American Slavery, for the education of
65 Colored Americans, and to forward in every way, the interests of humanity.

1

Over the course of the passage, Douglass's focus shifts from

A) a recognition of the efforts made against American slavery to a narration of his experiences after publishing his narrative.

B) a brief summary of his argument against slavery to a series of anecdotes depicting his treatment in America and abroad.

C) an earnest statement of gratitude to his audience to a synopsis of the oppression he has encountered in countries outside America.

D) an illustration of the state of affairs in America regarding slavery to a more optimistic outlook on the future of African Americans.

2

Based on the passage, Douglass's audience is most likely comprised of

A) former slaves.

B) free African Americans.

C) fellow abolitionists.

D) white slaveowners.

CONTINUE

3

Which choice provides the best answer for the answer to the previous question?

A) Lines 3-6 ("with those . . . emancipation")
B) Lines 22-24 ("Since . . . me")
C) Lines 38-39 ("This . . . revenge")
D) Lines 53-55 ("I saw . . . country")

4

According to Douglass, the primary purpose of his speech is

A) to clarify misconceptions the public might have about him and to speak against the spread of slavery.
B) to persuade the English to abolish slavery and to promote education among African American youths.
C) to recall his struggle for freedom and to recount his travels during his twenty-month absence.
D) to express his gratitude and appreciation to those who work towards the abolition of slavery.

5

Which choice provides the best evidence for the answer to the previous question?

A) Lines 11-15 ("have . . . overthrow")
B) Lines 16-20 ("to speak . . . Bondage")
C) Lines 24-27 ("I have . . . time")
D) Lines 62-66 ("to defend . . . humanity")

6

Douglass states that while racial relations during his visit to England were much better than those in America

A) he would not stay in England but would follow his duty to pursue equality and promote progress.
B) his circumstances while traveling were an exception among other instances of racial prejudice in England.
C) conditions in America had improved during his absence and it was now safe to return to the United States.
D) he was motivated to leave England upon noticing the heightened danger slaves faced in America.

7

In lines 47-51 ("Say . . . also"), Douglass primarily draws a contrast between

A) attitudes towards Douglass in America and attitudes towards Douglass in England.
B) his expectations of England before his visit and his circumstances after his arrival.
C) the supposed democracy of America and the democracy put into effect in England.
D) the dire social and economic state of England and the seemingly paradoxical racial equality he experienced.

8

As used in line 54, "perfect" most nearly means

A) absolute.
B) sublime.
C) ideal.
D) exact.

9

As used in line 55, "with which we are pursued" most nearly means

A) which binds us.
B) which we seek.
C) which defines us.
D) which has persisted.

10

Douglass mentions his trip to England for all of the following reasons EXCEPT:

A) to show the contrast between the racial discrimination in America and the lack thereof in England.
B) to provide an explanation of his prolonged absence after the publication of his memoir.
C) to contrast the English to Americans who are aware of the horrors of slavery but allow it to continue.
D) to indicate that he has advocated and spoken against slavery in countries other than America.

CONTINUE

Questions 1-10 are based on the following passage.
2.07
Adapted from Henry David Thoreau, "Resistance to Civil Government" (1849), an essay more commonly known as "Civil Disobedience."

    I heartily accept the motto, "That government is best which governs least"; and I should like to see it acted up to more rapidly and systematically. Carried out, it finally amounts to
Line this, which also I believe—"That government is best which
5 governs not at all"; and when men are prepared for it, that will be the kind of government which they will have. Government is at best but an expedient; but most governments are usually, and all governments are sometimes, inexpedient. The objections which have been brought against a standing army, and they
10 are many and weighty, and deserve to prevail, may also at last be brought against a standing government. The standing army is only an arm of the standing government. The government itself, which is only the mode which the people have chosen to execute their will, is equally liable to be abused and perverted
15 before the people can act through it. Witness the present Mexican war, the work of comparatively a few individuals using the standing government as their tool; for in the outset, the people would not have consented to this measure.
    This American government—what is it but a tradition,
20 though a recent one, endeavoring to transmit itself unimpaired to posterity, but each instant losing some of its integrity? It has not the vitality and force of a single living man; for a single man can bend it to his will. It is a sort of wooden gun to the people themselves. But it is not the less necessary for this; for
25 the people must have some complicated machinery or other, and hear its din, to satisfy that idea of government which they have. Governments show thus how successfully men can be imposed upon, even impose on themselves, for their own advantage. It is excellent, we must all allow. Yet this government never of
30 itself furthered any enterprise, but by the alacrity with which it got out of its way. It does not keep the country free. It does not settle the West. It does not educate. The character inherent in the American people has done all that has been accomplished; and it would have done somewhat more, if the government had
35 not sometimes got in its way. For government is an expedient, by which men would fain succeed in letting one another alone; and, as has been said, when it is most expedient, the governed are most let alone by it. Trade and commerce, if they were not made of India-rubber, would never manage to bounce over
40 obstacles which legislators are continually putting in their way; and if one were to judge these men wholly by the effects of their actions and not partly by their intentions, they would deserve to be classed and punished with those mischievous persons who put obstructions on the railroads.
45   But, to speak practically and as a citizen, unlike those who call themselves no-government men, I ask for, not at once no

government, but at once a better government. Let every man make known what kind of government would command his respect, and that will be one step toward obtaining it.
50   After all, the practical reason why, when the power is once in the hands of the people, a majority are permitted, and for a long period continue, to rule is not because they are most likely to be in the right, nor because this seems fairest to the minority, but because they are physically the strongest. But a
55 government in which the majority rule in all cases can not be based on justice, even as far as men understand it. Can there not be a government in which the majorities do not virtually decide right and wrong, but conscience?—in which majorities decide only those questions to which the rule of expediency is
60 applicable? Must the citizen ever for a moment, or in the least degree, resign his conscience to the legislator? Why has every man a conscience then? I think that we should be men first, and subjects afterward.

1

Thoreau's primary purpose in the passage is to

A) critically evaluate the relationship between the American government and the people it serves.
B) expose new ideologies that threaten to disrupt the basic functions of American society.
C) demonstrate why American elected officials have become oblivious to the wishes of their constituents.
D) characterize the American government as an increasingly belligerent institution.

2

Thoreau would agree with the "no-government men" (line 46) that

A) a government should not impede economic activity.
B) a government should not be able to wage war.
C) all governments are heavily reliant on propaganda.
D) all governments should be systematically abolished.

3

In the second paragraph, Thoreau indicates that the American government is often

A) ineffectual, even though it fulfills a psychological need.
B) useful, even though its workings are not well understood.
C) ineffectual, and is undergoing a series of major reforms.
D) useful, and has enabled Americans to take greater initiative in commerce and exploration.

61

CONTINUE

4

As used in line 14, "execute" most nearly means

A) assess.

B) eliminate.

C) enact.

D) nominate.

5

Thoreau indicates that the citizens of the United States

A) are extremely hostile to any effort to radically change how they live.

B) could have been more successful if the government had been less restrictive.

C) participate in the government only in order to achieve personal gain.

D) are in agreement that the influence of the government must be drastically reduced.

6

Which choice provides the best evidence for the answer to the previous question?

A) Lines 4-6 ("That government . . . have")

B) Lines 21-23 ("It has . . . will")

C) Lines 32-35 ("The character . . . way")

D) Lines 45-49 ("But, to . . . obtaining it")

7

With which of the following general statements would Thoreau most likely agree?

A) The legislators in democratic governments are often interested in redistributing wealth.

B) Democratic governments tend to make foreign policy choices based on short-term gain.

C) The citizens of democratic governments are seldom interested in moral disputes.

D) Democratic governments are not necessarily based on moral principles.

8

Which choice provides the best evidence for the answer to the previous question?

A) Lines 15-18 ("Witness the . . . measure")

B) Lines 38-41 ("Trade and . . . way")

C) Lines 50-54 ("After all . . . strongest")

D) Lines 61-63 ("Why has . . . afterward")

9

As used in line 57, "virtually" most nearly means

A) deceptively.

B) effectually.

C) fleetingly.

D) imaginatively.

10

In the final paragraph (lines 50-63), Thoreau transitions from

A) describing an oppressive government to praising its surprising potential to improve.

B) explaining a broad situation to articulating a specific principle.

C) paraphrasing an established political theory to offering a new speculation.

D) questioning a longstanding tradition to praising a new policy.

CONTINUE

Questions 1-10 are based on the following passages.
2.08
Starting in the summer of 1858, Senator Stephen A. Douglas of Illinois and Congressman Abraham Lincoln, also of Illinois, engaged in a series of debates regarding slavery, legislation, and Constitutional rights. Passage 1 is from a speech by Douglas, while Passage 2 is from Lincoln's immediate response to Douglas's remarks. Both passages refer to the 1854 Kansas-Nebraska Act, which allowed the territories of Kansas and Nebraska to determine whether they would enter the Union as free states or slave states.

Passage 1

If there is any one principle dearer and more sacred than all others in free governments, it is that which asserts the exclusive right of a free people to form and adopt their own fundamental
Line law, and to manage and regulate their own internal affairs and
5 domestic institutions.

When I found an effort being made during the recent session of Congress to force a slave state Constitution upon the people of Kansas against their will, and to force that State into the Union with a Constitution which her people had
10 rejected by more than 10,000, I felt bound as a man of honor and a representative of Illinois, bound by every consideration of duty, of fidelity, and of patriotism, to resist to the utmost of my power the consummation of that fraud. With others I did resist it, and resisted it successfully until the attempt was
15 abandoned. We forced them to refer that Constitution back to the people of Kansas, to be accepted or rejected as they shall decide at an election, which is fixed for the first Monday in August next. It is true that the mode of reference, and the form of the submission, was not such as I could sanction with my
20 vote, for the reason that it discriminated between Free States and Slave States; providing that if Kansas consented to come in under the Lecompton Constitution it should be received with a population of 35,000; but that if she demanded another Constitution, more consistent with the sentiments of her people
25 and their feelings, that it should not be received into the Union until she has 93,420 inhabitants. I did not consider that mode of submission fair, for the reason that any election is a mockery which is not free, that any election is a fraud upon the rights of the people which holds out inducements for affirmative votes,
30 and threatens penalties for negative votes.

Passage 2

I am not master of language; I have not a fine education; I am not capable of entering into a disquisition upon dialectics, as I believe you call it; but I do not believe the language I employed bears any such construction as Judge Douglas puts
35 upon it. But I don't care about a quibble in regard to words. I know what I mean, and I will not leave this crowd in doubt, if I can explain it to them, what I really mean.

I am not, in the first place, unaware that this government has endured eighty-two years half slave and half free. I know
40 that. I am tolerably well acquainted with the history of the country, and I know that it has endured eighty-two years half slave and half free. I believe—and that is what I meant to allude to there—I believe it has endured because during all that time, the public mind did rest all the time in the belief that
45 slavery was in course of ultimate extinction. That was what gave us the rest that we had through that period of eighty-two years—at least, so I believe. I have always hated slavery, I think, as much as any Abolitionist—I have been an Old Line Whig—I have always hated it; but I have always been quiet
50 about it until this new era of the introduction of the Kansas-Nebraska Bill began. I always believed that everybody was against it, and that it was in course of ultimate extinction. The great mass of the nation have rested in the belief that slavery was in course of ultimate extinction. They had reason so to
55 believe.

The adoption of the Constitution and its attendant history led the people to believe so; and that such was the belief of the framers of the Constitution itself, why did those old men, about the time of the adoption of the Constitution, decree that
60 slavery should not go into the new Territory, where it had not already gone? Why declare that within twenty years the African slave trade, by which slaves are supplied, might be cut off by Congress? Why were all these acts? I might enumerate more of these acts; but enough. What were they but a clear indication
65 that the framers of the Constitution intended and expected the ultimate extinction of that institution?

1

The "fraud" that Douglass condemns in line 13 of Passage 1 is best understood to be

A) the misrepresentation of recent voting statistics by Kansas officials.

B) the promotion of slavery in new states by an order of Congress.

C) the creation of a Kansas state constitution that promotes immoral behavior.

D) the adoption of a measure that is not wanted by a majority of Kansas voters.

CONTINUE

2

The author of Passage 2 would most likely interpret Passage 1 as

A) a "quibble in regard to words" (line 35).

B) a foreshadowing of slavery's "ultimate extinction" (line 45).

C) evidence of a discordant "new era" (line 50).

D) a condemnation of the "framers of the Constitution" (line 58).

3

As used in lines 10 and 11, "bound" most nearly means

A) obligated.

B) restricted.

C) forced.

D) secured.

4

The author of Passage 2 suggests that the idea that slavery would disappear was

A) articulated in the Constitution.

B) unpopular for many decades.

C) at one point almost universal.

D) misinterpreted by earlier politicians.

5

Which choice provides the best evidence for the answer to the previous question?

A) Lines 35-37 ("I know what . . . mean")

B) Lines 38-40 ("I am not . . . that")

C) Lines 52-55 ("The great . . . believe")

D) Lines 56-58 ("The adoption . . . itself")

6

As used in line 45, "ultimate" most nearly means

A) powerful.

B) eventual.

C) quintessential.

D) exaggerated.

7

What principles, respectively, are promoted by the author of Passage 1 and the author of Passage 2?

A) The acceptance of slavery as a permanent institution; the abolition of slavery as a moral necessity

B) Self-determination at the local level; elimination of injustice at the national level

C) Expansion into new territories; acceptance of America's present boundaries as final

D) Voting based primarily on economic self-interest; voting based primarily on party loyalty

8

The author of each passage presents himself as

A) a defender of state law as more important than federal law.

B) a supporter of a concerted movement for humanitarian reform.

C) an opponent of measures that would make slavery more prevalent.

D) a strict adherent to the principles laid out in the federal Constitution.

9

In Passage 2, Lincoln does which of the following in presenting his argument?

A) Sums up a specific viewpoint using rhetorical questions

B) Praises his opponent before offering a more assertive stance

C) Criticizes those who would attack him as uneducated

D) Acknowledges that his viewpoint has become a political liability

10

Which choice provides the best evidence for the answer to the previous question?

A) Lines 31-33 ("I am not . . . call it")

B) Lines 33-35 ("I do not . . . words")

C) Lines 49-51 ("I have always hated . . . began")

D) Lines 63-66 ("Why were . . . institution?")

CONTINUE

Questions 1-10 are based on the following passage.
2.09
Adapted from the English Edition of the *Communist Manifesto* (1888) by Karl Marx and Friedrich Engels. In Marx's terminology, the "bourgeoisie" is the materialistic middle class of society, while the "proletariat" is the working or laboring class that serves the bourgeoisie.

The history of all hitherto existing societies is the history of class struggles.

Freeman and slave, patrician and plebeian, lord and
Line serf, guild-master and journeyman, in a word, oppressor and
5　oppressed, stood in constant opposition to one another, carried on an uninterrupted, now hidden, now open fight, a fight that each time ended, either in a revolutionary re-constitution of society at large, or in the common ruin of the contending classes.

10　In the earlier epochs of history, we find almost everywhere a complicated arrangement of society into various orders, a manifold gradation of social rank. In ancient Rome we have patricians, knights, plebeians, slaves; in the Middle Ages, feudal lords, vassals, guild-masters, journeymen, apprentices, serfs; in
15　almost all of these classes, again, subordinate gradations.

The modern bourgeois society that has sprouted from the ruins of feudal society has not done away with class antagonisms. It has but established new classes, new conditions of oppression, new forms of struggle in place of the old ones.
20　Our epoch, the epoch of the bourgeoisie, possesses, however, this distinctive feature: it has simplified the class antagonisms. Society as a whole is more and more splitting up into two great hostile camps, into two great classes, directly facing each other: Bourgeoisie and Proletariat.
25　From the serfs of the Middle Ages sprang the chartered burghers of the earliest towns. From these burgesses the first elements of the bourgeoisie were developed.

The discovery of America, the rounding of the Cape, opened up fresh ground for the rising bourgeoisie. The East-
30　Indian and Chinese markets, the colonisation of America, trade with the colonies, the increase in the means of exchange and in commodities generally, gave to commerce, to navigation, to industry, an impulse never before known, and thereby, to the revolutionary element in the tottering feudal society, a rapid
35　development.

The feudal system of industry, under which industrial production was monopolised by closed guilds, now no longer sufficed for the growing wants of the new markets. The manufacturing system took its place. The guild-masters were
40　pushed on one side by the manufacturing middle class; division of labour between the different corporate guilds vanished in the face of division of labour in each single workshop.

Meantime the markets kept ever growing, the demand ever rising. Even manufacture no longer sufficed. Thereupon, steam
45　and machinery revolutionised industrial production. The place of manufacture was taken by the giant, Modern Industry, the place of the industrial middle class, by industrial millionaires, the leaders of whole industrial armies, the modern bourgeois.

Modern industry has established the world-market,
50　for which the discovery of America paved the way. This market has given an immense development to commerce, to navigation, to communication by land. This development has, in its time, reacted on the extension of industry; and in proportion as industry, commerce, navigation, railways
55　extended, in the same proportion the bourgeoisie developed, increased its capital, and pushed into the background every class handed down from the Middle Ages.

We see, therefore, how the modern bourgeoisie is itself the product of a long course of development, of a series of
60　revolutions in the modes of production and of exchange. . .

. . . The bourgeoisie, historically, has played a most revolutionary part.

The bourgeoisie, wherever it has got the upper hand, has put an end to all feudal, patriarchal, idyllic relations. It has
65　pitilessly torn asunder the motley feudal ties that bound man to his "natural superiors," and has left remaining no other nexus between man and man than naked self-interest, than callous "cash payment." It has drowned the most heavenly ecstasies of religious fervour, of chivalrous enthusiasm, of philistine
70　sentimentalism, in the icy water of egotistical calculation. It has resolved personal worth into exchange value, and in place of the numberless and indefeasible chartered freedoms, has set up that single, unconscionable freedom—Free Trade. In one word, for exploitation, veiled by religious and political illusions,
75　naked, shameless, direct, brutal exploitation.

1

Which statement best describes the developmental pattern of the passage?

A) A conflict is described, and attempts to permanently resolve that conflict are investigated.

B) A theory is formulated, and examples that could disprove that theory are assessed.

C) An improved state of society is imagined, and the factors that prevent that state from being attained are listed.

D) A principle is presented, and specific historical phenomena are linked to that principle.

CONTINUE

2

As used in line 8, "common" most nearly means

A) unremarkable.

B) majority-based.

C) mutual.

D) normal.

3

The information in lines 10-15 ("In the earlier . . . gradations") primarily serves to

A) present a scheme of organization that sets the context for Marx's later discussion.

B) show how the proletariat and bourgeoisie evolved from earlier social classes.

C) imply that earlier systems of organizing society were needlessly complicated.

D) indicate that the Middle Ages successfully emulated Rome's political system.

4

According to Marx, the bourgeoisie is notable for

A) oppressing the populations of newly-discovered lands.

B) treating successful businessmen as heroic figures.

C) relying on dishonest trade negotiations.

D) disrupting traditional forms of loyalty.

5

Which choice provides the best evidence for the answer to the previous question?

A) Lines 28-29 ("The discovery . . . bourgeoisie")

B) Lines 45-48 ("The place . . . bourgeois")

C) Lines 58-60 ("We see . . . exchange")

D) Lines 64-66 ("It has . . . superiors")

6

Which of the following, according to the passage, is a characteristic of the modern era?

A) The promotion of travel and infrastructure spending

B) The satisfactory resolution of most class conflicts

C) The creation of two classes that do not have any goals in common

D) A declining number of functioning religious institutions

7

Which choice provides the best evidence for the answer to the previous question?

A) Lines 16-18 ("The modern . . . antagonisms")

B) Lines 22-24 ("Society . . . Proletariat")

C) Lines 52-55 ("This development . . . extended")

D) Lines 68-70 ("It has drowned . . . calculation")

8

Which of the following developments does Marx link to the rise of the "manufacturing middle class" (line 40)?

A) The expansion of commerce well beyond Europe

B) The pursuit of greater profits by the guild-masters

C) A widespread decline in moral standards

D) A breakthrough in steam engine technology

9

In the final paragraph, what does Marx suggest about the relationship between the bourgeoisie and religion?

A) The bourgeoisie is forced to hide its own strong religious sentiments for the sake of material gain.

B) The bourgeoisie has often used traditional religious terminology to explain its new materialistic mentality.

C) The bourgeoisie is mostly indifferent to religion, but will manipulate religious notions for practical gain.

D) The bourgeoisie has found a way to promote public morals without promoting formal religion.

10

As used in lines 45 and 47, "place" most nearly means

A) function.

B) location.

C) assignment.

D) identity.

CONTINUE

Questions 1-10 are based on the following passage.
2.10
Adapted from *Our Androcentric Culture* (or *The Man-Made World*, first published in 1911) by Charlotte Perkins Gilman.

The origin of education is maternal. The mother animal is seen to teach her young what she knows of life, its gains and losses; and, whether consciously done or not, this is education.
Line In our human life, education, even in its present state, is the
5 most important process. Without it we could not maintain ourselves, much less dominate and improve conditions as we do; and when education is what it should be, our power will increase far beyond present hopes.

In lower animals, speaking generally, the powers of the
10 race must be lodged in each individual. No gain of personal experience is of avail to the others. No advantages remain, save those physically transmitted. The narrow limits of personal gain and personal inheritance rigidly hem in sub-human progress. With us, what one learns may be taught to the others. Our
15 life is social, collective. Our gain is for all, and profits us in proportion as we extend it to all. As the human soul develops in us, we become able to grasp more fully our common needs and advantages; and with this growth has come the extension of education to the people as a whole. Social functions are
20 developed under natural laws, like physical ones, and may be studied similarly.

In the evolution of this basic social function, what has been the effect of wholly masculine influence?

The original process, instruction of individual child by
25 individual mother, has been largely neglected in our man-made world. That was considered as a subsidiary sex-function of the woman, and as such, left to her "instinct." This is the main reason why we show such great progress in education for older children, and especially for youths, and so little comparatively
30 in that given to little ones.

We have had on the one side the natural current of maternal education, with its first assistant, the nursemaid, and its second, the "dame-school"; and on the other the influence of the dominant class, organized in university, college, and public
35 school, slowly filtering downward.

Educational forces are many. The child is born into certain conditions, physical and psychic, and "educated" thereby. He grows up into social, political and economic conditions, and is further modified by them. All these conditions, so far, have
40 been of androcentric character; but what we call education as a special social process is what the child is deliberately taught and subjected to; and it is here we may see the same dominant influence so clearly.

This conscious education was, for long, given to boys
45 alone, the girls being left to maternal influence, each to learn what her mother knew, and no more. This very clear instance of the masculine theory is glaring enough by itself to rest a case on. It shows how absolute was the assumption that the world was composed of men, and men alone were to be fitted for it.
50 Women were no part of the world, and needed no training for its uses. As females they were born and not made; as human beings they were only servants, trained as such by their servant mothers.

This system of education we are outgrowing more swiftly
55 with each year. The growing humanness of women, and its recognition, is forcing an equal education for boy and girl. When this demand was first made, by women of unusual calibre, and by men sufficiently human to overlook sex-prejudice, how was it met? What was the attitude of woman's
60 "natural protector" when she began to ask some share in human life?

Under the universal assumption that men alone were humanity, that the world was masculine and for men only, the efforts of the women were met as a deliberate attempt to
65 "unsex" themselves and become men. To be a woman was to be ignorant, uneducated; to be wise, educated, was to be a man. Women were not men, visibly; therefore they could not be educated, and ought not to want to be.

Under this androcentric prejudice, the equal extension
70 of education to women was opposed at every step, and is still opposed by many. Seeing in women only sex, and not humanness, they would confine her exclusively to feminine interests. This is the masculine view, par excellence. In spite of it, the human development of women, which so splendidly
75 characterizes our age, has gone on; and now both woman's colleges and those for both sexes offer "the higher education" to our girls, as well as the lower grades in school and kindergarten.

1

Over the course of the first two paragraphs (lines 1-21), Gilman shifts from

A) noting a parallel between humans and other animals to describing a distinction between humans and other animals.

B) outlining a recently-developed theory in the study of human culture to explaining why that theory cannot apply to the study of animals.

C) stating the presumed benefits of education to demonstrating why modern forms of education are so often counterproductive.

D) analyzing nurturing and maternal influences to arguing that masculine social norms completely undermine these influences.

CONTINUE

2

Gilman's main purpose in writing this passage is to

A) criticize specific groups of men who have questioned the value of women's education.

B) describe a series of practical improvements that are taking place in women's education.

C) persuade her audience to support a radical new proposal in women's education.

D) explain the origins of specific perceptions surrounding women and women's education.

3

With which of the following statements about the "masculine influence" (line 23) would Gilman most likely agree?

A) Its prevalence leads men to show little affection for the women in their families.

B) It is wrongly idealized by women and does not have any useful social functions.

C) Its negative effects have not prevented women from making measurable progress.

D) It is a fallacy promoted mainly by those who wish to limit opportunities for women.

4

Which choice provides the best evidence for the answer to the previous question?

A) Lines 24-26 ("The original . . . world")

B) Lines 44-46 ("This conscious . . . more")

C) Lines 62-65 ("Under the universal . . . men")

D) Lines 74-78 ("the human . . . kindergarten")

5

Which of the following, according to Gilman, was traditionally regarded as a defining characteristic of women?

A) Spirituality

B) Obedience

C) Practicality

D) Impulsiveness

6

As used in line 9, "lower" most nearly means

A) shorter.

B) humbler.

C) less advanced.

D) less rebellious.

7

As used in line 57, "unusual" most nearly means

A) remarkable.

B) outlandish.

C) idiosyncratic.

D) puzzling.

8

According to Gilman, "equal education for boy and girl" (line 56) is

A) a radical departure from earlier practices.

B) an idea supported by new social research.

C) a reform supported mainly by influential men.

D) a foreshadowing of even greater progress for women.

9

Overall, Gilman understands education as

A) segregated on the basis of both class and gender.

B) not purely reliant on formal institutions.

C) a reliable route to respect and prosperity.

D) a means of inhibiting women's progress.

10

Which choice provides the best evidence for the answer to the previous question?

A) Lines 14-16 ("With us, what . . . to all")

B) Lines 36-37 ("Educational . . . thereby")

C) Lines 54-56 ("This system . . . and girl")

D) Lines 69-71 ("Under this . . . many")

CONTINUE

Questions 1-10 are based on the following passage.
2.11
Adapted from Susan B. Anthony, "Women's Right to the Suffrage" (1873).

Friends and fellow citizens: I stand before you tonight under indictment for the alleged crime of having voted at the last presidential election, without having a lawful right to vote.
Line It shall be my work this evening to prove to you that in thus
5 voting, I not only committed no crime, but, instead, simply exercised my citizen's rights, guaranteed to me and all United States citizens by the National Constitution, beyond the power of any state to deny.

The preamble of the Federal Constitution says:
10 "We, the people of the United States, in order to form a more perfect union, establish justice, insure domestic tranquillity, provide for the common defense, promote the general welfare, and secure the blessings of liberty to ourselves and our posterity, do ordain and establish this Constitution for
15 the United States of America."

It was we, the people; not we, the white male citizens; nor yet we, the male citizens; but we, the whole people, who formed the Union. And we formed it, not to give the blessings of liberty, but to secure them; not to the half of ourselves and
20 the half of our posterity, but to the whole people—women as well as men. And it is a downright mockery to talk to women of their enjoyment of the blessings of liberty while they are denied the use of the only means of securing them provided by this democratic-republican government—the ballot.
25 For any state to make sex a qualification that must ever result in the disfranchisement of one entire half of the people, is to pass a bill of attainder, or, an ex post facto law, and is therefore a violation of the supreme law of the land. By it the blessings of liberty are forever withheld from women and their
30 female posterity.

To them this government has no just powers derived from the consent of the governed. To them this government is not a democracy. It is not a republic. It is an odious aristocracy; a hateful oligarchy of sex; the most hateful aristocracy ever
35 established on the face of the globe; an oligarchy of wealth, where the rich govern the poor. An oligarchy of learning, where the educated govern the ignorant, or even an oligarchy of race, where the Saxon rules the African, might be endured; but this oligarchy of sex, which makes father, brothers, husband,
40 sons, the oligarchs over the mother and sisters, the wife and daughters, of every household—which ordains all men sovereigns, all women subjects, carries dissension, discord, and rebellion into every home of the nation.

Webster, Worcester, and Bouvier* all define a citizen to be
45 a person in the United States, entitled to vote and hold office.

The only question left to be settled now is: Are women persons? And I hardly believe any of our opponents will have the hardihood to say they are not. Being persons, then, women are citizens; and no state has a right to make any law, or to
50 enforce any old law, that shall abridge their privileges or immunities. Hence, every discrimination against women in the constitutions and laws of the several states is today null and void, precisely as is every one against Americans of African heritage.

* Three dictionaries that would be familiar to audiences of Anthony's era

---

1

In line 2, Anthony uses the word "alleged" to suggest that

A) she is not fully aware of the laws surrounding women's suffrage.

B) she has faced widespread criticism for her actions.

C) her actions have not been officially documented.

D) her actions should not be interpreted as unlawful.

2

As used in line 6, "exercised" most nearly means

A) strengthened.

B) invigorated.

C) utilized.

D) agitated.

3

In lines 10-24 ("We, the people . . . ballot"), Anthony transitions from

A) praising the writers of the Constitution to condemning the politicians of her own era.

B) presenting an ideal state of society to encouraging women to make that ideal a reality.

C) citing a set of national principles to explaining how those principles are being transgressed.

D) quoting an important American document to urging a dramatic revision to that document.

4

As used in line 46, "settled" most nearly means

A) pacified.

B) evened out.

C) resolved.

D) nullified.

CONTINUE

5

Anthony uses which of the following devices in her discussion of the oppression of women in the United States?

A) Extended analysis of the virtues and intellectual capacities of women

B) Comparison to other forms of society that are premised on inequality

C) Refutation of an unflattering stereotype

D) A concession to opponents of women's suffrage

6

Which choice provides the best evidence for the answer to the previous question?

A) Lines 5-8 ("I not only . . . deny")

B) Lines 21-24 ("And it is . . . ballot")

C) Lines 33-36 ("It is an . . . poor")

D) Lines 46-48 ("The only . . . are not")

7

Anthony considers the answer to the "question" in lines 46-47 to be

A) controversial.

B) complex.

C) obvious.

D) boring.

8

According to Anthony, instituting inequality between men and women is dangerous because it can lead to

A) tension and conflict in everyday domestic life.

B) criticism from nations otherwise friendly to America.

C) discrimination based on race.

D) discrimination based on class and education.

9

With which statement about African-Americans would Anthony most likely agree?

A) They should be allowed to enjoy voting rights and civil rights alongside women.

B) The Federal Constitution must be altered in order to fully protect their civil rights.

C) There is an ongoing controversy as to whether they are defined as citizens.

D) Their rights have been promoted in a manner that undermines women's rights.

10

Which choice provides the best evidence for the answer to the previous question?

A) Lines 16-18 ("It was we . . . Union")

B) Lines 36-38 ("An oligarchy . . . endured")

C) Lines 44-45 ("Webster . . . office")

D) Lines 51-54 ("Hence, every . . . heritage")

CONTINUE

Questions 1-10 are based on the following passage.
2.12

This reading is adapted from The *Red Cross in Peace and War* by Clara Barton (1898). Here, Barton offers an excerpt from an 1881 address in which she urged the creation of Red Cross emergency relief societies in the United States.

In attempting to present to the people of this country the plan of the Red Cross societies, it is proper to explain that originally and as operating in other countries these
Line societies recognize only the miseries arising from war. Their
5 humanities, although immense, are confined to this war centre. The treaty does not cover more than this, but the resolutions for the establishment of societies under the treaty, permit them to organize in accordance with the spirit and needs of their nationalities. By our geographical position and isolation
10 we are far less liable to the disturbances of war than the nations of Europe, which are so frequently called upon that they do well to keep in readiness for the exigencies of war alone. But no country is more liable than our own to great overmastering calamities, various, widespread and terrible.
15 Seldom a year passes that the nation from sea to sea is not, by the shock of some sudden, unforeseen disaster, brought to utter consternation, and stands shivering like a ship in a gale, powerless, horrified, and despairing. Plagues, cholera, fires, flood, famine, all bear upon us with terrible force. Like war
20 these events are entirely out of the common course of woes and necessities. Like death they are sure to come in some form and at some time, and like it no mortal knows where, how or when.

What have we in readiness to meet these emergencies save
25 the good heart of our people and their impulsive, generous gifts? Certainly no organized system for collection, reception nor distribution; no agents, nurses nor material, and, worst of all, no funds; nowhere any resources in *reserve* for use in such an hour of peril and national woe; every movement crude,
30 confused and unsystematized, every thing as unprepared as if we had never known a calamity before and had no reason to expect one again.

Meanwhile the suffering victims wait! True, in the shock we bestow most generously, lavishly even. Men "on Change"
35 plunge their hands into their pockets and throw their gold to strangers, who may have neither preparation nor fitness for the work they undertake, and often no guaranty for honesty. Women, in the terror and excitement of the moment and in their eagerness to aid, beg in the streets and rush into fairs,
40 working day and night, to the neglect of other duties in the present, and at the peril of all health in the future—often an enormous outlay for very meagre returns. Thus our gifts fall far short of their best, being hastily bestowed, irresponsibly received and wastefully applied. We should not, even if to

45 some degree we might, depend upon our ordinary charitable and church societies to meet these great catastrophes; they are always overtaxed. Our communities abound in charitable societies, but each has its specific object to which its resources are and must be applied; consequently they cannot
50 be relied upon for prompt and abundant aid in a great and sudden emergency. This must necessarily be the case with all societies which organize to work for a specific charity. And this is as it should be; it is enough that they do constantly bestow.
55 Charity bears an open palm, to give is her mission. But I have never classed these Red Cross societies with charities, I have rather considered them as a wise national provision which seeks to garner and store up something against an hour of sudden need. In all our land we have not one
60 organization of this nature and which acts upon the system of conserved resources. Our people have been more wise and thoughtful in the establishment of means for preventing and arresting the destruction of property than the destruction of human life and the lessening of consequent suffering.
65 They have provided and maintain at an immense cost, in the aggregate, a system of fire departments with their expensive buildings and apparatus, with their fine horses and strong men kept constantly in readiness to dash to the rescue at the first dread clang of the fire bell. Still, while the electric
70 current may flash upon us at any moment its ill tidings of some great human distress, we have no means of relief in readiness such as these Red Cross societies would furnish.

1

The contrast between Europe and America that Barton establishes is premised on the different types of

A) ideologies that are popular in these regions.
B) diseases that proliferate in these regions.
C) governments that prevail in these regions.
D) disasters that are likely in these regions.

2

As used in line 26, "system" most nearly means

A) set of procedures.
B) code of beliefs.
C) theoretical explanation.
D) grand bureaucracy.

CONTINUE

3

As used in line 48, "object" most nearly means

A) obstacle.

B) goal.

C) possession.

D) device.

4

Which of the following best describes the developmental structure of the second and third paragraphs (lines 24-54)?

A) A general deficiency is indicated and flawed approaches are outlined.

B) A dilemma is explained and a new measure is described at great length.

C) An idealistic perspective is depicted and its advantages are elaborated.

D) A defunct institution is explained and its reasons for failure are put in perspective.

5

Which of the following best describes the main purpose of the passage?

A) To describe American society using a series of ironies.

B) To imply that existing institutions should replaced.

C) To offer a specific solution to a broad national problem.

D) To explain why the United States is not threatened by war.

6

According to Barton, relief efforts in the United States have tended to be

A) promising.

B) poorly publicized.

C) innovative.

D) inept.

7

Which choice provides the best evidence for the answer to the previous question?

A) Lines 9-13 ("By our geographical . . . alone")

B) Lines 29-32 ("every movement . . . again")

C) Lines 47-49 ("Our communities . . . applied")

D) Line 55 ("Charity . . . mission")

8

Barton uses the image of an "electric current" (lines 69-70) to suggest

A) the moral vigor of the Red Cross societies.

B) the enormous public response to even distant tragedies.

C) the suddenness with which calamity can strike.

D) the high efficiency of most modern fire departments.

9

It can be reasonably inferred that the Red Cross societies proposed by Barton for the United States are

A) unprecedented.

B) impractical.

C) much-anticipated.

D) controversial.

10

Which choice provides the best evidence for the answer to the previous question?

A) Lines 6-9 ("The treaty . . . nationalities")

B) Lines 19-23 ("Like war . . . or when")

C) Lines 59-61 ("In all our . . . resources")

D) Lines 61-64 ("Our people . . . suffering")

CONTINUE

Questions 1-10 are based on the following passages.
2.13
Passage 1 is adapted from *Random Reminiscences of Men and Events* (1909) by John D. Rockefeller; Passage 2 is adapted from *How the Other Half Lives: Studies Among the Tenements of New York* (1890) by Jacob Riis.

Passage 1

The best philanthropy, the help that does the most good and the least harm, the help that nourishes civilization at its very root, that most widely disseminates health, righteousness,
Line and happiness, is not what is usually called charity. It is, in my
5 judgment, the investment of effort or time or money, carefully considered with relation to the power of employing people at a remunerative wage, to expand and develop the resources at hand, and to give opportunity for progress and healthful labour where it did not exist before. No mere money-giving is
10 comparable to this in its lasting and beneficial results.

If, as I am accustomed to think, this statement is a correct one, how vast indeed is the philanthropic field! It may be urged that the daily vocation of life is one thing, and the work of philanthropy quite another. I have no sympathy with this
15 notion. The man who plans to do all his giving on Sunday is a poor prop for the institutions of the country.

The excuse for referring so often to the busy man of affairs is that his help is most needed. I know of men who have followed out this large plan of developing work, not as
20 a temporary matter, but as a permanent principle. These men have taken up doubtful enterprises and carried them through to success often at great risk, and in the face of great scepticism, not as a matter only of personal profit, but in the larger spirit of general uplift.

Passage 2

25 The practical question is what to do with the tenement. I watched a Mott Street landlord, the owner of a row of barracks that have made no end of trouble for the health authorities for twenty years, solve that question for himself the other day. His way was to give the wretched pile a coat of paint, and
30 put a gorgeous tin cornice on with the year 1890 in letters a yard long. From where I stood watching the operation, I looked down upon the same dirty crowds camping on the roof, foremost among them an Italian mother with two stark-naked children who had apparently never made the acquaintance of a
35 wash-tub. That was a landlord's way, and will not get us out of the mire.

The "flat" is another way that does not solve the problem. Rather, it extends it. The flat is not a model, though it is a modern, tenement. It gets rid of some of the nuisances of the
40 low tenement, and of the worst of them, the overcrowding—if it gets rid of them at all—at a cost that takes it at once out of the catalogue of "homes for the poor," while imposing some of the evils from which they suffer upon those who ought to escape from them.

45 There are three effective ways of dealing with the tenements in New York:

I. By law.
II. By remodelling and making the most out of the old houses.
50 III. By building new, model tenements.

Private enterprise—conscience, to put it in the category of duties, where it belongs—must do the lion's share under these last two heads. Of what the law has effected I have spoken already. The drastic measures adopted in
55 Paris, in Glasgow, and in London are not practicable here on anything like as large a scale. Still it can, under strong pressure of public opinion, rid us of the worst plague-spots. The Mulberry Street Bend will go the way of the Five Points when all the red tape that binds the hands of
60 municipal effort has been unwound. Prizes were offered in public competition, some years ago, for the best plans of modern tenement-houses. It may be that we shall see the day when the building of model tenements will be encouraged by subsidies in the way of a rebate of taxes. Meanwhile
65 the arrest and summary punishment of landlords, or their agents, who persistently violate law and decency, will have a salutary effect. If a few of the wealthy absentee landlords, who are the worst offenders, could be got within the jurisdiction of the city, and by arrest be compelled to employ
70 proper overseers, it would be a proud day for New York.

1

As used in line 5, "judgment" most nearly means

A) accusation.
B) carefulness.
C) cleverness.
D) assessment.

2

In Passage 1, Rockefeller argues that effective philanthropy is

A) inseparable from day-to-day considerations.
B) indistinguishable from acts of charitable giving.
C) almost entirely due to the activity of the wealthy.
D) exciting but widely misunderstood.

CONTINUE

3

Which choice provides the best evidence for the answer to the previous question?

A) Lines 1-4 ("The best . . . charity")

B) Lines 11-12 ("If, as I am . . . field!")

C) Lines 12-15 ("It may be . . . notion")

D) Lines 17-18 ("The excuse . . . needed")

4

In analyzing philanthropy efforts, the two passages differ in that Passage 1

A) analyzes the general causes of poverty, while Passage 2 depicts the effect of poverty on a single city.

B) calls for new political measures, while Passage 2 attests that legal and legislative action are ineffectual.

C) raises the possibility of creating employment, while Passage 2 focuses on basic living necessities.

D) praises powerful and industrious Americans, while Passage 2 argues that the wealthy only worsen the condition of the poor.

5

According to Passage 2, it is difficult to hold some tenement owners accountable because they

A) hold important government positions.

B) live far from the tenement jurisdictions.

C) have earned the loyalty of their tenants.

D) use bribes to avoid legal penalties.

6

Which choice provides the best evidence for the answer to the previous question?

A) Lines 29-31 ("His way . . . long")

B) Lines 56-58 ("Still it can . . . spots")

C) Lines 62-64 ("It may be . . . taxes")

D) Lines 67-70 ("If a few . . . New York")

7

Unlike Rockefeller in Passage 1, Riis in Passage 2 builds his argument by presenting

A) a statistical survey.

B) a series of faulty assumptions.

C) a broad recommendation.

D) a personal anecdote.

8

In Passage 2, Riis indicates that a practical approach to American tenement reform

A) cannot emulate foreign models.

B) will involve wealth redistribution.

C) should use the "flat" model as a starting point.

D) is underway outside New York.

9

As used in line 59, "binds" most nearly means

A) gathers.

B) restricts.

C) creates affection among.

D) exhibits loyalty to.

10

The authors of the two passages would be in clear agreement that

A) those who have prospered should actively help the disadvantaged.

B) better education can be used to combat a variety of social problems.

C) initiatives that improve job conditions can address the broader problem of poverty.

D) the greatest form of suffering in poor communities is the unsanitary lifestyle of their inhabitants.

CONTINUE

Questions 1-10 are based on the following passage.
2.14

Adapted from *Hero Tales from American History* (1895), co-authored by Henry Cabot Lodge and Theodore Roosevelt.

To understand George Washington at all we must first strip off all the myths which have gathered about him. We must cast aside into the dust-heaps all the wretched inventions
Line of the cherry-tree variety, which were fastened upon him
5 nearly seventy years after his birth. We must look at him as he looked at life and the facts about him, without any illusion or deception . . .

Washington did not refuse the opportunity to take control of the country, because he feared heavy responsibility, but
10 solely because, as a high-minded and patriotic man, he did not believe in meeting the situation in that way. He was, moreover, entirely devoid of personal ambition, and had no vulgar longing for personal power. After resigning his commission once the Revolution had run its course he returned quietly to
15 Mount Vernon, but he did not hold himself aloof from public affairs. On the contrary, he watched their course with the utmost anxiety. He saw the feeble Confederation breaking to pieces, and he soon realized that that form of government was an utter failure. In a time when no American statesman
20 except Hamilton had yet freed himself from the local feelings of the colonial days, Washington was thoroughly national in all his views. Out of the thirteen jarring colonies he meant that a nation should come, and he saw—what no one else saw—the destiny of the country to the westward. He wished
25 a nation founded which should cross the Alleghanies, and, holding the mouths of the Mississippi, take possession of all that vast and then unknown region. For these reasons he stood at the head of the national movement, and to him all men turned who desired a better union and sought to bring order
30 out of chaos. With him Hamilton and Madison consulted in the preliminary stages which were to lead to the formation of a new system. It was his vast personal influence which made that movement a success, and when the convention to form a constitution met at Philadelphia, he presided over its
35 deliberations, and it was his commanding will which, more than anything else, brought a constitution through difficulties and conflicting interests which more than once made any result seem well-nigh hopeless. When the Constitution formed at Philadelphia had been ratified by the States, all men turned to
40 Washington to stand at the head of the new government. As he had borne the burden of the Revolution, so he now took up the task of bringing the government of the Constitution into existence. For eight years he served as president. He came into office with a paper constitution, the heir of a bankrupt,
45 broken-down confederation. He left the United States, when he went out of office, an effective and vigorous government.

When he was inaugurated, we had nothing but the clauses of the Constitution as agreed to by the Convention. When he laid down the presidency, we had an organized government,
50 an established revenue, a funded debt, a high credit, an efficient system of banking, a strong judiciary, and an army. We had a vigorous and well-defined foreign policy; we had recovered the western posts, which, in the hands of the British, had fettered our march to the west; and we
55 had proved our power to maintain order at home, to repress insurrection, to collect the national taxes, and to enforce the laws made by Congress. Thus Washington had shown that rare combination of the leader who could first destroy by revolution, and who, having led his country through a great
60 civil war, was then able to build up a new and lasting fabric upon the ruins of a system which had been overthrown. . .

Washington stands among the greatest men of human history, and those in the same rank with him are very few. Whether measured by what he did, or what he was, or
65 by the effect of his work upon the history of mankind, in every aspect he is entitled to the place he holds among the greatest of his race. Few men in all time have such a record of achievement. Still fewer can show at the end of a career so crowded with high deeds and memorable victories a life
70 so free from spot, a character so unselfish and so pure, a fame so void of doubtful points demanding either defense or explanation.

1

The authors point out the "myths" (line 2) that are associated with Washington in order to

A) introduce a method that will improve how biographies are written.

B) suggest that Washington's popularity is explained mostly by popular delusions.

C) criticize earlier ideas and introduce their own project.

D) summarize the views of Washington's peers.

2

As used in line 28, "movement" most nearly means

A) uprising.

B) initiative.

C) pilgrimage.

D) retreat.

CONTINUE

3

The main purpose of the passage is to

A) explain how the American statesmen of a new era can fulfill the high moral standards set by Washington.

B) demonstrate why few statesmen have attained Washington's level of renown.

C) argue that strengthening and expanding the federal government is the best course for a struggling nation.

D) clarify Washington's pivotal role in the formation of the early United States government.

4

In the development of the passage as a whole, the second paragraph (lines 8-61) is important mainly because it presents

A) biography combined with analysis.

B) chronology combined with speculation.

C) a critique of Washington's successors.

D) a description of Washington's personal life.

5

According to the passage, Washington was motivated to re-enter public life by

A) personal ambitions.

B) deep-seated concerns.

C) respect for his peers.

D) patriotic idealism.

6

According to the passage, Washington's virtues were

A) multi-faceted and for the most part unparalleled.

B) the product of his belief in settling new territory.

C) unexpected in a former military leader.

D) only capable of finding expression within a democratic society.

7

Which choice provides the best evidence for the answer to the previous question?

A) Lines 8-11 ("Washington did . . . that way")

B) Lines 24-27 ("He wished . . . region")

C) Lines 40-43 ("As he had . . . existence")

D) Lines 64-67 ("Whether measured . . . race")

8

As used in line 60, "fabric" most nearly means

A) commodity.

B) textile.

C) way of life.

D) means of protection.

9

As described in the passage, Washington and Hamilton are similar in that both of these men

A) mentored Madison and promoted his career.

B) were proponents of westward expansion.

C) were popular and often-mythologized leaders.

D) prioritized federal over regional interests.

10

Which choice provides the best evidence for the answer to the previous question?

A) Lines 19-22 ("In a time . . . views")

B) Lines 22-24 ("Out of the . . . westward")

C) Lines 27-30 ("For these . . . chaos")

D) Lines 30-32 ("With him . . . system")

CONTINUE

Questions 1-10 are based on the following passage.
2.15

Adapted from *The Souls of Black Folk* (1903) by African-American author and activist W.E.B. Du Bois.

The problem of the twentieth century is the problem of the color-line—the relation of the darker to the lighter races of men in Asia and Africa, in America and the islands of the sea.
Line It was a phase of this problem that caused the Civil War; and
5 however much they who marched South and North in 1861 may have fixed on the technical points, of union and local autonomy, all nevertheless knew, as we know, that the question of Negro slavery was the real cause of the conflict. Curious it was, too, how this deeper question ever forced itself to the
10 surface despite effort and disclaimer. No sooner had Northern armies touched Southern soil than this old question, newly guised, sprang from the earth,—What shall be done with Negroes? Peremptory military commands this way and that, could not answer the query; the Emancipation Proclamation
15 seemed but to broaden and intensify the difficulties; and the War Amendments made the Negro problems of today.

It is the aim of this essay to study the period of history from 1861 to 1872 so far as it relates to the American Negro. In effect, this tale of the dawn of Freedom is an account of
20 that government of men called the Freedmen's Bureau,—one of the most singular and interesting of the attempts made by a great nation to grapple with vast problems of race and social condition.

The war has naught to do with slaves, cried Congress,
25 the President, and the Nation; and yet no sooner had the armies, East and West, penetrated Virginia and Tennessee than fugitive slaves appeared within their lines. They came at night, when the flickering camp-fires shone like vast unsteady stars along the black horizon: old men and thin, with
30 gray and tufted hair; women with frightened eyes, dragging whimpering hungry children; men and girls, stalwart and gaunt,—a horde of starving vagabonds, homeless, helpless, and pitiable, in their dark distress. Two methods of treating these newcomers seemed equally logical to opposite sorts
35 of minds. Ben Butler, in Virginia, quickly declared slave property contraband of war, and put the fugitives to work; while Fremont, in Missouri, declared the slaves free under martial law. Butler's action was approved, but Fremont's was hastily countermanded, and his successor, Halleck, saw things
40 differently. "Hereafter," he commanded, "no slaves should be allowed to come into your lines at all; if any come without your knowledge, when owners call for them deliver them." Such a policy was difficult to enforce; some of the black refugees declared themselves freemen, others showed that their
45 masters had deserted them, and still others were captured with forts and plantations. Evidently, too, slaves were a source of strength to the Confederacy, and were being used as laborers

and producers. "They constitute a military resource," wrote Secretary Cameron, late in 1861; "and being such, that
50 they should not be turned over to the enemy is too plain to discuss." So gradually the tone of the army chiefs changed; Congress forbade the rendition of fugitives, and Butler's "contrabands" were welcomed as military laborers. This complicated rather than solved the problem, for now the
55 scattering fugitives became a steady stream, which flowed faster as the armies marched.

Then the long-headed man with care-chiselled face who sat in the White House saw the inevitable, and emancipated the slaves of rebels on New Year's, 1863. A month later
60 Congress called earnestly for the Negro soldiers whom the act of July, 1862, had half grudgingly allowed to enlist. Thus the barriers were levelled and the deed was done. The stream of fugitives swelled to a flood, and anxious army officers kept inquiring: "What must be done with slaves, arriving
65 almost daily? Are we to find food and shelter for women and children?"

. . . This much all men know: despite compromise, war, and struggle, the Negro is not free. In the backwoods of the Gulf States, for miles and miles, he may not leave the
70 plantation of his birth; in well-nigh the whole rural South the black farmers are peons, bound by law and custom to an economic slavery, from which the only escape is death or the penitentiary. In the most cultured sections and cities of the South the Negroes are a segregated servile caste, with
75 restricted rights and privileges. Before the courts, both in law and custom, they stand on a different and peculiar basis. Taxation without representation is the rule of their political life.

1

As used in line 6, "fixed on" most nearly means

A) attached.
B) emphasized.
C) repaired.
D) embellished.

2

It can be inferred that Du Bois would respond to the idea that "The war has naught to do with slaves" (line 24) with

A) unabashed mockery.
B) measured skepticism.
C) respectful tolerance.
D) vigorous disagreement.

CONTINUE

3

Which choice provides the best evidence for the answer to the previous question?

A) Lines 7-8 ("all nevertheless . . . the conflict")

B) Lines 13-16 ("Peremptory . . . today")

C) Lines 33-35 ("Two methods . . . minds")

D) Lines 53-56 ("This complicated . . . marched")

4

In describing fugitive slaves, Du Bois calls attention primarily to their

A) bravery and endurance.

B) secrecy and calculation.

C) desperation and poverty.

D) exhaustion and distrust.

5

According to Du Bois, the conditions faced by the African Americans of his own era

A) are disturbingly similar to the conditions faced by slaves.

B) can only be improved through legal and political reform.

C) are slowly being improved by organizations modeled on the Freedmen's Bureau.

D) have been neglected by all but a few American scholars.

6

Which choice provides the best evidence for the answer to the previous question?

A) Lines 1-3 ("The problem . . . the sea")

B) Lines 19-23 ("In effect . . . condition")

C) Lines 68-73 ("In the backwoods . . . penitentiary")

D) Lines 75-78 ("Before the . . . life")

7

The passage suggests that the Northern army decided not to return fugitive slaves primarily for what reason?

A) Slavery was regarded as unjust by the soldiers.

B) Returning escaped slaves was complicated and time-consuming.

C) Fugitive slaves possessed knowledge of Southern terrain and tactics.

D) Returned fugitive slaves could help the Southern war effort.

8

The "policy" mentioned in line 43 could not be effectively enforced because it

A) was strongly opposed on moral grounds by Ben Butler.

B) led to a rebellion among the fugitive slaves.

C) did not account for the different circumstances of the fugitive slaves.

D) required an enormous amount of planning and manpower to be put into practice.

9

One of the main problems that Du Bois addresses is that

A) even momentous efforts to aid African Americans have had unsatisfactory results.

B) the history of American military policy is not well understood.

C) African Americans have made greater social progress than is widely believed.

D) welfare and enrichment programs that benefit African Americans are being rapidly eliminated.

10

As used in line 50, "plain" most nearly means

A) disciplined.

B) austere.

C) evident.

D) honest.

Answer Key on Next Page

Answer Key: CHAPTER TWO

SAT

2.01	2.02	2.03	2.04	2.05
1. C	1. D	1. D	1. D	1. A
2. C	2. A	2. C	2. A	2. C
3. B	3. D	3. B	3. D	3. A
4. B	4. D	4. A	4. A	4. C
5. A	5. B	5. A	5. D	5. B
6. A	6. A	6. C	6. D	6. A
7. B	7. C	7. B	7. C	7. C
8. C	8. D	8. B	8. C	8. D
9. B	9. A	9. A	9. B	9. A
10. A	10. D	10. D	10. B	10. B

2.06	2.07	2.08	2.09	2.10
1. A	1. A	1. D	1. D	1. A
2. C	2. A	2. C	2. C	2. D
3. A	3. A	3. A	3. A	3. C
4. D	4. C	4. C	4. D	4. D
5. B	5. B	5. C	5. D	5. B
6. A	6. C	6. B	6. A	6. C
7. D	7. D	7. B	7. C	7. A
8. A	8. C	8. C	8. A	8. A
9. D	9. B	9. A	9. C	9. B
10. C	10. B	10. D	10. A	10. B

2.11	2.12	2.13	2.14	2.15
1. D	1. D	1. D	1. C	1. B
2. C	2. A	2. A	2. B	2. D
3. C	3. B	3. C	3. D	3. A
4. C	4. A	4. C	4. A	4. C
5. B	5. C	5. B	5. B	5. A
6. C	6. D	6. D	6. A	6. C
7. C	7. B	7. D	7. D	7. D
8. A	8. C	8. A	8. C	8. C
9. A	9. A	9. B	9. D	9. A
10. D	10. C	10. A	10. A	10. C

Answer Explanations

Chapter 02 | Emerging Democracy

2.01 | Anna Laetitia Barbauld

1) CORRECT ANSWER: C
In lines 12-15, Barbauld explains that "national religion" is a quality of regard and guidance "extending to those affairs in which we act in common": it is not an actual form of religion, but a spirit of devotion and moral principle that extends to public life. C is thus the best answer. Although Barbauld does criticize some societies and individuals, she does not state that national religion is a rarity OVERALL (eliminating A). National religion is also separable from religious customs, with which it can coexist (and is not really a replacement for them, eliminating B), and, as a form of morality in public life, should guide responses to international affairs (eliminating D).

2) CORRECT ANSWER: C
See above for the explanation of the correct answer. A presents an assumption a reader might make (not an idea of Barbauld's own), B describes what a national religion is not (but does NOT offer a direct definition), and D describes how the vices of states may be understood, but does not address the topic of national religion.

3) CORRECT ANSWER: B
The word "affairs" refers to instances in which the members of society "act in common and as a body" (lines 13-14): these affairs involve the positive public spirit of "national religion". B, "situations", is an appropriate choice for describing such specific instances: A, however, wrongly introduces a negative, since a few types of "intrigues" are often "scandals" and "conspiracies". C (which assumes that people are negotiating, rather than simply AGREEING) and D (which introduces the topic of business) are both out of context.

4) CORRECT ANSWER: B
In the relevant lines, Barbauld explains that individuals are kind to their neighbors but aggressive in political matters: for instance, people who would never think of plundering "a private dwelling" (line 23) would not object to "joining with a confederacy of princes to plunder a province" (lines 24-25). This information supports B and can be used to eliminate C (since the people in fact RESPECT local property rights) and D (since the people are more aggressive on account of MAJOR political movements). A is a trap answer: Barbauld is only interested in what people DO in practical terms, not in whether they SEE themselves as patriotic or not.

5) CORRECT ANSWER: A
In lines 31-35, Barbauld notes that the proper conduct (or national religion) in certain states is "very much assisted" by the contemplation of "pains and penalties": in other

words, fear of repercussions causes people to act properly. A is thus the best answer, while C and D name positive influences and are contradicted by the idea that fear of NEGATIVES is most important. B is a trap answer: Barbauld discusses the general virtue of national religion, not ACTUAL religion, in relation to social wrongs.

6) CORRECT ANSWER: A

See above for the explanation of the correct answer. B indicates that religious traditions are not compatible with true morality, and C and D both speak of the benefits of a mild and stable government. While B raises strong negatives, none of these answers directly address the topic of how to avoid social wrongs as demanded by the previous question.

7) CORRECT ANSWER: B

Barbauld notes that "good government is the first of national duties" (line 59) and warns against the "indolent and passive happiness" (line 64) that can undermine good government over time; instead, people must act to preserve and maintain good governments. These ideas align with B, while Barbauld does not provide sufficient information for C: she is convinced that good government must be maintained, but HOW to maintain it is never precisely defined. A distorts the emphasis of the passage (avoiding social wrongdoing, not reporting wrongdoing AFTER it has been committed), while D distorts one of Barbauld's arguments (that actual religion can coexist with national religion, NOT that religious rituals must be replaced).

8) CORRECT ANSWER: C

The word "mild" describes a particular type of "government" (line 54): the happiness of living under this government is like "the happiness of living under an indulgent climate" (line 55). C is thus an effective answer, since such a government does not harm its people. A describes a level of complexity (not a positive effect), B is wrongly negative, and D would best refer to a person or a relationship, not to a government.

9) CORRECT ANSWER: B

In the final paragraph, Barbauld argues that "a people born under a good government, will probably not die under one" (lines 62-63) unless they actively work to keep their government just: in other words, because a good government needs such purposeful maintenance, it is fragile, uncertain, or precarious. This information supports B and can be used to eliminate A (which states the opposite) and C (since Barbauld has in fact defined good government and how it works throughout the passage). D is a trap answer: people may not successfully maintain good government, but to assume that they do not VALUE good government would be incorrect.

10) CORRECT ANSWER: A

In presenting the idea of "national religion", Barbauld draws a distinction between this idea and traditional religious practices (lines 6-15); she then goes on to explain distinctions between how members of the public act "As private individuals" (line 25) and "as a people" (line 26). This information supports A, while Barbauld's focus on the broadly applicable principle of national religion (not on narratives or her own stage of history) can be used to eliminate C and D. B is a trap answer: in endorsing "national religion", Barbauld recommends specific ATTITUDE, not a series of practical REFORMS that would change how government is structured.

2.02 | Benjamin Franklin and Thomas Paine

1) CORRECT ANSWER: D
While Passage 1 argues that "Freedom of speech is a pillar of free government" (lines 1-2) and goes on to consider both an "evil magistrate" (line 15) and a Roman "law" (line 23) against libel, Passage 2 mainly considers "the licentiousness of the press" (line 37) and the practices "common with printers" (line 53). This information supports D and can be used to eliminate A, since Passage 1 considers history and Passage 2 considers the author's own life. B is inaccurate because Passage 2, though often negative, argues that the character of a country for either good or bad can be ascertained "from the character of its press" (lines 49-50): it is possible that a good nation will exhibit good uses of freedom of speech. C is inaccurate because Passage 1 considers freedom of the press in relation to HISTORY, not in relation to the foreign affairs of the writer's own time.

2) CORRECT ANSWER: A
The word "constitution" refers to a feature of a free society that is "dissolved" (line 3) when the important "support" (line 2) of free speech is taken away: a constitution in this case is thus a fundamental condition, or foundation. A is the best answer, while B refers to a literal government document (not to a broad social condition), C refers to a shape or a process of evolution, and D would only be appropriate to organisms, not to governments.

3) CORRECT ANSWER: D
In lines 23-26, the author of Passage 1 describes a problematic Roman law against libel: for every mischief that this law prevented, "ten thousand evils, horrible and afflicting, sprung up in its place". This qualifies the claim in Passage 2 that freedom of the press and restraint of the press are equally destructive, so that D is the best answer. The fact that Passage 1 accepts abuses of freedom of speech as harmful, persistent realities can be used to eliminate A and B, while C (though perhaps true in reality) introduces topics (education and the arts) that are not considered directly in Passage 1.

4) CORRECT ANSWER: D
See above for the explanation of the correct answer. A notes the importance of freedom of speech, B notes that freedom of speech will always be abused, and C expresses ambivalence about the bad effects of free expression. Note that the negative answers B and C can be used to help you eliminate positive answers such as Question 3 A and Question 3 B.

5) CORRECT ANSWER: B
The comparison occurs in the context of the author's discussion of freedom of speech: according to the passage, robbing another of "his moral reputation" deserves stronger punishment than plundering the actual wealth contained in a "purse". B is thus the best answer, while A criticizes the wrong force: the POWER of freedom of speech is what makes the injustice described in the comparison possible. C and D both misdirect the author's ideas: here, general injustices involved in freedom of speech are being considered, while a particular type of magistrate is only mentioned earlier, and a particular Roman law is only mentioned later.

6) CORRECT ANSWER: A
Although the Federal papers can be rightly described as "vulgarly abusive" (line 35),

their tactics are oddly ineffective, since the "majority of the elections always go against the Federal papers" (line 44). This information supports A. B wrongly indicates that the Federal papers are against freedom of speech (when in fact they use free speech for negative ends), C distorts the passage's COMPARISON between English and American papers to wrongly argue that the Federal papers are CAUSING America's reputation to decline, and D is inaccurate in light of the current popularity of the Federal papers over the Republican papers. (Previous figures for these papers are never in fact discussed.)

7) CORRECT ANSWER: C
See above for the explanation of the correct answer. A indicates that freedom of the press and suppression of the press can have equally negative effects, B compares the number of Federal papers to the number of Republican papers, and D notes that a press reflects the character of the nation where it is located. A and D are both general statements, while B should not wrongly be taken as evidence for Question 6 D.

8) CORRECT ANSWER: D
While Passage 1 explains that freedom of speech can define "a free government" (lines 1-2), and is to some extent also present in "Republics and limited monarchies" (line 4), Passage 2 argues that "the manners of a nation" (line 48) are directly reflected in "the character of its press" (lines 49-50). D is thus the best answer. A is contradicted by the strong negative tone that Passage 2 applies to American uses of free speech, B presents an issue that is not explicitly considered in Passage 2, and C refers to an idea that is only articulated in Passage 1.

9) CORRECT ANSWER: A
The word "character" refers to the elements of a national "press" (line 50) that allow people to discern "the manners of a nation, or of a party" (lines 48-49). This kind of "character" would involve understanding qualities, manners of acting, or traits, so that A is the best answer. While B and C would best refer to specific people (not, in context, to a country), D is a positive that is inappropriate in the at times highly critical discussion in Passage 2.

10) CORRECT ANSWER: D
In this passage, Paine has already established the viciousness and "licentiousness" (line 45) of the papers that he is discussing; this paragraph explains how the ideal of "Liberty of the Press" (line 54) is used by printers to justify their powers, both positive and negative. This information supports D and can be used to eliminate A (since other professions are never mentioned) and C (since Paine is only noting a general tendency, not a specific case). B is a trap answer because printers have claimed privileges on their own, not with the cooperation of the public.

2.03 | Mary Wollstonecraft

1) CORRECT ANSWER: D
In this passage, Wollstonecraft explains that men are empowered to have "various employments and pursuits" (lines 7-8), while women are only allowed to develop "the most insignificant part of themselves" (lines 10-11). This information, along with the later discussion of possible abuses of power (lines 38-51), makes D the best answer. Wollstonecraft does not link this power dynamic specifically to economics (eliminating A) and is most interested in developing her own ideas: past theories and past efforts are

never considered at length, thus eliminating B and C.

2) CORRECT ANSWER: C
This sentence indicates that women are kept in a "deplorable state" (line 1) in which ignorance and artificiality are the imposed characteristics; Wollstonecraft supports this idea later on with her argument that women are only allowed to develop "the most insignificant part of themselves" (lines 10-11). C is thus the best answer, while the same information can be used to eliminate B and D (since Wollstonecraft is presenting a single strong idea, not a flawed assumption or a different perspective from her own). A is also problematic, because the sentence in the line reference does not refer to men, even though the PARAGRAPH that contains it does.

3) CORRECT ANSWER: B
In lines 7-10, Wollstonecraft explains that men are given great scope in choosing their pursuits, while women are "confined to one". This information supports B, while A overstates the powers given to men (who would need to, at the very least, compromise with ONE ANOTHER over exercising power). C and D both overstate the power given to women (who in fact appear to have very little according to the passage).

4) CORRECT ANSWER: A
See above for the explanation of the correct answer. B describes how women's powers are confined but may be emancipated, C indicates that men have been conditioned to accept problematic leaders (but not that women have rejected this idea), and D indicates that society continues to exert an oppressive influence (but does not draw a distinction between men and women). Be careful not to wrongly take B as a justification for Question 3 D: both mention tyrants, yet B uses these references figuratively.

5) CORRECT ANSWER: A
In describing how men have led society, Wollstonecraft notes in the third paragraph that men can become monarchs and ministers "whose deadly grasp stops the progress of the human mind" (lines 36-37); such leaders are followed by "tribes of men, like flocks of sheep" (line 28). This information indicates that B, C, and D are present in the passage. A misstates one of Wollstonecraft's ideas, since FOLLOWERS are greedy people, "enervated by luxury and sloth" (lines 31-32), not leaders.

6) CORRECT ANSWER: C
The word "solve" is used to draw a link between why people "quietly follow" (line 29) poor leaders and why they exhibit "present enjoyment and narrowness of understanding" (line 30): the latter quality would link to or explain the former, since both are related negatives. C is the best answer, while A and D are both positives and B wrongly refers to a transformation (not a fundamental link).

7) CORRECT ANSWER: B
While Wollstonecraft spends lines 1-37 describing the subordinate position of women and the problematic activities of men, she uses the remainder of her passage to indicate the necessity of "a revolution in female manners" (line 52). This information supports B and can be used to eliminate A and D (which both assume that Wollstonecraft is uncertain in the early stages of her writing). C is problematic because BOTH stages of the passage consider the status of women in Wollstonecraft's own time, even though the history of society is surveyed in parts of the first three paragraphs.

8) CORRECT ANSWER: B

The word "lost" refers to the "dignity" (line 53) of women, which Wollstonecraft believes must be restored through "a revolution in female manners" (line 52). Thus, the dignity of women has been undermined or compromised and needs to be made a focus once again: B is the best answer. A wrongly refers to thought, C wrongly refers literally to movement, and D is illogical in context: if the dignity of women CAN be restored, such dignity is not absolutely irretrievable.

9) CORRECT ANSWER: A

In lines 53-55, Wollstonecraft explains how women can prove their worth to society by "reforming themselves to reform the world": this idea contrasts with the abuses of male power described in lines 23-37 and, in context, justifies A and can be used to eliminate D. B is inaccurate because Wollstonecraft advocates actions that women can take on their own, while C is problematic because individual virtue (not formal legislation) is the focus of Wollstonecraft's argument.

10) CORRECT ANSWER: D

See above for the explanation of the correct answer. A describes the negative effect of men's power (without referring directly to women), B criticizes women who obtain power by unjust means, and C notes that unjust power has similar effects on men and women. Make sure not to misread B or C as evidence for Question 9 D.

2.04 | Thomas Jefferson

1) CORRECT ANSWER: D

While Jefferson begins the paragraph by referring to "the honor, the happiness, and the hopes" (line 6) of the United States, he goes on to state that men charged with "the sovereign functions of legislation" (lines 14-15) will help the country to navigate "a troubled world" (line 18). This information supports D and can be used to eliminate C, since Jefferson begins on a positive note. A is problematic because Jefferson only addresses legislators as a broad group (rather than pinpointing specific politics), while B is problematic because only the legislators (the "you" in line 15), NOT the members of the populace, are addressed.

2) CORRECT ANSWER: A

In lines 31-34, Jefferson promotes the ideals of unity, "harmony and affection" among his listeners or "fellow-citizens", making A a highly effective answer and C a problematic negative. Note that Jefferson focuses on broad moral values as opposed to specific policies (eliminating B) and that he emphasizes cooperation rather than describing his own life (eliminating D).

3) CORRECT ANSWER: D

See above for the explanation of the correct answer. A records Jefferson's optimism about America's prospects, B indicates Jefferson's trust in other government officials, and C notes that a recent, energetic political contest may strike some onlookers as unusual or alienating. No answer aligns directly with an answer to the previous question, though be cautious of aligning C with the much more strongly negative Question 2 C.

4) CORRECT ANSWER: A

Jefferson notes that the potentially off-putting contest of opinion has "passed" (line 20) and that people will now abandon their earlier animation to "unite in common efforts for the common good" (line 26). This information supports A and eliminates B, since America seems to have more potential for progress AFTER the contest. C overstates the negative effects of the contest, while D wrongly assumes that Jefferson would like to return to this earlier state (instead of developing the current, superior state of national unity).

5) CORRECT ANSWER: D
In lines 60-63, Jefferson continues his analysis of the "republican form" (line 49) of government by stating that "every man" would treat "invasions of the public order as his own personal concern": citizens are thus extremely dedicated to or loyal to this type of government, so that D is the best answer. Throughout the passage, Jefferson's main focus is on civic virtues such as unity and cooperation: military power (A), intellectualism (B), and commerce (C) are not among his focuses and thus are not reasons why republican government is "especially" potent.

6) CORRECT ANSWER: D
See above for the explanation of the correct answer. A describes a spreading state of chaos from earlier history (not Jefferson's present republican government), B notes that people may have the same principles yet still be divided, and C notes the fear that some people have concerning the weakness of republican government. Note that all these answers are negative, while the previous question calls for a positive reason why republican government is POTENT.

7) CORRECT ANSWER: C
The word "charged with" refers to "gentlemen" (line 14) who are responsible for legislation and may be looked to for "guidance and support" (line 16). These men can thus be trusted, making C an appropriate answer and A and B inappropriate negatives. D refers to the act of literally charging a price and is thus out of context.

8) CORRECT ANSWER: C
The word "monuments" refers to the "any among us who would wish to dissolve this Union" (lines 48-49) and with whom Jefferson disagrees. These individuals are specimens of people with a specific strong opinion: C is thus an effective answer, while A and B both offer literal meanings of the word "monuments" and D is too positive for the context.

9) CORRECT ANSWER: B
In the final paragraph, Jefferson notes that "some honest men fear that a republican government can not be strong" (lines 52-53), but contrasts this idea with his conviction that a republican model is "the strongest Government on earth" (line 60). This information directly supports B, while A (dictatorship) and D (publicity) raise issues that are not part of Jefferson's analysis of effective government. C is a trap answer: Jefferson is not comparing spirituality and practicality, but is concerned exclusively with whether republican government is practical or not.

10) CORRECT ANSWER: B
In lines 34-38, Jefferson notes that religious intolerance has been eliminated and expresses the hope that "political intolerance", which is similarly destructive, will also be banished. This information can be used to justify B and to eliminate A. C is a problematic answer because political intolerance and differences of opinion are not synonymous: it is

possible for people to disagree, but still TOLERATE one another's political opinions. D is also problematic because Jefferson strongly supports patriotism as a form of devotion to the Union, so that this answer distorts one of his actual points.

2.05 | Alexis de Tocqueville

1) CORRECT ANSWER: A
In this passage, Tocqueville explains that great political parties "cling to principles more than to their consequences" (line 31), while minor political parties "are, on the other hand, generally deficient in political faith" (lines 40-41). This information supports A, while B and C should be eliminated because Tocqueville declares that "America has already lost the great parties which once divided the nation" (lines 53-54). D is problematic because political structures, not economic practices, are Tocqueville's main concern.

2) CORRECT ANSWER: C
The word "course" refers to "time" (line 16), which does not stop for either nations or men: time would naturally continue or pass in this manner. C is the best answer, while A and D refer to activities undertaken by humans and B refers to space, not to time.

3) CORRECT ANSWER: A
Earlier in the passage, Tocqueville notes that men and nations are "all advancing towards a goal with which they are unacquainted" (lines 17-18); however, the "men" mentioned in the question fallaciously assume the exact opposite, that their condition is final. A is thus the best answer, while B (though negative) wrongly refers to a more detailed emotional state, C is too harshly critical, and D is incorrectly positive.

4) CORRECT ANSWER: C
In lines 30-32, Tocqueville explains that the political parties "which I style great" are based on broad principles, not on smaller and somewhat more specific conditions or leaders. Such a political party, in Tocqueville's construction, would CONTRAST directly with a policy- and leader-oriented minor political party, so that C is the best answer. While a minor party may result from a major party, Tocqueville never argues that this is the ONLY way that a minor party can be created (eliminating A). Great political parties (not minor ones, eliminating B) are linked to insecurity and upheaval, while minor parties appear in peaceful times (but are not defined as creating peaceful times, eliminating D).

5) CORRECT ANSWER: B
See above for the explanation of the correct answer. A refers to parties generally (not to either great or minor political parties in particular), C notes that great parties accompany greater disturbances than minor parties, and D notes that parties in America have been much less violent than parties elsewhere. Make sure not to wrongly take trap answer C as evidence for an answer to the previous question, since this answer compares the EFFECTS of parties rather than providing stable DEFINITIONS.

6) CORRECT ANSWER: A
In lines 58-63, Tocqueville explains that there were two major opinions among the political parties in America, "the one tending to limit, the other to extend indefinitely, the power of the people". This information supports A, while the absence of violence

among American parties can be used to eliminate B. Although Tocqueville notes that the great parties have been dissolved, he never explains exactly how or on what timeline this happened: thus, C and D introduce specifics that are nowhere substantiated by the passage.

7) CORRECT ANSWER: C
See above for the explanation of the correct answer. A describes great parties generally (not American great parties), B notes that America's great parties have disappeared (but never indicates which one disappeared first), and D notes the consensus existing between the important American parties. Make sure not to wrongly take B as a justification for Question 6 D.

8) CORRECT ANSWER: D
The word "private" refers to a person's "interest" (line 35) or involvement in politics, which is contrasted with the idea of "public good" (line 37) as a motive. The idea of what interests an "individual" would effectively contrast with the idea of the "public", so that D is the best answer. Both A and B refer to things that are sensitive or hidden and do not build the contrast as effectively, while C is too negative in context.

9) CORRECT ANSWER: A
In the first paragraph, Tocqueville explains that political parties arise due to "different opinions upon subjects which affect the whole country alike" (lines 1-2): thus, he defines a fundamental condition of parties, so that A is the best answer. Although political parties are defined as a "necessary evil" (line 5), the idea that they do not have ANY good effects is too extreme (eliminating B). Moreover, Tocqueville does not at this point present DISTINCTIONS between political parties, as he does later in the passage: C and D both imply that such distinctions are raised in the first paragraph, and must thus be eliminated.

10) CORRECT ANSWER: B
Although Tocqueville is often critical of minor political parties, he does note that minor parties are associated with "a calm state of things" (line 46), while major parties are associated with historical change and upheaval. This information supports B and can be used to eliminate A, C, and even D: a declining country may, after all, be in the changing or "convulsed" (line 49) state associated with great political parties.

2.06 | Frederick Douglass

1) CORRECT ANSWER: A
Early in the passage, Douglass refers to "my efforts and the efforts of others" (line 19) in fighting slavery: then, he explains that he "had written a book giving a history of that portion of my life spent in the gall and bitterness and degradation of Slavery" (lines 34-36) and recounts his travels immediately afterwards, when he went abroad to spread a message of liberty. This information supports A and can be used to eliminate B, since Douglass's audience is already opposed to slavery and does not need to be convinced by an argument against it, and C, since Douglass speaks FAVORABLY of the "anti-Prejudice" (line 60) countries he visited. D also misdirects the tone of the passage: while describing foreign countries such as England positively, Douglass does not definitively or optimistically say that the situation in America WILL improve, only that it CAN with English guidance.

2) CORRECT ANSWER: C

Douglass's audience has worked with him in trying to bring slaves liberty and in "hastening the day of their emancipation" (lines 5-6): however, Douglass's audience is never described as PART of Douglass's ethnic brethren, and Douglass sets out to describe forms of racial prejudice that his audience might never have encountered. This information supports C, since Douglass is speaking to ideological allies (eliminating D) but not to people of his own race (eliminating A and B).

3) CORRECT ANSWER: A

See above for the explanation of the correct answer. B indicates that Douglass has been through much since an earlier speaking engagement, C notes Douglass's antagonism towards slave-owners, and D indicates that Douglass was favorably received outside the United States. Only B refers to Douglass's audience, and does not directly define either its beliefs or its ethnicity.

4) CORRECT ANSWER: D

In lines 16-20, Douglass declares that his speech is meant to deliver "sober truths" and celebrates his audience as a "noble" band that supports him in his efforts against slavery. This information supports D, while A is wrongly negative about Douglass himself and B makes it seem that slavery in England needs to be abolished, when in fact Douglass seeks English aid in eliminating American slavery. C is a trap answer: while Douglass does mention his struggle and his travels, discussing these ideas is not the primary purpose of the speech "According to Douglass".

5) CORRECT ANSWER: B

See above for the explanation of the correct answer. A alludes to Douglass's experiences and expresses his strong opposition to slavery, C refers to Douglass's travels (which he DECLINES to discuss at length), and D refers to Douglass's hope that England can help America to combat slavery. Be especially careful of mistaking D as a justification for Question 4 B.

6) CORRECT ANSWER: A

In context, Douglass is speaking to an audience gathered in America and hopes for "English aid and English sympathy for the overthrow of American Slavery" (lines 63-64): thus, he has returned to the United States in order to continue his efforts to promote racial justice. A is the best answer, while the same information can be used to eliminate the positive tone towards America in C. B and D both distort actual observations from Douglass's travels: "anti-Prejudice" (line 60) is a general condition in England, while Douglass returned to America because he needed to continue his work and because slaves faced ongoing oppression, not "heightened" danger.

7) CORRECT ANSWER: D

In lines 47-51, Douglass calls attention to the apparent "degradation" and "poverty" in England, but notes that even this troubling state offers freedom for both "the white man" and "the black man". This information supports D, while A and C both mention America (which is not actually mentioned in the line reference) and must thus be eliminated. B is problematic because the line reference states a fact from ONE timeframe, rather than comparing two different time signatures.

8) CORRECT ANSWER: A

The word "perfect" refers to the "absence" (line 54) of hatred that Douglass encountered abroad: he looked around "in vain" (line 56) and could find no sign of hatred whatsoever. This context supports A. B, C, and D are all positives, but do not directly fit the context, which should indicate that the absence was "total", not simply that it was praiseworthy.

9) CORRECT ANSWER: D

The phrase "with which we are pursued" refers to the "hate" (line 55) that is present in America and which is an ongoing condition, in contrast to the racial hatred that has been eliminated in England. D is the best answer, while B is wrongly positive and A and C are incorrect in context: although some people in America are bound or defined by hate, Douglass and his allies are not.

10) CORRECT ANSWER: C

Douglass notes a level of freedom "for the black man" (line 51) that is present in England but not in America, explains that he went to England to "preserve" (line 41) his liberty "until the excitement occasioned by the publication of my Narrative had subsided" (lines 42-44), and construes his trip as an effort "to get rid of Democratic Slavery" (lines 44-45). This information can be used to eliminate A, B, and D, respectively. C states the wrong contrast: Douglass contrasts the English with Americans who actively display "disgusting hate" (lines 54-55), not with Americans who passively accept the injustices of slavery.

2.07 | Henry David Thoreau

1) CORRECT ANSWER: A

Although Thoreau believes that the government should not invade the lives of its people and endorses the idea that "That government is best which governs not at all" (lines 4-5), he later declares that "the people must have some complicated machinery or other" (line 25) to satisfy their expectations of government. This information and its cynical tone supports A. B and D are both contradicted by Thoreau's positive belief that there can be "better government" (line 47) and that America is not fated for disaster; C distorts Thoreau's idea that officials DISREGARD the will of their citizens and argues, instead, that officials are UNAWARE of the will of their citizens.

2) CORRECT ANSWER: A

In the second paragraph, Thoreau indicates that trade and commerce face "obstacles which legislators are continually putting in their way" (lines 40-41): he is critical of such intervention, while no-government men are critical of ALL functions of government. A is thus the best answer, while B misstates an idea from the first paragraph (in which Thoreau criticizes the Mexican War, not ALL wars), C introduces a factor (propaganda) that is not considered in the passage, and D states the position of the no-government men (not the more moderate position taken by Thoreau).

3) CORRECT ANSWER: A

In the relevant paragraph, Thoreau compares the government to a "wooden gun" (line 23) and lists the many things it does not actually do (lines 29-32); however, people need a formal government "to satisfy that idea of government which they have" (line 26). This information supports A and can be used to eliminate positive answers B and D. C, though rightly negative, calls attention to the false topic of "reforms": although such changes may be desirable, Thoreau never mentions that any reforms are in fact underway.

4) CORRECT ANSWER: C

The word "execute" refers to an action that the government takes in response to the "will" (line 14) of the people, who hope to "act through" (line 15) the government. To "execute" in this context would mean to put into practice or "enact": C is thus an effective answer, while B is wrongly negative. A refers to judgment and D refers to a position or a responsibility, not to the act of directly putting an idea into practice.

5) CORRECT ANSWER: B

In lines 32-35, Thoreau notes that even though the American populace has done much, it "would have done somewhat more, if the government had not sometimes got in its way". This information supports B and eliminates C, since the government actually works AGAINST personal gain. A is problematic because, in light of these negative circumstances, the American people MIGHT support changing the presence of government in their lives: however, D wrongly assumes that all Americans DEFINITELY want to reduce the role of government (when in fact only Thoreau definitely voices such an idea) and must thus be eliminated.

6) CORRECT ANSWER: C

See above for the explanation of the correct answer. A notes Thoreau's belief that the role of government should be reduced, B notes that the government can easily be manipulated, and D indicates that Thoreau wants the American government to be improved. None of these answers offers a clear statement about the "citizens of the United States", so that all should be readily eliminated.

7) CORRECT ANSWER: D

In lines 50-54, Thoreau argues that, even in a government in which power is "in the hands of the people", members of a majority may rule "not because they are most likely to be in the right" but because they outnumber their opponents. This information supports D, while other answers distort a few of Thoreau's actual arguments. Legislators impede economic progress (but do not actually redistribute resources, eliminating A), some foreign policy choices such as the Mexican War have been suspect (but not ALL foreign policy choices are made for short-term gain, eliminating B), and the citizens of a democratic government may be interested in little more than the shallow appearance of official government (but may be interested in moral disputes in OTHER areas, eliminating C).

8) CORRECT ANSWER: C

See above for the explanation of the correct answer. A indicates that the Mexican War was undertaken without genuine democratic consent, B indicates that government can inhibit trade and commerce, and D indicates that people should take moral initiative. None of these offers a direct analysis of democratic government that aligns with an answer to the previous question, though make sure not to align A with Question 7 B, B with Question 7 A, or D with Question 7 C.

9) CORRECT ANSWER: B

The word "virtually" refers to how majorities "decide right and wrong" (line 58): in majority government, the more popular position more or less determines the nation's sense of what is right, while genuine morality is ineffectual. Thus, the majorities actually or "effectually" decide right and wrong, so that B is the best answer. In context, A, C, and

D would all indicate that the majorities actually do not have power or privileges: thus, these answer must be readily eliminated.

10) CORRECT ANSWER: B
Thoreau begins the final paragraph by considering why "a majority are permitted, and for a long period continue, to rule" (lines 51-52); then, in relation to his discussion of government, he voices support for the idea that "we should be men first, and subjects afterward" (lines 62-63). This information supports B and can be used to eliminate A (since Thoreau is critical of government throughout) and C (since his ideas, though opposed to common practices, may have in fact been taken from a fairly old source). D is a trap answer, since Thoreau praises the possible acts of individuals, not the policies of a government.

2.08 | Stephen Douglas and Abraham Lincoln

1) CORRECT ANSWER: D
In the second paragraph, Douglas is discussing an attempt "to force a slave state Constitution upon the people of Kansas against their will" (lines 7-8): the similarly negative "fraud" that he addresses and opposes is this attempt. D is thus the best answer, while A is problematic because it does not refer to any sort of legislation. B is incorrect because only one state, Kansas, is discussed, while C is out of scope because the Kansas state constitution only allows slavery and does not actively promote any other forms of immoral behavior. (Oddly enough, Douglas never argues that slavery is immoral at this point in the passage.)

2) CORRECT ANSWER: C
Passage 1 describes a dispute surrounding the Kansas state constitution that pitted pro-slavery and anti-slavery lawmakers against one another: this tone of conflict supports the idea that there is a "new era" of slavery disputes in areas such as Kansas and Nebraska. C is thus the best answer, while A focuses on the wrong issue ("words") and wrongly makes Passage 1 seem insignificant, B indicates certainty instead of conflict, and D condemns the wrong group (earlier American leaders, not the pro-slavery advocates targeted in Passage 2).

3) CORRECT ANSWER: A
The word "bound" describes the author of Passage 1, who objects to the slave state Constitution and resists it "to the utmost of my power" (lines 12-13). He thus feels a strong need or obligation to resist the Constitution: A is an effective choice, while B and C, in context, both wrongly indicate that he DID NOT have a choice in whether to resist or not. D refers to a physical position or a physical object, not to a strong decision.

4) CORRECT ANSWER: C
In lines 53-55, Lincoln explains that "The great mass of the nation" reasonably believed that slavery "was in course of ultimate extinction". This information supports C and can be used to eliminate B and D, which wrongly take negative stances on the idea that slavery would become extinct. Trap answer A distorts one of Lincoln's own arguments: while events surrounding the Constitution and the actions of the framers of the Constitution indicated that slavery would disappear, it is never stated that the Constitution ITSELF records this idea.

5) CORRECT ANSWER: C

See above for the explanation of the correct answer. A expresses Lincoln's certainty in his own ideas, B expresses his awareness of the longevity of slavery, and D indicates that the extinction of slavery was associated with the Constitution (but not actually PHRASED in the Constitution). Note that A and B do not refer directly to the extinction of slavery: thus, eliminate these answers.

6) CORRECT ANSWER: B

The word "ultimate" describes the "extinction" (line 45) of slavery, which Lincoln had once seen as a historical certainty because he "believed that everybody was against" (lines 51-52) slavery. Slavery would thus after a time, or eventually, be eliminated thanks to such strong opposition: B is the best answer, while A and C describe abilities or virtuous status (not the course of events) and D is an inappropriate negative.

7) CORRECT ANSWER: B

While the author of Passage 1 believes that the Kansas state constitution should "be accepted or rejected" (line 16) according to the will of the people of Kansas, the author of Passage 2 declares that he has "always hated slavery" (line 47) and links antipathy to slavery to the national Constitution. This information supports B and can be used to eliminate A, since Passage 1 argues that a pro-slavery constitution should in fact be REJECTED. C raises the issue of America's boundaries (a topic that, unlike the spread of slavery WITHIN those boundaries, is never discussed), while D raises the topic of party loyalty (which, in the context of Passage 2, is not discussed at all in relation to slavery).

8) CORRECT ANSWER: C

The author of Passage 1 opposes measures that would "force a slave state Constitution upon the people of Kansas" (lines 7-8); for his part, the author of Passage 2 has "always hated slavery" (line 47) and feels moved to take action by the "introduction of the Kansas-Nebraska Bill" (lines 50-51). This information supports C. Passage 2 prioritizes federal law by speaking positively of the Constitution (eliminating A), Passage 1 supports voters' interests but not any "humanitarian" initiatives (eliminating B), and only Passage 2 discusses the federal Constitution at all (eliminating D).

9) CORRECT ANSWER: A

In arguing against slavery in lines 63-66, Lincoln asks whether anti-slavery acts were necessary and whether the framers of the Constitution really intended to eliminate slavery: the implied answers to his inquiries are clear. These rhetorical questions justify A. Other answers distort Lincoln's other tactics: he calls his own eloquence into question (but does not praise Douglas, eliminating A), indicates that he might be relatively uneducated (but does not criticize those who would make this assumption, eliminating C), and acknowledges that anti-slavery viewpoints are now less popular (but not that they weaken his OWN political position, eliminating D).

10) CORRECT ANSWER: D

See above for the explanation of the correct answer. A sums up some of Lincoln's personal drawbacks, B questions Douglas's interpretation of Lincoln's ideas, and C indicates that Lincoln dislikes slavery and has modified his approach. Make sure not to align A with Question 9 C, B with Question 9 B, or C with Question 9 D.

2.09 | Karl Marx and Friedrich Engels

1) CORRECT ANSWER: D
At the beginning of the passage, Marx and Engels directly state that "The history of all hitherto existing societies is the history of class struggles" (lines 1-2); from there, the authors explain the "gradation of social rank" (line 12) that preceded the development of the evolving conflict between the proletariat and the bourgeoisie (which is the main topic of the passage). This information supports D and can be used to eliminate B, which assumes that the authors QUESTION their own theory. However, because the passage suggests that class conflict has not been resolved (and that the bourgeoisie continues to be a brutally exploitative class), both A and C must be rejected as envisioning positives (resolutions and social improvements) that the authors never consider.

2) CORRECT ANSWER: C
The word "common" refers to the "ruin" (line 8) of contending classes after a historical upheaval: the other alternative would be that both classes re-constitute society. Thus, both classes would be ruined under the worse alternative, so that their ruin would be shared or "mutual". Choose C and eliminate A as introducing an irrelevant negative, B as referring to the wrong factor (since EVERYONE, not simply a majority, would be ruined), and D as introducing a slight negative and a false meaning (since society is not normally subjected to revolutions and ruined).

3) CORRECT ANSWER: A
In the relevant paragraph, the "arrangement of society into various orders" (line 11) is described for ancient Rome and the Middle Ages: modern society has maintained the overall principle of "class antagonisms" (lines 17-18) exhibited earlier, although some of the antagonisms themselves have changed. A is thus the best answer, while B is out of scope (since the proletariat and bourgeoisie are not mentioned at all in lines 10-15). C is inaccurate, since the COMPLEXITY of earlier society is not being criticized, while D creates a faulty comparison, since Rome and the Middle Ages societies both expressed the same general idea of class differences using DIFFERENT specific classifications.

4) CORRECT ANSWER: D
In lines 64-61, Marx explains that the bourgeoisie has disrupted the "feudal ties" that once united different classes and has made "naked self-interest" the only real form of connection. D is an effective answer, while A and C mistake the DESCRIPTION of the role of commerce and travel in the development of the bourgeoisie for a CRITICISM of the bourgeoisie. B is similarly misdirected: the bourgeoisie makes money a general priority, but does not necessarily spend the same energy promoting specific businessmen.

5) CORRECT ANSWER: D
See above for the explanation of the correct answer. A explains that new discoveries promoted the rise of the bourgeoisie, B explains that bourgeois industry transformed society, and C explains that the modern bourgeoisie was created by a process of historical change and revolution. Be especially careful of aligning A with Question 4 A or Question 4 C, and of aligning B with Question 4 B.

6) CORRECT ANSWER: A
In lines 52-55, Marx describes the modern era (when the bourgeoisie developed) as a time when "industry, commerce, navigation, railways extended", thus indicating that

travel and infrastructure were major investments. This information supports A. B is contradicted by the passage (since class conflict remains, even though the bourgeoisie has the upper hand), C is inaccurate (since the bourgeoisie and proletariat, though antagonistic, may have common goals such as earning money), and D is out of scope (since the focus throughout the passage is on economics, not on religious institutions).

7) CORRECT ANSWER: C

See above for the explanation of the correct answer. A indicates that class antagonisms persist in the modern era (contradicting Question 6 B), B indicates that the bourgeoisie and the proletariat are the two main social classes (not aligning with any answer to the previous question), and D indicates that overall religious spirit (not the number of religious INSTITUTIONS) has declined in the modern era.

8) CORRECT ANSWER: A

According to Marx, aggressive exploration "opened up fresh ground for the rising bourgeoisie" (line 29), and the "growing wants of the new markets" (line 38) led directly to the rise of the manufacturing middle class. This information supports A and can be used to eliminate B, since the same forces led to the elimination of guilds as an economic force. C (morality) and D (technology) refer to factors that are not directly related to economics and exploration in Marx's discussion, and must thus be eliminated as irrelevant.

9) CORRECT ANSWER: C

In the relevant paragraph, Marx notes that the bourgeoisie has replaced "the most heavenly ecstasies of religious fervor" (lines 68-69) with "egotistical calculation" (line 70), but that the aims of the bourgeoisie are often "veiled by religious and political illusions" (line 74). Thus, the bourgeoisie is not truly religious, but uses religion for practical purposes: C is the best answer while A and D wrongly assume that the bourgeoisie is truly religious or moral. B is a trap answer: the bourgeoisie uses religion to practically promote its aims, but is never described as using religious terminology to EXPLAIN what it is up to.

10) CORRECT ANSWER: A

In the passage, the word "place" occurs in the context of manufacture being replaced by Modern Industry, then in the context of the industrial middle class being replaced by industrial millionaires. These new classes replace, or take on the essential role or function, of earlier groups: A is thus the best answer. B wrongly assumes that the new and old classes live in the same place (a possibility never presented), C refers to a formal duty (not a general role), and D wrongly indicates, in context, that the classes are all EXACTLY the same, when in fact new classes have simply assumed some of the functions of the old.

2.10 | Charlotte Perkins Gilman

1) CORRECT ANSWER: A

In the first paragraph, Gilman notes that education is essential for animals and further observes that education "is the most important process" (lines 4-5) for humans. However, while in animals "the powers of the race must be lodged in each individual" (lines 9-10), people can cooperate to a greater extent and make greater gains because "Our life is social, collective" (lines 14-15). This information supports A and eliminates C and D, which wrongly attribute critical tones to the second paragraph of the passage. B is a trap answer: although Gilman is outlining a theory, there is no context to indicate WHEN the theory was developed.

2) CORRECT ANSWER: D
In the passage, Gilman explains that "The origin of education is maternal" (line 1), but then discusses an educational system under which men are perceived as largely superior to women. However, people increasingly recognize the "humaneness of women" (line 55) and are reacting anew to "the universal assumption that men alone were humanity" (lines 62-63). This information supports D but can also be used to eliminate A, because Gilman focuses on broad social classifications such as "men" and "women" rather than targeting small groups of men. B and C, though rightly positive about women, wrongly neglect the long explanatory and critical portions of Gilman's passage and should thus be eliminated.

3) CORRECT ANSWER: C
In lines 74-78, Gilman states that the "human development" of women has proceeded and calls attention to the educational opportunities available to women at both basic and advanced levels. This information supports the positive answer C, since women have made progress despite "masculine influence", and can be used to eliminate B (which assumes that women have not overcome oppressive male influences) and D (which wrongly assumes that masculine influence does not in fact exist). A is a trap answer: masculine influence may be linked to male opposition to outspoken women's roles, but is not clearly linked to conflict with the more traditional, domestic women's roles that masculine influence in fact allows.

4) CORRECT ANSWER: D
See above for the explanation of the correct answer. A indicates that mother-to-child instruction has been widely neglected, B indicates that girls were once solely educated by their mothers, and C indicates that masculine influence has led to opposition to the efforts of women to assert themselves. Make sure not to wrongly take C as evidence for one of the negative answers to the previous question.

5) CORRECT ANSWER: B
In lines 52-53, Gilman states that women were traditionally regarded as "only servants, trained as such by their servant mothers". This information supports B and can be used to eliminate D. Although even a subservient woman could be spiritual or practical in some of her actions, the qualities mentioned in A and C are not directly mentioned in the passage: these answers should thus be eliminated.

6) CORRECT ANSWER: C
The word "lower" refers to "animals" (line 9), which are defined as "sub-human" (line 13) in nature. Compared to humans, these animals would be less advanced, so that C is the best answer. A wrongly refers to size, while B and D refer to temperament or personality, not to stages of advancement or sophistication.

7) CORRECT ANSWER: A
The word "unusual" refers to the "calibre [quality]" (line 58) of women who were aware of women's "humaneness" (line 55) and wanted equal education for boys and girls. These

women who wanted such privileges would logically be virtuous or excellent people themselves: A is the best answer, while B, C, and D all introduce negatives that would criticize the women as having strange or confusing personalities.

8) CORRECT ANSWER: A
Gilman explains that traditional education was based on the ideas that "men alone were to be fitted" (line 49) for the world and that women "were only servants" (line 52): equal education for both sexes is a radical departure from exactly this setup. A is the best answer, while the efforts of both men and women, not the influence of new research (B) or of men primarily (C), have made equal education more acceptable. However, because Gilman does not link the expansion of equal education to OTHER forms of progress for women, D must be eliminated as out of scope.

9) CORRECT ANSWER: B
In lines 36-37, Gilman indicates that "certain conditions, physical and psychic" into which a child is born can be forms of education: education, thus, is not only the product of formal institutions. B is an effective answer, while A introduces the issue of "class" (which is not a major consideration of the passage) and D is wrongly negative about education, which can be adapted to PROMOTE women's progress. C, however, is a trap answer, since education may enable progress and prosperity but is not CERTAIN to do so.

10) CORRECT ANSWER: B
See above for the explanation of the correct answer. A indicates that education is a collective endeavor in human societies, C indicates that the idea of equal education is gaining popularity, and D indicates that men have opposed women's education in the past. Make sure not to take A as evidence for Question 9 C or D as evidence for Question 9 D.

2.11 | Susan B. Anthony

1) CORRECT ANSWER: D
The word "alleged" refers to the "crime of having voted" (line 2); as Anthony later explains, she in fact "not only committed no crime, but, instead, simply exercised my citizens' rights" (lines 5-6). She does not see her "crime" as truly unlawful or problematic, making D the best answer and eliminating A (since Anthony in fact appeals to laws to make her argument). B (criticism) and C (documentation) refer to issues that are not within the scope of this discussion of whether Anthony, in her own regard, has truly committed a crime.

2) CORRECT ANSWER: C
The word "exercised" refers to the "citizens' rights" (line 6) that Anthony sees as guaranteed to her and that are "beyond the power of any state to deny" (lines 7-8). She is thus allowed to make use of these rights and cast a vote, so that C is the best answer. D is a problematic negative while A and B, in context, would both indicate that the rights are being reinforced or improved: however, the rights are ALREADY strong in Anthony's mind and can thus be put to practical use.

3) CORRECT ANSWER: C
In lines 10-15, Anthony explains how "the people of the United States" committed to

principles such as justice and liberty in the Constitution: in lines 16-24, she explains that the principles of the Constitution are being wrongly confined to "male citizens" and calls attention to a "downright mockery" of the Constitution's values. This information supports C and can be used to eliminate B and D, which do not indicate that lines 16-24 are strongly negative. A is problematic because Anthony does not single out specific "politicians" for criticism: instead, she indicates that the values of her entire era are unjust.

4) CORRECT ANSWER: C
The word "settled" refers to a "question" (line 46) that Anthony raises in the course of her decisive defense of women's rights: she would thus want to firmly answer or resolve this question. C is the best answer, while A and B both refer to soothing or physical actions and D is problematic in context. To "nullify" would be to cancel out or disregard the question: instead, Anthony wants to arrive at an answer that helps to build her case.

5) CORRECT ANSWER: B
In lines 33-36, Anthony compares the "hateful oligarchy of sex" that women face to an "oligarchy of wealth, where the rich govern the poor", thus creating a parallel between two negative social structures. B is the best answer, while Anthony's thorough advocacy of women and their rights can be used to eliminate answers C and D, which are wrongly negative towards women. A is a trap answer: while Anthony may have great respect for other women, her argument is premised mostly on the CIVIC and LEGAL ideas behind women's rights as voters and citizens, not on in-depth analysis of virtues and intellect.

6) CORRECT ANSWER: C
See above for the explanation of the correct answer. A justifies Anthony's actions in voting, B criticizes those who would not grant women the power to vote, and D argues that denying women the status of persons is nonsensical. Make sure not to misread any of these answers as taking a positive stance towards women's opponents, or a critical stance towards women.

7) CORRECT ANSWER: C
After posing the question "Are women persons?" (lines 46-47), Anthony declares that not even "opponents" (line 47) of suffrage would deny that women are persons, and then definitively states that "Being persons, then, women are citizens" (lines 48-49). The answer to this question is extremely clear and is not open to dispute, justifying C and eliminating both A and B. D is a trap answer: though the question and its answer are not complex, they are not boring because they are part of Anthony's energetic and important effort to secure voting rights for women.

8) CORRECT ANSWER: A
Anthony states that the "oligarchy of sex" (line 39) that renders men and women unequal would divide the members "of every household" (line 41) and cause problems in "every home of the nation" (line 43). This information supports A. Anthony never mentions foreign nations directly (eliminating B), mentions racial discrimination as a point of comparison (not as a CAUSE, eliminating C), and is concerned with members of the same household and therefore of the SAME class (eliminating D).

9) CORRECT ANSWER: A
In lines 51-54, Anthony declares that "discrimination against women" is null and void according to logical principles: as she points out, discriminations "against Americans of

African heritage" have been successfully fought. Thus, these two groups should enjoy the same voting rights, once women have achieved the recognition they deserve. A is the best choice, while African Americans are depicted as ALREADY having considerable rights (eliminating B and C) and are shown as SIMILAR to women, not as UNDERMINING women (eliminating D).

10) CORRECT ANSWER: D
See above for the explanation of the correct answer. A indicates the people of the United States as a whole were involved in forming the country, B indicates that racial inequality might be allowed in some forms of society, and C offers a definition of a "citizen". Only B describes people of African descent directly, yet this choice does not align with an answer to the previous question.

2.12 | Clara Barton

1) CORRECT ANSWER: D
While Barton argues that America is "far less liable to the disturbances of war than the nations of Europe" (lines 10-11), she notes that problems such as "Plagues, cholera, fires, flood, famine" are prominent in the United States. This information supports D, while A and C both consider political issues that are unrelated to Barton's emphasis on disaster relief. B is problematic because specific diseases in Europe are never named, so that there is no basis for comparison with the United States.

2) CORRECT ANSWER: A
The "system" mentioned in the passage is described as "organized" (line 26) and involves activities such as collection, reception, and distribution. Such a system would involve practical measures or procedures, so that A is the best answer. B and C wrongly focus on ideas, not on practical actions, while D overstates the extent and nature of the system: a bureaucracy is an overbearing system that involves much paperwork, and is unlike the efficient, pragmatic system that Barton envisions.

3) CORRECT ANSWER: B
The word "object" refers to something "specific" (line 48) and to which "resources are and must be applied" (line 49). Such an object would thus be a precise aim or goal that requires effort. B is an effective choice, while A is wrongly negative and C and D both refer to concrete ITEMS, not to the kind of AIM that Barton envisions.

4) CORRECT ANSWER: A
In these paragraphs, Barton calls attention to the lack of an "organized system" (line 26) that results in "crude, confused and unsystematized" (lines 29-30) efforts: as a result of this lack of order, people haphazardly bestow charity and attempt to do good works "to the neglect of other duties in the present, and at the peril of all health in the future" (lines 40-41). This negative information supports A and can be used to eliminate B (new measure) and C (idealistic), which both introduce irrelevant positives. D is problematic because Barton is focusing on a WIDESPREAD social failing, not on the problems involved in a SPECIFIC institution.

5) CORRECT ANSWER: C
In the course of her passage, Barton calls attention to the civic dangers that the United

States might face, points out deficiencies in existing institutions, and argues for the adoption of Red Cross societies because "we have no means of relief in readiness such as these Red Cross societies would furnish" (lines 71-72). This information supports C and can be used to eliminate B, since Barton is most interested in creating a new institution, not in creating REPLACEMENTS that would function like the old ones. Although Barton does use irony (A) and does explain that the United States is not threatened by war (D), these are secondary points in her main argument about the Red Cross societies: thus, these answers do not properly describe the main idea.

6) CORRECT ANSWER: D
In lines 29-32, Barton argues that American relief efforts are "crude, confused, and unsystematized" and that Americans seem "unprepared" for further tragedies. This information supports D and can be used to eliminate positive answers A and C. B, though negative, departs from Barton's main concern: she objects to the practical effects of American relief efforts, not to the publicity that such efforts have received.

7) CORRECT ANSWER: B
See above for the explanation of the correct answer. A indicates that war is a greater threat to Europe than to America, C indicates that existing charitable institutions are limited in scope, and D indicates that charity is meant to be generous. Only C directly describes American aid societies, but does not align directly with an answer to the previous question.

8) CORRECT ANSWER: C
Barton indicates that the "electric current" may bring "at any moment its ill tidings of some great human distress" (lines 70-71): thus, the current communicates misfortunes that are sudden and most likely unexpected. C is thus the best answer, while A, B, and D describe not the current itself (which signifies calamities) but possible and desirable RESPONSES to the misfortunes signified by the current.

9) CORRECT ANSWER: A
In lines 59-61, Barton describes the Red Cross societies by noting that "In all our land we have not one organization of this nature": this information supports A, while the adoption of relief methods very DIFFERENT from those used by the societies makes C incorrect. B and D both wrongly introduce negatives, since Barton promotes the societies as a beneficial measure in providing disaster relief.

10) CORRECT ANSWER: C
See above for the explanation of the correct answer. A indicates that the Red Cross societies can adapt to the conditions of specific countries, B indicates that the United States will face unpredictable disasters, and D indicates that attempts to combat the loss of property have been more effective than attempts to prevent to the loss of life in the United States. Only A refers directly to the societies, yet the trait indicated by this line reference (adaptability) is not an available answer to the previous question.

2.13 | John D. Rockefeller and Jacob Riis

1) CORRECT ANSWER: D
The word "judgment" occurs in the context of Rockefeller's analysis of "The best

philanthropy" (line 1), which he sees as a matter of providing opportunity instead of as a matter of merely giving money. He is thus forming an opinion, or an assessment, of the best form of philanthropy: D is an effective choice. A wrongly introduces a negative, while B and C wrongly refer to personality traits instead of to analysis.

2) CORRECT ANSWER: A
In lines 12-15, Rockefeller rejects the idea that "the daily vocation of life is one thing, and the work of philanthropy quite another". He thus believes the opposite, making A the best answer and eliminating C, since people other than the wealthy could perform good works in "the daily vocation of life". B is contradicted by the first paragraph (which distinguishes giving money from the best forms of philanthropy), while D is out of scope: Rockefeller does argue against misconceptions about philanthropy, but how WIDELY such misconceptions are accepted is never explained.

3) CORRECT ANSWER: C
See above for the explanation of the correct answer. A distinguishes between philanthropy and charity, B notes that there are many opportunities for philanthropy, and D indicates that businessmen can play pivotal roles in philanthropy. Be careful of taking B as a justification for Question 2 D or D as a justification for the more absolute Question 2 C.

4) CORRECT ANSWER: C
While Passage 1 focuses on a form of philanthropy that involves "the power of employing people at a remunerative wage" (lines 6-7), Passage 2 is devoted to the issue of "what to do with the tenement" (line 25) and considers "effective ways of dealing with the tenements in New York" (lines 45-46). This information supports C, while other answers refer to topics that are never raised. Passage 1 only discusses how to deal with hardship (not its causes, eliminating A) and never calls for new political measures (only for a new general approach to philanthropy, eliminating B), while Passage 2 indicates that some of the wealthy have worsened the condition of the poor (not that ALL of the wealthy do so, eliminating D).

5) CORRECT ANSWER: B
In lines 67-70, Passage 2 calls attention to the corrective actions that could be taken "If a few of the wealthy absentee landlords" could be "got within the jurisdiction of the city": these landlords are thus not present to face effective judgment. B is the best answer, while A (positions) and D (bribes) refer to topics that, though negative, are never directly raised. The passage also indicates the opposite of C, since tenants in a poorly-kept tenement would be unlikely to be loyal to their landlord.

6) CORRECT ANSWER: D
See above for the explanation of the correct answer. A indicates that some landlords use superficial decorations when managing their properties, B indicates that the law can unite with public opinion to solve housing problems, and C indicates that financial incentives can be given for the creation of improved tenements. Only A refers to tenement owners as demanded by the previous question, but does not actually align with any of the critical answer choices to Question 5.

7) CORRECT ANSWER: D
While Rockefeller is a businessman talking about business, he does not actually describe events from his own life: in contrast, Riis describes how "I watched a Mott Street Landlord" (lines 25-26) early in Passage 2. This information supports D, while neither

passage makes use of statistics (eliminating A). In Passage 1, Rockefeller does in fact present faulty assumptions (concerning the idea that charity and philanthropy are the same, eliminating B) and does make a broad recommendation (philanthropy as a form of employment and investment, eliminating C).

8) CORRECT ANSWER: A
In his discussion of housing reform in Passage 2, Riis notes that "The drastic measures adopted in Paris, in Glasgow, and in London" (lines 54-55) are "not practicable" (line 55) on a similar scale in the United States. This information supports A, while Riis's focus on housing improvement (not wealth redistribution) within New York (not other American cities) can be used to eliminate B and D. Because Riis argues AGAINST the "flat" model in lines 37-38, C must be eliminated as contradicted by the passage.

9) CORRECT ANSWER: B
The word "binds" refers to the "red tape [bureaucratic restriction]" (line 59) that makes a "municipal effort" (line 60) problematic. Because the effort is not yet effectual, it has been impeded or restricted: B is the best answer, while A, C, and D all create faulty positives.

10) CORRECT ANSWER: A
In Passage 1, Rockefeller speaks of the "busy man of affairs" (lines 17-18) as an important figure in the philanthropic "large plan of developing work" (line 19); Riis in Passage 2, though more critical of the wealthy, argues that "wealthy absentee landlords" (line 67) should be made to help the poor by employing "proper overseers" (line 70). This information supports A, while neither passage focuses on education (eliminating B), only Passage 1 focuses on job creation (eliminating C), and only Passage 2 focuses on sanitation (eliminating D).

2.14 | Henry Cabot Lodge and Theodore Roosevelt

1) CORRECT ANSWER: C
The authors declare that they must "strip off" (line 2) all the myths that surround Washington: instead, they want to consider the facts of his life "without any illusion or deception" (lines 6-7). This information supports C. The authors are only considering their own project on Washington, not biographies generally (eliminating A) or the views of Washington's peers (eliminating D). B is a trap answer: while some of Washington's popularity may have a questionable basis, this answer neglects the fact that the "myths" strongly contrast with the authors' OWN project.

2) CORRECT ANSWER: B
The word "movement" refers to a phase of "national" (line 28) life led by Washington: this movement involved "a better union" (line 29) and bringing "order out of chaos" (lines 29-30). Such a movement would be a positive effort or initiative: B is the best answer, while A and D are negative and C refers to religion and devotion, not to politics and action.

3) CORRECT ANSWER: D
In surveying the facts of Washington's life, the authors argue that Washington was "thoroughly national in all his views" (lines 21-22) and explain how this mentality helped him "to build up a new and lasting fabric upon the ruins of a system which had been

overthrown" (lines 60-61). This information supports D and can be used to eliminate A and B (which wrongly assume that the passage describes other statesmen at length) and C (which completely neglects the central topic of Washington's role).

4) CORRECT ANSWER: A
The relevant paragraph describes Washington's activities after "the Revolution" (line 14) and his response to the "Constitution formed at Philadelphia" (lines 38-39), but also shows how Washington's presidency and overall engagement in public life were motivated by the desire to create a strong government. This information supports A and can be used to eliminate B (which assumes that some of the authors' discussion is speculative or uncertain). C refers to Washington's successors (not to Washington himself) while D neglects this biographical passage's emphasis on Washington's PUBLIC life.

5) CORRECT ANSWER: B
Although Washington did temporarily leave public life to live at Mount Vernon, he watched public affairs with "utmost anxiety" (line 17) and was motivated to place himself "at the head of the national movement" (line 28) in order to address political troubles. B is the best answer, while A is contradicted by the passage's depiction of Washington as devoted to his nation (not his own career) and C and D are wrongly positive.

6) CORRECT ANSWER: A
In lines 64-67, the authors note that Washington was among the greatest men according to different criteria: "what he did, or what he was, or by the effect of his work upon the history of mankind". This multi-sided, unmatched influence supports A. The authors trace Washington's accomplishments to his remarkable character and strong system of values, not to a belief in expansion (eliminating B), his military background (eliminating C), or the society he lived in (eliminating D).

7) CORRECT ANSWER: D
See above for the explanation of the correct answer. A explains Washington's principled reluctance to exercise great authority, B indicates Washington's enthusiasm for national expansion, and C describes how Washington shifted his efforts directly from fighting the Revolution to forming the Constitution. Only A refers directly to Washington's virtues, but does not in fact align with an answer to the previous question.

8) CORRECT ANSWER: C
The word "fabric" refers to the new conditions that, thanks to Washington, were created "upon the ruins of a system which had been overthrown" (line 61). Because the authors in context are describing how Washington brought new social and political structures into being, C is the best answer. A and B both present wrongly literal meanings of "fabric", while D refers to an issue that is too narrow: although a nation may need means of protection, the relevant portions of the passage describe how Washington helped the nation in a BROADER sense.

9) CORRECT ANSWER: D
In lines 19-22, the authors explain that Hamilton had "freed himself from the local feelings of the colonial days" and that Washington, similarly, "was thoroughly national in all of his views". This similarity supports D. The only other direct mention of Hamilton occurs in lines 30-32: here, Hamilton is simply described as a colleague of Madison (not a mentor, eliminating A). B and C refer to qualities related to Washington in the passage,

NOT explicitly to Hamilton, and must thus be eliminated.

10) CORRECT ANSWER: A
See above for the explanation of the correct answer. B indicates Washington's belief in westward expansion (not Hamilton's), C indicates that Washington led a national movement (but makes no mention of Hamilton), and D indicates that Hamilton and Madison worked with Washington. Make sure not to wrongly take D as evidence for Question 9 A, since both answers mention Madison.

2.15 | W.E.B. Du Bois

1) CORRECT ANSWER: B
The phrase "fixed on" refers to how people have responded to "technical points, of union and local autonomy" (line 6-7) in analyzing the causes of the Civil War: according to Du Bois, these points have been given too much attention or have been too strongly emphasized, since the Civil War was more closely related to slavery. B is thus the best answer, while A, C, and D all refer to physical or decorative actions, not to the matters of INTERPRETATION that are the focus of this part of the passage.

2) CORRECT ANSWER: D
In lines 7-8, Du Bois asserts that, in the Civil War, "the question of Negro slavery was the real cause of the conflict". This strong stance supports D and can be used to eliminate B and C, which assume that Du Bois would be somewhat accepting of the idea that slavery was not a root cause of the Civil War. A is both too negative and out of scope: while Du Bois would vigorously disagree with the denial that slavery and the Civil War were linked, there is no indication that he would personally mock or insult the people behind this viewpoint.

3) CORRECT ANSWER: A
See above for the explanation of the correct answer. B indicates that race relations have remained problematic since the Civil War (but does not discuss slavery), C discusses responses to slaves (but not the reasons behind the Civil War), and D indicates that fugitive slaves were a problem for the Union army (but, again, does not actually discuss whether or not slavery motivated the Civil War).

4) CORRECT ANSWER: C
According to Du Bois, fugitive slaves were "a horde of starving vagabonds, hopeless, helpless, and pitiable, in their dark distress" (lines 32-33). This information directly supports C and can be used to eliminate the positives in A. While the slaves faced problems and were encountering the Union forces for the first time, Du Bois never explicitly describes the fugitive slaves as suspicious: thus, eliminate B and D.

5) CORRECT ANSWER: A
In lines 68-73, Du Bois notes that a typical African American of his time "may not leave the plantation of his birth" and is bound by "economic slavery". This information supports A and can be used to eliminate B (since economic progress may be ANOTHER way to improve conditions) and C (since the situation of African Americans in the South is thoroughly negative). D is a trap answer: Du Bois objects to the fact that the needs and dignity of African Americans have been neglected, not to the fact that African Americans have been insufficiently studied.

6) CORRECT ANSWER: C

See above for the explanation of the correct answer. A indicates the prevalence of racial tensions in the twentieth century, B notes that the Freedmen's Bureau attempted to improve the lives of African Americans (but does not record the results of these efforts), and D indicates the legal and socioeconomic oppression that African Americans face. Make sure not to falsely align B with Question 5 C or D with Question 5 B.

7) CORRECT ANSWER: D

In his analysis, Du Bois notes that slaves "were a source of strength to the Confederacy, and were being used as laborers and producers" (lines 46-48): this fact was acknowledged by an official of the time, Secretary Cameron, who spoke against turning slaves over to the Confederacy. This information supports D and can be used to eliminate A (since only practical considerations are brought into focus) and C (since the slaves were a source of labor, not of knowledge). B is a trap answer: while it may seem likely that the act of returning slaves would take up time, Du Bois never explicitly makes this argument, so that this answer must be eliminated as out of scope.

8) CORRECT ANSWER: C

In lines 43-46, Du Bois explains why the policy was difficult to enforce: some refugees "declared themselves freemen, others showed that their masters had deserted them, and still others were captured with forts and plantations". These different and irreconcilable circumstances support C, while Butler is only discussed in an earlier stage of the passage (eliminating A) and the temperament of the slaves is never considered (eliminating B). D is a trap answer: while returning slaves to owners might in fact have required great attention and resources, this is not the main reason, according to the passage, why such a measure was problematic.

9) CORRECT ANSWER: A

Du Bois notes that "despite compromise, war, and struggle, the Negro is not free" (lines 67-68): in other words, significant efforts to change the status of African Americans have been ineffectual. A is thus the best answer, while the same information can be used to eliminate both C (which is much too positive) and D (which wrongly assumes that great benefits for African Americans WERE at one time prominent). B is a trap answer: Du Bois is interested throughout the passage in criticizing PRACTICAL problems faced by African Americans, not in criticizing a PERSPECTIVE different from his own.

10) CORRECT ANSWER: C

The word "plain" refers to the idea that a military resource (fugitive slaves) "should not be turned over to the enemy" (line 50): this idea does not deserve discussion and is thus apparently or evidently correct. C is the best answer, while A, B, and D all refer to matters of human TEMPERAMENT, not to measures of how VALID an idea is.

CHAPTER 3
Emerging Nationalism

Emerging Nationalism
1914-1945

In the early years of the twentieth century, America both transformed its own way of life and took an assertive new stance on the world stage. On the domestic front, lawmakers such as President Theodore Roosevelt ushered in an era of economic and humanitarian reform. Political life itself was further transformed when, in 1920, women were granted national voting rights for the first time: proponents of women's suffrage such as Carrie Chapman Catt would see years of effort and protest finally rewarded. Female intellectuals also proved to be astute commentators on this era of rapid change. Novelist Edith Wharton reported on the progress and ramifications of World War I, while Elizabeth Morris documented the materialistic consumer culture of the 1910s and 1920s.

While women's life seemed to be taking assertive new directions, the proper uses of America's global influence remained in dispute. President Woodrow Wilson urged participation in World War I, only to meet the principled objections of legislators such as Robert M. La Follette. And after the hostilities, when Wilson advocated American involvement in the League of Nations, his policies ran up against the inward-looking approach of politicians such as Warren G. Harding, his successor as President. For the 1920s at least, Harding's approach won out. The era was seen as a time of opportunity in business, technology, and the arts: industrialist Henry Ford and educator William Osler tried to reconcile this spirit of enterprise with high ethical standards. But on the whole, this was an era of both cultural dynamism and political stability, presided over by limited-government politicians such as President Calvin Coolidge.

All that ended with the onset of the Great Depression. Americans renounced the Republican Party of Harding and Coolidge and once again embraced large and proactive government—this time in the person of Democratic President Franklin D. Roosevelt and his "New Deal" reform and relief programs. Roosevelt was a beloved leader, even though his interventions did not go far enough for some of the other lawmakers of the 1930s. Senator Huey Long of Louisiana, for instance, proposed pension creation and wealth redistribution programs more radical than any New Deal measures. But Roosevelt's vision of government as an implement of justice and order would meet its greatest test with the outbreak of World War II. An America emboldened by its new world stature but humbled by economic crisis would pit its values against the authoritarianism of Nazi Germany, Fascist Italy, and Imperial Japan.

Questions 1-10 are based on the following passage.
3.01
Adapted from *Fighting France: From Dunkirk to Belport*
(1915), an account of the German invasion of France
written by American author Edith Wharton.

The war has been a calamity unheard of; but France has
never been afraid of the unheard of. No race has ever yet so
audaciously dispensed with old precedents; as none has ever
Line so revered their relics. It is a great strength to be able to walk
5 without the support of analogies; and France has always shown
that strength in times of crisis. The absorbing question, as the
war went on, was to discover how far down into the people this
intellectual audacity penetrated, how instinctive it had become,
and how it would endure the strain of prolonged inaction.

10   There was never much doubt about the army. When a
warlike race has an invader on its soil, the men holding back
the invader can never be said to be inactive. But behind the
army were the waiting millions to whom that long motionless
line in the trenches might gradually have become a mere
15 condition of thought, an accepted limitation to all sorts of
activities and pleasures. The danger was that such a war—
static, dogged, uneventful—might gradually cramp instead of
enlarging the mood of the lookers-on. Conscription, of course,
was there to minimize this danger. Every one was sharing
20 alike in the glory and the woe. But the glory was not of a kind
to penetrate or dazzle. It requires more imagination to see
the halo around tenacity than around dash; and the French
still cling to the view that they are, so to speak, the patentees
and proprietors of dash, and much less at home with his dull
25 drudge of a partner. So there was reason to fear, in the long
run, a gradual but irresistible disintegration, not of public
opinion, but of something subtler and more fundamental:
public sentiment. It was possible that civilian France, while
collectively seeming to remain at the same height, might
30 individually deteriorate and diminish in its attitude toward the
war.

The French would not be human, and therefore would
not be interesting, if one had not perceived in them occasional
symptoms of such a peril. There has not been a Frenchman or
35 a Frenchwoman—save a few harmless and perhaps nervous
theorizers—who has wavered about the military policy of the
country; but there have naturally been some who have found
it less easy than they could have foreseen to live up to the
sacrifices it has necessitated. Of course there have been such
40 people: one would have had to postulate them if they had not
come within one's experience. There have been some to whom
it was harder than they imagined to give up a certain way of
living, or a certain kind of breakfast-roll; though the French,
being fundamentally temperate, are far less the slaves of the
45 luxuries they have invented than are the other races who have
adopted these luxuries.

There have been many more who found the sacrifice of
personal happiness—of all that made life livable, or one's
country worth fighting for—infinitely harder than the most
50 apprehensive imagination could have pictured. There have
been mothers and widows for whom a single grave, or the
appearance of one name on the missing list, has turned the
whole conflict into an idiot's tale. There have been many
such; but there have apparently not been enough to deflect
55 by a hair's breadth the subtle current of public sentiment;
unless it is truer, as it is infinitely more inspiring, to suppose
that, of this company of blinded baffled sufferers, almost
all have had the strength to hide their despair and to say of
the great national effort which has lost most of its meaning
60 to them: "Though it slay me, yet will I trust in it." That
is probably the finest triumph of the tone of France: that
its myriad fiery currents flow from so many hearts made
insensible by suffering, that so many dead hands feed its
undying lamp.

65 This does not in the least imply that resignation is the
prevailing note in the tone of France. The attitude of the
French people, after fourteen months of trial, is not one of
submission to unparalleled calamity. It is one of exaltation,
energy, the hot resolve to dominate the disaster. In all classes
70 the feeling is the same: every word and every act is based
on the resolute ignoring of any alternative to victory. The
French people no more think of a compromise than people
would think of facing a flood or an earthquake with a white
flag.

1

The passage as a whole can best be described as

A) a darkly humorous commentary based on the author's
travels through France.

B) a series of general statements about a single
nationality.

C) a set of concrete examples that proves a central point.

D) a consideration of the advisability of a new military
strategy.

CONTINUE

2

Which of the following assumptions about the French is present in Wharton's discussion?

A) They chose war even though doing so would cripple their economy.

B) They are almost unanimous in their stance regarding the war.

C) Their war effort is sustained by their belief in democratic government.

D) They trust their leaders even though most of their military campaigns have failed.

3

As used in line 26, "irresistible" means

A) alluring.

B) convincing.

C) impulsive.

D) overwhelming.

4

In this passage, Wharton's purpose is to characterize the French as

A) unconcerned about the outcome of the war.

B) unwilling to acknowledge any form of weakness.

C) determined to prevail in their efforts.

D) irreverent towards most traditions.

5

Which choice provides the best evidence for the answer to the previous question?

A) Lines 2-4 ("No race has . . . relics")

B) Lines 32-34 ("The French . . . peril")

C) Lines 39-41 ("Of course . . . experience")

D) Lines 66-69 ("The attitude . . . disaster")

6

As used in line 66, "note" most nearly means

A) comment.

B) reminder.

C) element.

D) allusion.

7

The "undying lamp" mentioned in line 64 is best understood to symbolize

A) France's vigorous military effort.

B) France's many wartime casualties.

C) France's methods of honoring its heroes.

D) France's self-sacrificing political elite.

8

The "peril" that Wharton mentions in line 34 can best be defined as

A) the use of innovative propaganda by France's enemies.

B) the possibility of a decline in morale among the French populace.

C) disobedience and insubordination in the French army.

D) an emphasis on heroic gestures instead of practical strategic gains.

9

According to Wharton, which of the following was a source of uncertainty?

A) How stratified French society had become

B) How exactly the French army would be funded

C) How easily the French would find wartime allies

D) How French civilians would react to warfare

10

Which choice provides the best evidence for the answer to the previous question?

A) Lines 10-12 ("When a warlike . . . inactive")

B) Lines 16-18 ("The danger . . . lookers on")

C) Lines 18-20 ("Conscription . . . the woe")

D) Lines 47-50 ("There have . . . pictured")

CONTINUE

Questions 1-10 are based on the following passages.
3.02
These two readings discuss the early stages of American involvement in World War I. Passage 1 is adapted from the 1917 "War Message to Congress" delivered by President Woodrow Wilson, while Passage 2 is taken from a response delivered only days later by Senator Robert M. La Follette.

Passage 1

With a profound sense of the solemn and even tragical character of the step I am taking and of the grave responsibilities which it involves, but in unhesitating
Line obedience to what I deem my constitutional duty, I advise that
5 the Congress declare the recent course of the Imperial German Government to be in fact nothing less than war against the government and people of the United States; that it formally accept the status of belligerent which has thus been thrust upon it, and that it take immediate steps not only to put the country
10 in a more thorough state of defense but also to exert all its power and employ all its resources to bring the Government of the German Empire to terms and end the war.

What this will involve is clear. It will involve the utmost practicable cooperation in counsel and action with the
15 governments now at war with Germany, and, as incident to that, the extension to those governments of the most liberal financial credit, in order that our resources may so far as possible be added to theirs. It will involve the organization and mobilization of all the material resources of the country to
20 supply the materials of war and serve the incidental needs of the Nation in the most abundant and yet the most economical and efficient way possible. It will involve the immediate full equipment of the navy in all respects but particularly in supplying it with the best means of dealing with the enemy's
25 submarines. It will involve the immediate addition to the armed forces of the United States already provided for by law in case of war at least five hundred thousand men, who should, in my opinion, be chosen upon the principle of universal liability to service, and also the authorization of subsequent
30 additional increments of equal force so soon as they may be needed and can be handled in training.

Passage 2

Mr. President, I had supposed until recently that it was the duty of senators and representatives in Congress to vote and act according to their convictions on all public matters
35 that came before them for consideration and decision. Quite another doctrine has recently been promulgated by certain newspapers, which unfortunately seems to have found considerable support elsewhere, and that is the doctrine of "standing back of the President" without inquiring whether the
40 President is right or wrong.

For myself, I have never subscribed to that doctrine and never shall. I shall support the President in the measures he proposes when I believe them to be right. I shall oppose measures proposed by the President when I believe them
45 to be wrong. The fact that the matter which the President submits for consideration is of the greatest importance is only an additional reason why we should be sure that we are right and not to be swerved from that conviction or intimidating in its expression by any influence of its power
50 whatsoever.

If it is important for us to speak and vote our convictions in matters of internal policy, though we may unfortunately be in disagreement with the President, it is infinitely more important for us to speak and vote our
55 convictions when the question is one of peace or war, certain to involve the lives and fortunes of many of our people and, it may be, the destiny of all of them and of the civilized world as well. If, unhappily, on such momentous questions the most patient research and conscientious consideration
60 we could give to them leave us in disagreement with the President, I know of no course to take except to oppose, regretfully but not the less firmly, the demands of the Executive. . . .

Mr. President, many of my colleagues on both sides of
65 this floor have from day to day offered for publication in the *Record* messages and letters received from their constituents I have received some 15,000 letters and telegrams. They have come from forty-four states in the Union. They have been assorted according to whether they speak in criticism or
70 commendation of my course in opposing war.

Assorting the 15,000 letters and telegrams by states in that way, 9 out of 10 are an unqualified endorsement of my course in opposing war with Germany on the issue presented.

1

The main purpose of Passage 1 is to

A) explain the origins of the conflict with Germany.
B) argue for the moral validity of America's position.
C) urge Congress to debate a complex issue.
D) propose a series of new government efforts.

CONTINUE

2

As used in line 10, "state" most nearly means

A) position.

B) nation.

C) government.

D) appearance.

3

In Passage 1, Wilson supports the idea that the United States should

A) increase enlistment in its navy.

B) increase enlistment in its military.

C) penalize companies linked to the German economy.

D) begin a new round of diplomacy with Germany.

4

Which choice provides the best evidence for the answer to the previous question?

A) Lines 9-12 ("that it take . . . the war")

B) Lines 13-18 ("What this will . . . theirs")

C) Lines 22-25 ("It will involve . . . submarines")

D) Lines 25-29 ("It will involve . . . service")

5

Which aspect of the proposed declaration of war is emphasized in both Passage 1 and Passage 2?

A) Its unprecedented nature

B) Its support in the press

C) Its grave consequences

D) Its direct impact on America's allies

6

Both Wilson in Passage 1 and La Follette in Passage 2 argue that their stances are based on

A) American principles of sound government.

B) consideration of international rather than domestic affairs.

C) the will of their constituents.

D) the majority opinion within Congress.

7

It can be reasonably inferred that the information presented in lines 13-31 of Passage 1 ("What this . . . training") would

A) make the author of Passage 2 more likely to support the war.

B) have no influence on the opinions of the author of Passage 2.

C) make the "constituents" (line 66) less likely to support the war.

D) have no influence on the opinions of the "constituents" (line 66).

8

As used in line 69, "assorted" most nearly means

A) organized.

B) ranked.

C) diversified.

D) randomized.

9

In opposing American involvement in war against Germany, La Follette takes a stance that can best be described as

A) informed yet cynical.

B) thoughtful yet decisive.

C) pragmatic yet uncommitted.

D) principled yet self-doubting.

10

Which choice provides the best evidence for the answer to the previous question?

A) Lines 35-40 ("Quite another . . . wrong")

B) Lines 51-55 ("If it is . . . or war")

C) Lines 58-63 ("If unhappily . . . executive")

D) Lines 71-74 ("Assorting the . . . presented")

112

CONTINUE

Questions 1-10 are based on the following passage.
3.03
Adapted from an address to the United States Congress by Carrie Chapman Catt, an outspoken proponent of voting rights for women. Catt's speech was delivered in November of 1917; women were granted suffrage by the 19th Amendment to the Constitution only a few years later.

Your party platforms have pledged women suffrage. Then why not be honest, frank friends of our cause, adopt it in reality as your own, make it a party program, and "fight with
Line us?" As a party measure—a measure of all parties—why not
5 put the amendment through Congress and the legislatures? We shall all be better friends, we shall have a happier nation, we women will be free to support loyally the party of our choice, and we shall be far prouder of our history.

"There is one thing mightier than kings and armies"—
10 aye, than Congresses and political parties—"the power of an idea when its time has come to move." The time for woman suffrage has come. The woman's hour has struck. If parties prefer to postpone action longer and thus do battle with this idea, they challenge the inevitable. The idea will not perish;
15 the party which opposes it may. Every delay, every trick, every political dishonesty from now on will antagonize the women of the land more and more, and when the party or parties which have so delayed woman suffrage finally let it come, their sincerity will be doubted and their appeal to the new
20 voters will be met with suspicion. This is the psychology of the situation. Can you afford the risk? Think it over.

We know you will meet opposition. There are a few "women haters" left, a few "old males of the tribe," as Vance Thompson calls them, whose duty they believe it to be to keep
25 women in the places they have carefully picked out for them. Treitschke, made world famous by war literature, said some years ago, "Germany, which knows all about Germany and France, knows far better what is good for Alsace-Lorraine than that miserable people can possibly know." . . . There
30 are women, too, with "slave souls" and "clinging vines" for backbones. There are female dolls and male dandies. But the world does not wait for such as these, nor does liberty pause to heed the plaint of men and women with a grouch. She does not wait for those who have a special interest to serve, nor a selfish
35 reason for depriving other people of freedom. Holding her torch aloft, liberty is pointing the way onward and upward and saying to America, "Come."

To you and the supporters of our cause in Senate and House, and the number is large, the suffragists of the nation
40 express their grateful thanks. This address is not meant for you. We are more truly appreciative of all you have done than any words can express. We ask you to make a last, hard fight for the amendment during the present session. Since last we asked a vote on this amendment, your position has been
45 fortified by the addition to suffrage territory of Great Britain, Canada, and New York.

Some of you have been too indifferent to give more than casual attention to this question. It is worthy of your immediate consideration. A question big enough to engage
50 the attention of our allies in wartime is too big a question for you to neglect.

Some of you have grown old in party service. Are you willing that those who take your places by and by shall blame you for having failed to keep pace with the world and
55 thus having lost for them a party advantage? Is there any real gain for you, for your party, for your nation by delay? Do you want to drive the progressive men and women out of your party?

Some of you hold to the doctrine of states' rights as
60 applying to woman suffrage. Adherence to that theory will keep the United States far behind all other democratic nations upon this question. A theory which prevents a nation from keeping up with the trend of world progress cannot be justified.
65 Gentlemen, we hereby petition you, our only designated representatives, to redress our grievances by the immediate passage of the Federal Suffrage Amendment and to use your influence to secure its ratification in your own state, in order that the women of our nation may be endowed with political
70 freedom before the next presidential election, and that our nation may resume its world leadership in democracy.

Woman suffrage is coming—you know it. Will you, Honorable Senators and Members of the House of Representatives, help or hinder it?

1

Catt's main point is that women's suffrage

A) is morally just, but that it remains unpopular in many regions of America.

B) is widely supported, and that it will give women a new role in the American workforce.

C) is bound to be accepted, and that those who have opposed it will be marginalized.

D) is still being debated, and that it is impossible to say what form women's suffrage will take.

2

Catt's apparent aim in delivering this speech is to

A) redefine women's suffrage.

B) explain the worldwide situation of women's suffrage.

C) thank her allies in the women's suffrage movement.

D) engage those who do not promote women's suffrage.

CONTINUE

3

Which choice provides the best evidence for the answer to the previous question?

A) Lines 9-11 ("There is . . . move")

B) Lines 38-41 ("To you and . . . for you")

C) Lines 43-46 ("Since last we . . . New York")

D) Lines 62-64 ("A theory . . . justified")

4

As used in line 38, "cause" most nearly means

A) pretext.

B) origins.

C) effort.

D) dispute.

5

As used in line 47, "indifferent" most nearly means

A) ordinary.

B) fair.

C) uninteresting.

D) uninvolved.

6

In what respect do the quotations in the first and second paragraphs (lines 1-21) differ from the quotations that begin the third paragraph (lines 22-37)?

A) The quotations that begin the third paragraph have named sources.

B) The quotations that begin the third paragraph weaken Catt's argument.

C) The quotations that begin the third paragraph are not ironic or sarcastic.

D) The quotations that begin the third paragraph are from publications, not speeches.

7

The Congressmen that Catt is addressing are open to which of the following allegations?

A) They have helped to perpetuate negative stereotypes about women.

B) They are more preoccupied with small domestic issues than important international issues.

C) The endorse ideas that are not complemented by their actions.

D) They condone the corrupt tactics used by opponents of suffrage.

8

Which choice provides the best evidence for the answer to the previous question?

A) Lines 1-4 ("Your party . . . us?")

B) Lines 15-20 ("Every delay . . . suspicion")

C) Lines 31-33 ("There are . . . grouch")

D) Lines 49-51 ("A question . . . neglect")

9

In line 33, "She" is best understood as

A) one of Catt's fellow activists.

B) Catt herself.

C) a personification of an ideal valued by Catt.

D) a reference to a type of woman despised by Catt.

10

In lines 47-64, Catt argues in favor of women's suffrage by calling attention to America's

A) history of innovation.

B) international status.

C) founding principles.

D) economic power.

CONTINUE

Questions 1-10 are based on the following passages.
3.04

Passage 1 is adapted from President Woodrow Wilson's 1919 Address in Favor of the League of Nations; Passage 2 is adapted from a speech delivered in 1920 by Warren G. Harding, who served as President immediately after Wilson.

Passage 1

We must see that all the questions which have disturbed the world, all the questions which have eaten into the confidence of men toward their governments, all the
Line questions which have disturbed the processes of industry,
5 shall be brought out where men of all points of view, men of all attitudes of mind, men of all kinds of experience, may contribute their part of the settlement of the great questions which we must settle and cannot ignore.

At the front of this great treaty is put the Covenant of the
10 League of Nations. It will also be at the front of the Austrian, treaty and the Hungarian treaty and the Bulgarian treaty and the treaty with Turkey. Every one of them will contain the Covenant of the League of Nations, because you cannot work any of them without the Covenant of the League of Nations.
15 Unless you get the united, concerted purpose and power of the great Governments of the world behind this settlement, it will fall down like a house of cards. There is only one power to put behind the liberation of mankind, and that is the power of mankind. It is the power of the united moral forces of the
20 world, and in the Covenant of the League of Nations the moral forces of the world are mobilized. For what purpose?

Reflect, my fellow citizens, that the membership of this great League is going to include all the great fighting nations of the world, as well as the weak ones. It is not for the present
25 going to include Germany, but for the time being Germany is not a great fighting country. All the nations that have power that can be mobilized are going to be members of this League, including the United States.

And what do they unite for? They enter into a solemn
30 promise to one another that they will never use their power against one another for aggression; that they never will impair the territorial integrity of a neighbour; that they never will interfere with the political independence of a neighbour; that they will abide by the principle that great populations are
35 entitled to determine their own destiny and that they will not interfere with that destiny.

Passage 2

There isn't anything the matter with world civilization, except that humanity is viewing it through a vision impaired in a cataclysmal war. Poise has been disturbed, and nerves have
40 been racked, and fever has rendered men irrational; sometimes there have been draughts upon the dangerous cup of barbarity,

and men have wandered far from safe paths, but the human procession still marches in the right direction.

America's present need is not heroics, but healing; not
45 nostrums, but normalcy; not revolution, but restoration; not agitation, but adjustment; not surgery, but serenity; not the dramatic, but the dispassionate; not experiment, but equipoise; not submergence in internationality, but sustainment in triumphant nationality. . .
50 This republic has its ample tasks. If we put an end to false economics which lure humanity to utter chaos, ours will be the commanding example of world leadership today. If we can prove a representative popular government under which a citizenship seeks what it may do for the government
55 rather than what the government may do for individuals, we shall do more to make democracy safe for the world than all armed conflict ever recorded.

The world needs to be reminded that all human ills are not curable by legislation, and that quantity of statutory
60 enactment and excess of government offer no substitute for quality of citizenship.

The problems of maintained civilization are not to be solved by a transfer of responsibility from citizenship to government, and no eminent page in history was ever drafted
65 by the standards of mediocrity. More, no government is worthy of the name which is directed by influence on the one hand, or moved by intimidation on the other . . .

My best judgment of America's needs is to steady down, to get squarely on our feet, to make sure of the right
70 path. Let's get out of the fevered delirium of war, with the hallucination that all the money in the world is to be made in the madness of war and the wildness of its aftermath. Let us stop to consider that tranquillity at home is more precious than peace abroad, and that both our good fortune and our
75 eminence are dependent on the normal forward stride of all the American people.

1

Respectively, Passage 1 and Passage 2 deal with initiatives that are

A) theoretical versus practical.

B) international versus domestic.

C) conciliatory versus aggressive.

D) simplistic versus complicated.

CONTINUE

2

Which of the following does the author of Passage 1 envision as a necessary function of the League of Nations?

A) The promotion of new civil liberties by all world governments

B) Systematic methods for punishing belligerent nations

C) The gradual reduction of military forces among all world powers

D) Vigorous debate that can produce broad consensus

3

Which choice provides the best evidence for the answer to the previous question?

A) Lines 5-8 ("men of all points . . . ignore")

B) Lines 15-17 ("Unless you . . . cards")

C) Lines 24-26 ("It is not . . . country")

D) Lines 29-31 ("They enter . . . aggression")

4

In Passage 2, Harding explains his view of how America should act by presenting

A) the viewpoints of war heroes.

B) a series of sharp ideological contrasts.

C) a new theory of politics and economics.

D) a brief chronology of the First World War.

5

According to both passages, which of the following was an effect of the recent war?

A) Increases in the industrial capacity of the United States

B) Decreases in the industrial capacity of Germany and its allies

C) Broader acceptance of democratic principles

D) Loss of confidence in political and social structures

6

How would the author of Passage 2 regard the measures outlined in the final paragraph of Passage 1 (lines 29-36)?

A) As advisable, because the recent war has caused Americans to lose faith in their government.

B) As advisable, because new arrangements will restore America to its former prosperity.

C) As problematic, because America must play a more active and direct role as an example for other nations.

D) As problematic, because the measures outlined in Passage 1 are designed to destabilize foreign governments.

7

Which choice provides the best evidence for the answer to the previous question?

A) Lines 37-39 ("There isn't . . . war")

B) Lines 44-45 ("America's . . . restoration")

C) Lines 50-52 ("This republic . . . today")

D) Lines 62-65 ("The problems . . . mediocrity")

8

As used in line 32, "integrity" most nearly means

A) honesty.

B) sovereignty.

C) isolation.

D) purity.

9

Which of the following does neither Passage 1 nor Passage 2 recommend?

A) Forming new international covenants

B) Observing high standards of morality and responsibility

C) Expanding the role of government in daily life

D) Prioritizing domestic issues over foreign affairs

10

As used in line 60, "substitute for" most nearly means

A) representation of.

B) counterfeit of.

C) alternative to.

D) deputy of.

CONTINUE ➡

Questions 1-10 are based on the following passage.
3.05
Adapted from Elizabeth Morris, "The Tyranny of Things"
(1917).

It is an age of things. As I walk through the shops at
Christmas time and survey their contents, I find it a most
depressing spectacle. All of us have too many things already,
Line and here are more! . . . It extends to all our doings. For every
5   event there is a "souvenir." We cannot go to luncheon and meet
our friends but we must receive a token to carry away. Even
our children cannot have a birthday party, and play games, and
eat good things, and be happy. The host must receive gifts from
every little guest, and provide in return some little remembrance
10   for each to take home. Truly, on all sides we are beset, and
we go lumbering along through life like a ship encrusted with
barnacles, which can never cut the waves clean and sure and
swift until she has been scraped bare again. And there seems
little hope for us this side our last port.

15   And to think that there was a time when folk had not even
that hope! When a man's possessions were burned with him,
so that he might, forsooth, have them all about him in the next
world! Suffocating thought! To think one could not even then
be clear of things, and make at least a fresh start! That must,
20   indeed, have been in the childhood of the race.

Once upon a time, when I was very tired, I chanced to go
away to a little house by the sea. "It is empty," they said, "but
you can easily furnish it." Empty! Yes, thank Heaven! Furnish
it? Heaven forbid! Its floors were bare, its walls were bare, its
25   tables (there were only two in the house) were bare. There was
nothing in the closets but books; nothing in the bureau drawers
but the smell of clean, fresh wood; nothing in the kitchen but
an oil stove, and a few, a very few dishes; nothing in the attic
but rafters and sunshine, and a view of the sea. After I had
30   been there an hour there descended upon me a great peace,
a sense of freedom, of infinite leisure. In the twilight I sat
before the flickering embers of the open fire, and looked out
through the open door to the sea, and asked myself, "Why?"
Then the answer came: I was emancipated from things. There
35   was nothing in the house to demand care, to claim attention,
to cumber my consciousness with its insistent, unchanging
companionship. There was nothing but a shelter, and outside,
the fields and marshes, the shore and the sea. These did not
have to be taken down and put up and arranged and dusted
40   and cared for. They were not things at all, they were powers,
presences.

And so I rested. While the spell was still unbroken, I came
away. For broken it would have been, I know, had I not fled
first. Even in this refuge the enemy would have pursued me,
45   found me out, encompassed me.

If we could but free ourselves once for all, how simple
life might become! One of my friends, who, with six young
children and only one servant, keeps a spotless house and a
soul serene, told me once how she did it. "My dear, once a
50   month I give away every single thing in the house that we do
not imperatively need. It sounds wasteful, but I don't believe it
really is. Sometimes Jeremiah mourns over missing old clothes,
or back numbers of the magazines, but I tell him if he doesn't
want to be mated to a gibbering maniac he will let me do as I
55   like."

The old monks knew all this very well. One wonders
sometimes how they got their power; but go up to Fiesole, and
sit a while in one of those little, bare, white-walled cells, and
you will begin to understand. If there were any spiritual force
60   in one, it would have to come out there.

I have not their courage, and I win no such freedom. I
allow myself to be overwhelmed by the invading host of things,
making fitful resistance, but without any real steadiness of
purpose. Yet never do I wholly give up the struggle, and in my
65   heart I cherish an ideal, remotely typified by that empty little
house beside the sea.

1

As used in line 2, "survey" most nearly means
A) gather the opinions of.
B) make an overview of.
C) record the positions of.
D) observe the behavior of.

2

Which of the following best describes the developmental
pattern of the passage?
A) A pervasive situation is described and a personal
response is offered.
B) A catastrophe is presented and a new explanation is put
forward.
C) A humorous anecdote gives way to an account of an
intense conflict.
D) A single strong example contradicts the author's
original argument.

3

For Morris, the "little house by the sea" (line 22) can be
understood to represent.
A) a misguided experiment.
B) an artistic inspiration.
C) an impossible imagining.
D) a desirable lifestyle.

CONTINUE ➡

4

As used in line 19, "clear of" most nearly means

A) unencumbered by.
B) elucidated by.
C) forgiven for.
D) expressed through.

5

Morris's discussion of the role of things in everyday life is ironic because

A) she has never attempted to follow her own advice.
B) she is unhappy as soon as she frees herself from things.
C) she has profited personally from the materialism of others.
D) she falls prey to the very influence she criticizes.

6

Which choice provides the best evidence for the answer to the previous question?

A) Lines 3-4 ("All of us . . . doings")
B) Lines 37-38 ("There was . . . the sea")
C) Lines 43-45 ("For broken . . . encompassed me")
D) Lines 61-64 ("I allow . . . purpose")

7

Morris mentions one of her "friends" (line 47) and the "monks" (line 56) as examples of people who

A) are oblivious to the ideas of others.
B) have successfully resisted materialism.
C) obey strict and well-known moral codes.
D) remain mostly secluded from society.

8

Morris states that people accumulate "things" in order to

A) honor their ancestors and traditions.
B) cope with personal losses.
C) showcase their wealth.
D) commemorate minor events.

9

Which choice provides the best evidence for the answer to the previous question?

A) Lines 4-6 ("For every . . . away")
B) Lines 10-14 ("Truly, on all . . . last port")
C) Lines 16-18 ("When a man's . . . world!")
D) Lines 52-55 ("Sometimes . . . as I like")

10

Morris repeats the word "bare" in lines 24-25 in order to

A) emphasize the thoroughness of the house's condition.
B) characterize the owners of the house as oblivious.
C) imply her disappointment with the state of the house.
D) call attention to her sole reason for staying in the house.

118

CONTINUE

Questions 1-10 are based on the following passage.
3.06
Adapted from *My Life and Work* (1922), the autobiography of Henry Ford, written in collaboration with Samuel Crowther.

We have only started on our development of our country—we have not as yet, with all our talk of wonderful progress, done more than scratch the surface. The progress has
Line been wonderful enough—but when we compare what we have
5 done with what there is to do, then our past accomplishments are as nothing. When we consider that more power is used merely in ploughing the soil than is used in all the industrial establishments of the country put together, an inkling comes of how much opportunity there is ahead. And now, with so many
10 countries of the world in ferment and with so much unrest every where, is an excellent time to suggest something of the things that may be done in the light of what has been done.

When one speaks of increasing power, machinery, and industry there comes up a picture of a cold, metallic sort of
15 world in which great factories will drive away the trees, the flowers, the birds, and the green fields. And that then we shall have a world composed of metal machines and human machines. With all of that I do not agree. I think that unless we know more about machines and their use, unless we better
20 understand the mechanical portion of life, we cannot have the time to enjoy the trees, and the birds, and the flowers, and the green fields.

I think that we have already done too much toward banishing the pleasant things from life by thinking that there
25 is some opposition between living and providing the means of living. We waste so much time and energy that we have little left over in which to enjoy ourselves.

Power and machinery, money and goods, are useful only as they set us free to live. They are but means to an end. For
30 instance, I do not consider the machines which bear my name simply as machines. If that was all there was to it I would do something else. I take them as concrete evidence of the working out of a theory of business, which I hope is something more than a theory of business—a theory that looks toward
35 making this world a better place in which to live. The fact that the commercial success of the Ford Motor Company has been most unusual is important only because it serves to demonstrate, in a way which no one can fail to understand, that the theory to date is right. Considered solely in this light I can
40 criticize the prevailing system of industry and the organization of money and society from the standpoint of one who has not been beaten by them. As things are now organized, I could, were I thinking only selfishly, ask for no change. If I merely want money the present system is all right; it gives money in
45 plenty to me. But I am thinking of service. The present system does not permit of the best service because it encourages

every kind of waste—it keeps many men from getting the full return from service. And it is going nowhere. It is all a matter of better planning and adjustment.
50 I have no quarrel with the general attitude of scoffing at new ideas. It is better to be skeptical of all new ideas and to insist upon being shown rather than to rush around in a continuous brainstorm after every new idea. Skepticism, if by that we mean cautiousness, is the balance wheel of
55 civilization. Most of the present acute troubles of the world arise out of taking on new ideas without first carefully investigating to discover if they are good ideas. An idea is not necessarily good because it is old, or necessarily bad because it is new, but if an old idea works, then the weight
60 of the evidence is all in its favor. Ideas are of themselves extraordinarily valuable, but an idea is just an idea. Almost any one can think up an idea. The thing that counts is developing it into a practical product.

1

The main ideas that Ford presents in this passage are premised on a principle of

A) individualism.
B) materialism.
C) loyalty.
D) balance.

2

As used in line 8, "establishments" most nearly means

A) accepted authorities.
B) places of hospitality.
C) facilities.
D) beginnings.

3

As used in line 48, "return" most nearly means

A) arrival.
B) benefit.
C) resurgence.
D) repetition.

CONTINUE

4

For Ford, machinery and industry are meaningful primarily because they

A) enhance overall quality of life.

B) serve educational purposes.

C) symbolize power and authority.

D) lifted Ford himself out of poverty.

5

Which choice provides the best evidence for the answer to the previous question?

A) Lines 9-12 ("And now . . . been done")

B) Lines 13-15 ("When one . . . world")

C) Lines 28-29 ("Power and . . . an end")

D) Lines 39-42 ("Considered . . . by them")

6

Which statement best describes the relationship between the first two paragraphs (lines 1-22)?

A) The first praises the growth of American industry, while the second laments the subsequent decline of American agriculture.

B) The first explains a project that could change society, while the second praises a prevailing attitude.

C) The first outlines new conditions, while the second promotes a certain attitude towards these conditions.

D) The first describes an international situation, while the second focuses only on domestic problems.

7

With which statement about current systems of production would Ford most likely agree?

A) They should be altered, because they are not as efficient as possible.

B) They should stay the same, because his successes are characteristic of the current system.

C) They should be altered, because people have begun to emphasize spirituality.

D) They should stay the same, because skepticism only leads to chaos.

8

The discussion of the "Ford Motor Company" (line 36) serves mainly to

A) introduce the argument that service-oriented businesses are often inefficient.

B) indicate that Ford intends to invest his wealth in new endeavors.

C) imply that the automotive industry will be profitable in the years to come.

D) illustrate that Ford's ideas can be implemented with excellent results.

9

In the final paragraph, Ford argues that skepticism is

A) widely unpopular.

B) socially useful.

C) easily underestimated.

D) purely theoretical.

10

Which choice provides the best evidence for the answer to the previous question?

A) Lines 50-51 ("I have . . . ideas")

B) Lines 53-55 ("Skepticism . . . civilization")

C) Lines 57-60 ("An idea is . . . favor")

D) Lines 60-61 ("Ideas are . . . just an idea")

CONTINUE

Questions 1-10 are based on the following passage.
3.07
Adapted from William Osler, "The Student Life" (1921).

Only steadfastness of purpose and humility enable the
student to shift his position to meet the new conditions in
which new truths are born, or old ones modified beyond
Line recognition. The honest heart will keep him in touch with his
5 fellow students, and furnish that sense of comradeship without
which he travels an arid waste alone. I say advisedly an honest
heart—the honest head is prone to be cold and stern, given
to judgment, not mercy, and not always able to entertain that
true charity which, while it thinketh no evil, is anxious to put
10 the best possible interpretation upon the motives of a fellow
worker. It will foster, too, an attitude of generous, friendly
rivalry untinged by the green peril, jealousy, that is the best
preventive of the growth of an aberrant scientific spirit, loving
seclusion and working in a lock-and-key laboratory, as timorous
15 of light as is a thief.
You have all become brothers in a great society, not
apprentices, since that implies a master, and nothing should be
further from the attitude of the teacher than much that is meant
in that word, used though it be in another sense, particularly
20 by our French brethren in a most delightful way, signifying
a bond of intellectual filiation. A fraternal attitude is not easy
to cultivate—the chasm between the chair and the bench is
difficult to bridge. Two things have helped to put up a cantilever
across the gulf. The successful teacher is no longer on a height,
25 pumping knowledge at high pressure into passive receptacles.
The new methods have changed all this. He is no longer Sir
Oracle, perhaps unconsciously by his very manner antagonizing
minds to whose level he cannot possibly descend, but he is
a senior student anxious to help his juniors. When a simple,
30 earnest spirit animates a college, there is no appreciable interval
between the teacher and the taught—both are in the same class,
the one a little more advanced than the other. So animated, the
student feels that he has joined a family whose honor is his
honor, whose welfare is his own, and whose interests should be
35 his first consideration.
The hardest conviction to get into the mind of a beginner
is that the education upon which he is engaged is not a college
course, not a medical course, but a life course, for which
the work of a few years under teachers is but a preparation.
40 Whether you will falter and fail in the race or whether you will
be faithful to the end depends on the training before the start,
and on your staying powers, points upon which I need not
enlarge. You can all become good students, a few may become
great students, and now and again one of you will be found
45 who does easily and well what others cannot do at all, or badly,
which is John Ferriar's excellent definition of a genius.
In the hurry and bustle of a business world, which is the
life of this continent, it is not easy to train first-class students.

Under present conditions it is hard to get the needful seclusion,
50 on which account it is that our educational market is so full
of wayside fruit. I have always been much impressed by the
advice of St. Chrysostom: "Depart from the highway and
transplant thyself in some enclosed ground, for it is hard for
a tree which stands by the wayside to keep her fruit till it
55 be ripe." The dilettante is abroad in the land, the man who
is always venturing on tasks for which he is imperfectly
equipped, a habit of mind fostered by the multiplicity of
subjects in the curriculum: and while many things are studied,
few are studied thoroughly. Men will not take time to get to
60 the heart of a matter. After all, concentration is the price the
modern student pays for success. Thoroughness is the most
difficult habit to acquire, but it is the pearl of great price, worth
all the worry and trouble of the search.

1

According to Osler, the ideal relationship between teacher
and student is one of

A) sympathetic collaboration.

B) unworried good humor.

C) unrelenting skepticism.

D) reverence for tradition.

2

As used in line 29, "senior" most nearly means

A) widely esteemed.

B) noticeably older.

C) clearly outdated.

D) vastly superior.

3

Throughout the passage, Osler uses the word "you" in
order to

A) profess his solidarity with other academics.

B) appeal to those who might be able to advance his
   career.

C) address students who would benefit from his advice.

D) imagine the academic successes of an ideal student.

CONTINUE ➤

4

Osler explains that one who wishes to become an outstanding student would do well to

A) study a very large number of subjects.

B) reject existing institutions.

C) seek out only the most celebrated instructors.

D) avoid a life of commerce and distraction.

5

Which choice provides the best evidence for the answer to the previous question?

A) Lines 21-23 ("A fraternal . . . bridge")

B) Lines 32-35 ("So animated . . . consideration")

C) Lines 47-48 ("In the hurry . . . students")

D) Lines 55-58 ("The dilettante . . . curriculum")

6

In the first paragraph, Osler presents a contrast between

A) the virtues of study and the drawbacks of leisure.

B) a private desire and a social initiative.

C) an impractical idea and a needed modification.

D) a possible excess and a more temperate approach.

7

As used in line 45, "badly" most nearly means

A) ineptly.

B) maliciously.

C) rebelliously.

D) fatally.

8

Which does Osler cite as a drawback of some of his recommendations?

A) Their incompatibility with the ideas of John Ferriar and other authority figures

B) The disdain that many students have expressed for them

C) The difficulty of comprehending the ideas behind them

D) The difficulty of putting them into practice in his society

9

Overall, Osler characterizes education as

A) valued mainly by elites.

B) a means of reforming society.

C) a detriment to modern business.

D) a long-term pursuit.

10

Which choice provides the best evidence for the answer to the previous question?

A) Lines 1-4 ("Only steadfastness . . . recognition")

B) Lines 36-39 ("The hardest . . . preparation")

C) Lines 59-61 ("Men will not . . . success")

D) Lines 61-63 ("Thoroughness is . . . the search")

CONTINUE

Questions 1-10 are based on the following passage.
3.08
Adapted from the 1924 State of the Union Address
delivered by President Calvin Coolidge.

Our country is almost unique in its ability to discharge
fully and promptly all its obligations at home and abroad,
and provide for all its inhabitants an increase in material
Line resources, in intellectual vigor and in moral power. The Nation
5 holds a position unsurpassed in all former human experience.
This does not mean that we do not have any problems. It
is elementary that the increasing breadth of our experience
necessarily increases the problems of our national life. But
it does mean that if all will but apply ourselves industriously
10 and honestly, we have ample powers with which to meet
our problems and provide for their speedy solution. I do not
profess that we can secure an era of perfection in human
existence, but we can provide an era of peace and prosperity,
attended with freedom and justice and made more and more
15 satisfying by the ministrations of the charities and humanities
of life.

Our domestic problems are for the most part economic.
We have our enormous debt to pay, and we are paying it.
We have the high cost of government to diminish, and we
20 are diminishing it. We have a heavy burden of taxation to
reduce, and we are reducing it. But while remarkable progress
has been made in these directions, the work is yet far from
accomplished. We still owe over $21,000,000,000, the cost of
the National Government is still about $3,500,000,000, and
25 the national taxes still amount to about $27 for each one of
our inhabitants. There yet exists this enormous field for the
application of economy.

In my opinion the Government can do more to remedy
the economic ills of the people by a system of rigid economy
30 in public expenditure than can be accomplished through any
other action. The costs of our national and local governments
combined now stand at a sum close to $100 for each inhabitant
of the land. A little less than one-third of this is represented
by national expenditure, and a little more than two-thirds by
35 local expenditure. It is an ominous fact that only the National
Government is reducing its debt. Others are increasing theirs at
about $1,000,000,000 each year. The depression that overtook
business, the disaster experienced in agriculture, the lack of
employment and the terrific shrinkage in all values which our
40 country experienced in a most acute form in 1920, resulted in
no small measure from the prohibitive taxes which were then
levied on all productive effort. The establishment of a system
of drastic economy in public expenditure, which has enabled
us to pay off about one-fifth of the national debt since 1919,
45 and almost cut in two the national tax burden since 1921, has
been one of the main causes in reestablishing a prosperity
which has come to include within its benefits almost every one
of our inhabitants. Economy reaches everywhere. It carries a
blessing to everybody.

50 The fallacy of the claim that the costs of government are
borne by the rich and those who make a direct contribution
to the National Treasury can not be too often exposed. No
system has been devised, I do not think any system could be
devised, under which any person living in this country could
55 escape being affected by the cost of our government. It has
a direct effect both upon the rate and the purchasing power
of wages. It is felt in the price of those prime necessities of
existence, food, clothing, fuel and shelter. It would appear
to be elementary that the more the Government expends
60 the more it must require every producer to contribute out of
his production to the Public Treasury, and the less he will
have for his own benefit. The continuing costs of public
administration can be met in only one way—by the work
of the people. The higher they become, the more the people
65 must work for the Government. The less they are, the more
the people can work for themselves.

1

As used in line 11, "speedy" most nearly means

A) impulsive.
B) exhilarating.
C) efficient.
D) effortless.

2

The second paragraph (lines 17-27) is notable for its use
of which pair of writing devices?

A) Extended analogy and ironic exaggeration
B) Concrete evidence and dry humor
C) Appeal to emotion and references to distant history
D) Collective voice and recurring sentence structure

3

Coolidge characterizes American government as

A) pervasive in its influence.
B) irresponsible in its expenditures.
C) committed to education.
D) undergoing vast reforms.

CONTINUE

4

Which choice provides the best evidence for the answer to the previous question?

A) Lines 1-4 ("Our country . . . power")

B) Lines 13-16 ("we can provide . . . of life")

C) Lines 31-33 ("The costs . . . land")

D) Lines 52-55 ("No system . . . government")

5

The "Economy" that Coolidge mentions in line 48 is best understood as

A) the new industrial capacities that have made America a world power.

B) the free market that has arisen despite America's national expenses.

C) a way of thinking that could alleviate America's problems.

D) a new theory that explains historical patterns of behavior.

6

In the final paragraph (lines 50-66), Coolidge

A) offers a proposal.

B) invokes a spirit of unity.

C) refutes a misconception.

D) praises an institution.

7

Coolidge takes an attitude towards America's future that can best be described as

A) vindictive.

B) dismayed.

C) detached.

D) optimistic.

8

As used in line 63, "work" most nearly means

A) earnings.

B) professionalism.

C) creativity.

D) drudgery.

9

With which of the following statements would Coolidge most likely agree?

A) America should spend more on national than on local efforts.

B) America is successfully recovering from a period of hardship.

C) America should place a much lower tax burden on the rich.

D) America will see an increase in patriotic sentiment if administrative costs are lowered.

10

Which choice provides the best evidence for the answer to the previous question?

A) Lines 33-35 ("A little less . . . expenditure")

B) Lines 42-48 ("The establishment . . . inhabitants")

C) Lines 50-52 ("The fallacy . . . exposed")

D) Lines 62-66 ("The continuing . . . themselves")

CONTINUE

Questions 1-10 are based on the following passages.
3.09
Both of these passages are from 1934 and address efforts to combat poverty in America during the Great Depression. Passage 1 is an excerpt from a speech by President Franklin Roosevelt, while Passage 2 is from a speech by Louisiana Senator Huey Long.

Passage 1

In meeting the problems of industrial recovery the chief agency of the government has been the National Recovery Administration. Under its guidance, trades and industries
Line covering over ninety percent of all industrial employees
5 have adopted codes of fair competition, which have been approved by the President. Under these codes, in the industries covered, child labor has been eliminated. The work day and the work week have been shortened. Minimum wages have been established and other wages adjusted toward a rising
10 standard of living. The emergency purpose of the N. R. A. was to put men to work and since its creation more than four million persons have been re-employed, in great part through the cooperation of American business brought about under the codes.
15   Benefits of the Industrial Recovery Program have come, not only to labor in the form of new jobs, in relief from over-work and in relief from under-pay, but also to the owners and managers of industry because, together with a great increase in the payrolls, there has come a substantial rise in the total of
20 industrial profits—a rise from a deficit figure in the first quarter of 1933 to a level of sustained profits within one year from the inauguration of N. R. A.

Now it should not be expected that even employed labor and capital would be completely satisfied with present
25 conditions. Employed workers have not by any means all enjoyed a return to the earnings of prosperous times; although millions of hitherto under-privileged workers are today far better paid than ever before.

Passage 2

Now, we have organized a society, and we call it "Share
30 Our Wealth Society," a society with the motto "every man a king."

Every man a king, so there would be no such thing as a man or woman who did not have the necessities of life, who would not be dependent upon the whims and caprices of the
35 financial martyrs for a living. What do we propose by this society? We propose to limit the wealth of big men in the country. There is an average of $15,000 in wealth to every family in America. That is right here today.

We do not propose to divide it up equally. We do not
40 propose a division of wealth, but we propose to limit poverty that we will allow to be inflicted upon any man's family. We

will not say we are going to try to guarantee any equality, or $15,000 to families. No; but we do say that one third of the average is low enough for any one family to hold, that
45 there should be a guaranty of a family wealth of around $5,000; enough for a home, and automobile, a radio, and the ordinary conveniences, and the opportunity to educate their children; a fair share of the income of this land thereafter to that family so there will be no such thing as merely the select
50 to have those things, and so there will be no such thing as a family living in poverty and distress.

We have to limit fortunes. Our present plan is that we will allow no one man to own more than $50,000,000. We think that with that limit we will be able to carry out the
55 balance of the program. It may be necessary that we limit it to less than $50,000,000. It may be necessary, in working out of the plans, that no man's fortune would be more than $10,000,000 or $15,000,000. But be that as it may, it will still be more than any one man, or any one man and his
60 children and their children, will be able to spend in their lifetimes; and it is not necessary or reasonable to have wealth piled up beyond that point where we cannot prevent poverty among the masses.

Another thing we propose is old-age pension of $30 a
65 month for everyone that is 60 years old. Now, we do not give this pension to a man making $1,000 a year, and we do not give it to him if he has $10,000 in property, but outside of that we do.

We will limit hours of work. There is not any necessity
70 of having over-production. I think all you have got to do, ladies and gentlemen, is just limit the hours of work to such an extent as people will work only so long as is necessary to produce enough for all of the people to have what they need.

1

One problem that is cited in both Passage 1 and Passage 2 is

A) the prevalence of child labor.

B) the exploitation of tax code loopholes.

C) demanding workday schedules.

D) ineffectual pension programs.

2

The primary purpose of Passage 1 is to

A) emphasize the need for private acts of charity.

B) encourage the development of American industry.

C) predict the impact of proposed legislation.

D) list the successes of a government program.

CONTINUE

3

Unlike the author of Passage 1, the author of Passage 2 employs which of the following in his writing?

A) A citation of recent economic statistics

B) An explanation of a major change in society

C) An acknowledgment of continuing challenges and drawbacks

D) A direct address to his supporters and allies

4

Historians see the proposals outlined in Passage 2 as both more radical and based on larger direct benefits than the proposals in Passage 1. The author of Passage 1 would argue that the popularity of such radical proposals can be explained by

A) a growing rift between the rich and the poor.

B) the belief that the government is incapable of addressing economic problems.

C) continued dissatisfaction with economic progress among employees.

D) a spreading ideology based on giving workers ownership in their companies.

5

The primary objective of the measures outlined in Passage 2 is to

A) limit the political influence of the most powerful Americans.

B) alleviate the suffering of the most disadvantaged Americans.

C) enable an even distribution of wealth across America.

D) gather new statistics on expenditures and working conditions.

6

Which choice provides the best evidence for the answer to the previous question?

A) Lines 35-37 ("What do we . . . country")

B) Lines 49-51 ("there will be . . . distress")

C) Lines 58-61 ("But be that . . . lifetimes")

D) Lines 70-73 ("I think all . . . need")

7

As used in line 5, "codes" most nearly means

A) signals.

B) secrets.

C) sequences.

D) standards.

8

As used in line 62, "piled up" most nearly means

A) constructed.

B) reinforced.

C) elevated.

D) accumulated.

9

In contrast to the policies presented in Passage 2, the policies presented in Passage 1

A) have clear advantages for the wealthy and powerful.

B) are already popular among the most affluent citizens.

C) are based on a well-defined set of moral principles.

D) continue a tradition established by earlier politicians.

10

Which choice provides the best evidence for the answer to the previous question?

A) Lines 3-6 ("Under its . . . President")

B) Lines 7-10 ("The work day . . . of living")

C) Lines 15-20 ("Benefits of the . . . profits")

D) Lines 27-28 ("millions of . . . before")

CONTINUE

Questions 1-10 are based on the following passage.
3.10
Adapted from the 1941 State of the Union Address, more commonly known as the "Four Freedoms" Speech, delivered by President Franklin D. Roosevelt.

Certainly this is no time for any of us to stop thinking about the social and economic problems which are the root cause of the social revolution which is today a supreme
Line factor in the world. For there is nothing mysterious about the
5 foundations of a healthy and strong democracy.

The basic things expected by our people of their political and economic systems are simple. They are:

Equality of opportunity for youth and for others.

Jobs for those who can work.

10 Security for those who need it.

The ending of special privilege for the few.

The preservation of civil liberties for all.

The enjoyment of the fruits of scientific progress in a wider and constantly rising standard of living.

15 These are the simple, the basic things that must never be lost sight of in the turmoil and unbelievable complexity of our modern world. The inner and abiding strength of our economic and political systems is dependent upon the degree to which they fulfill these expectations.

20 Many subjects connected with our social economy call for immediate improvement. As examples:

We should bring more citizens under the coverage of old-age pensions and unemployment insurance.

We should widen the opportunities for adequate medical
25 care.

We should plan a better system by which persons deserving or needing gainful employment may obtain it.

I have called for personal sacrifice, and I am assured of the willingness of almost all Americans to respond to that call. A
30 part of the sacrifice means the payment of more money in taxes. In my budget message I will recommend that a greater portion of this great defense program be paid for from taxation than we are paying for today. No person should try, or be allowed to get rich out of the program, and the principle of tax payments in
35 accordance with ability to pay should be constantly before our eyes to guide our legislation.

If the Congress maintains these principles the voters, putting patriotism ahead of pocketbooks, will give you their applause.

40 In the future days, which we seek to make secure, we look forward to a world founded upon four essential human freedoms.

The first is freedom of speech and expression—everywhere in the world.

45 The second is freedom of every person to worship God in his own way—everywhere in the world.

The third is freedom from want, which, translated into world terms, means economic understandings which will secure to every nation a healthy peacetime life for its
50 inhabitants—everywhere in the world.

The fourth is freedom from fear, which, translated into world terms, means a world-wide reduction of armaments to such a point and in such a thorough fashion that no nation will be in a position to commit an act of physical aggression against
55 any neighbor—anywhere in the world.

That is no vision of a distant millennium. It is a definite basis for a kind of world attainable in our own time and generation. That kind of world is the very antithesis of the so-called "new order" of tyranny which the dictators seek to create
60 with the crash of a bomb.

To that new order we oppose the greater conception—the moral order. A good society is able to face schemes of world domination and foreign revolutions alike without fear.

Since the beginning of our American history we have
65 been engaged in change, in a perpetual, peaceful revolution, a revolution which goes on steadily, quietly, adjusting itself to changing conditions without the concentration camp or the quicklime in the ditch. The world order which we seek is the cooperation of free countries, working together in a friendly,
70 civilized society.

This nation has placed its destiny in the hands and heads and hearts of its millions of free men and women, and its faith in freedom under the guidance of God. Freedom means the supremacy of human rights everywhere. Our support goes to
75 those who struggle to gain those rights and keep them. Our strength is our unity of purpose.

To that high concept there can be no end save victory.

1

According to Roosevelt, the "four essential human freedoms" (lines 41-42) are

A) outlined in a declaration of the United States Congress.

B) theoretical constructs seldom found in reality.

C) often wrongly confused with the principles of oppressive nations.

D) capable of being promoted in a practical way.

2

Which choice provides the best evidence for the answer to the previous question?

A) Lines 37-39 ("If the Congress . . . applause")

B) Lines 56-58 ("That is no . . .generation")

C) Lines 58-60 ("That kind . . . a bomb")

D) Lines 61-62 ("To that new . . . moral order")

CONTINUE

3

The "basic things" enumerated in lines 8-14 are meant to be understood as a list of

A) successes achieved earlier by Roosevelt.

B) legislative measures being proposed by Roosevelt.

C) specific yet unlikely goals.

D) realistic political objectives.

4

As used in line 14, "rising" most nearly means

A) ascending.

B) awakening.

C) enlarging.

D) improving.

5

In describing the third and fourth freedoms, Roosevelt

A) relates these principles to major objectives in international politics.

B) explains why so few nations have granted their citizens these freedoms.

C) implies that these freedoms are harder to protect than the first two freedoms.

D) implies that these freedoms are more widely valued than the first two freedoms.

6

According to Roosevelt, social change in America is exceptional because such change occurs

A) abruptly.

B) peacefully.

C) with little debate.

D) during wartime.

7

As used in line 74, "supremacy" most nearly means

A) elitism.

B) prioritization.

C) abundance.

D) conquest.

8

In lines 71-76 ("This nation . . . purpose"), Roosevelt does which of the following?

A) Praises a policy

B) Defines a concept

C) Dismisses an objection

D) Explains a paradox

9

In his speech, Roosevelt cautions Americans against

A) assuming that young people do not need assistance.

B) attempting to bar the most needy individuals from obtaining medical care.

C) manipulating new government policies for personal advantage.

D) mistaking other free countries for hostile nations.

10

Which choice provides the best evidence for the answer to the previous question?

A) Lines 6-9 ("The basic things . . . can work")

B) Lines 22-25 ("We should . . . care")

C) Lines 33-36 ("No person . . . legislation")

D) Lines 68-70 ("The world . . . society")

Answer Key on Next Page

Answer Key: CHAPTER THREE

SAT

3.01	3.02	3.03	3.04	3.05
1. B	1. D	1. C	1. B	1. B
2. B	2. A	2. D	2. D	2. A
3. D	3. B	3. B	3. A	3. D
4. C	4. D	4. C	4. B	4. A
5. D	5. C	5. D	5. D	5. D
6. C	6. A	6. A	6. C	6. D
7. A	7. B	7. C	7. C	7. B
8. B	8. A	8. A	8. B	8. D
9. D	9. B	9. C	9. C	9. A
10. B	10. C	10. B	10. C	10. A

3.06	3.07	3.08	3.09	3.10
1. D	1. A	1. C	1. C	1. D
2. C	2. B	2. D	2. D	2. B
3. B	3. C	3. A	3. D	3. D
4. A	4. D	4. D	4. C	4. D
5. C	5. C	5. C	5. B	5. A
6. C	6. D	6. C	6. B	6. B
7. A	7. A	7. D	7. D	7. B
8. D	8. D	8. A	8. D	8. B
9. B	9. D	9. B	9. A	9. C
10. B	10. B	10. B	10. C	10. C

Answer Explanations

Chapter 03 | Emerging Nationalism

3.01 | Edith Wharton

1) CORRECT ANSWER: B
Wharton begins the passage by observing that "France has never been afraid of the unheard of" (lines 1-2) and that "France has always shown" (line 5) strength in times of crisis: she then discusses how the French, who are "fundamentally temperate" (line 44), have reacted generally to World War I. This information supports B and can be used to eliminate C, which contradicts the use of general statements (not smaller, concrete incidents) as Wharton's central strategy. A introduces the idea of Wharton's travels (never discussed in this exclusively third-person passage), while D introduces the possibility of a single strategy (while Wharton is most focused on broader questions of national mood and morale).

2) CORRECT ANSWER: B
In describing how the French reacted to war conditions with energy and determination, Wharton notes that "In all classes the feeling is the same" (lines 69-70). This information supports B. France's main drawbacks have involved daily deprivations (not the weakening of the entire economy, eliminating A) and its effort is sustained by a spirit of determination and national pride (but not necessarily pride in democratic institutions, which are never analyzed, eliminating C). D is out of scope, since the results of past military campaigns (in contrast to a few of the civilian drawbacks of the present one) are never considered.

3) CORRECT ANSWER: D
The word "irresistible" refers to the possible "disintegration" (line 26) of public sentiment, which "there was reason to fear" (line 25) could not be avoided. Thus, it would be feared that this problem would become unavoidable or overwhelming, making D the best answer and eliminating the positives A and B. C, though somewhat negative, refers to a personality trait, not to a possibly negative turn of events.

4) CORRECT ANSWER: C
In lines 66-69, Wharton explains that the French have not exhibited "submission" in war, but have instead displayed "exaltation, energy, the hot resolve to dominate the disaster". This information supports C and can be used to eliminate A. While Wharton does acknowledge that French morale was at one point in doubt, and points out that the French have suffered inconveniences and losses, B and D call attention to negatives that are not anywhere present in her analysis.

5) CORRECT ANSWER: D
See above for the explanation of the correct answer. A indicates that French attitudes

towards the past can be paradoxical (not that the French disrespect tradition), B refers to the possibility that morale in France might decrease, and C indicates that some residents of France have found wartime sacrifices difficult. Make sure not to wrongly align A with Question 4 D.

6) CORRECT ANSWER: C
The word "note" refers to possible "resignation" (line 65), which is seen as a potential part of the "tone of France" (line 66) or of the way that the French act. C is thus the best answer, while A, B, and D all refer to LITERAL or VERBAL notes, not to an individual sentiment or note that would be an element of a LARGER tone.

7) CORRECT ANSWER: A
Wharton mentions the "fiery lamp" in the context of "hearts made insensible by suffering" (lines 62-63) during wartime: the lamp itself is an element of French life that is fed by "dead hands" (line 63). Wartime casualties ("dead hands") would thus enable a war effort, so that A is the best answer and B refers to what FEEDS the lamp, not to the lamp itself. Although France may honor its heroes and value sacrifice, the lamp represents the wartime effort that heroes and sacrifice enable, not the secondary factors described in C and D.

8) CORRECT ANSWER: B
In the lines immediately preceding the reference to the "peril", Wharton discusses the possibility that "civilian France" (line 28) might "individually deteriorate and diminish in its attitude toward the war" (lines 30-31): these are the negatives that she analyzes, referring to them as the "peril". B is the best answer, while France's enemies are not mentioned directly (eliminating A) and the work of the French military, as opposed to civilians, is considered much earlier in the passage (eliminating C and D).

9) CORRECT ANSWER: D
In lines 16-18, Wharton indicates that the French "lookers-on" during the war might have grown antagonistic to the French military efforts, rather than becoming engaged in them: the civilian reaction, thus, was a source of uncertainty. D is the best answer, while Wharton expresses certainty about the social structure of France (eliminating A) and mentions neither army funding (eliminating B) nor foreign allies (eliminating C) in the course of the passage.

10) CORRECT ANSWER: B
See above for the explanation of the correct answer. A describes the vigor of the French army in its opposition to invasion, C indicates that conscription could help to unify the French, and D indicates that some of the sacrifices experienced by the French were greater than expected. Make sure not to take D (which does not indicate uncertainty of any meaningful sort) as a justification for Question 9 D.

3.02 | Woodrow Wilson and Robert M. La Follette

1) CORRECT ANSWER: D
In describing a state of "war against the government and people of the United States" (lines 6-7), Wilson argues that a number of practical actions are necessary, including "counsel and action with the governments now at war with Germany" (lines 14-15) and investment in the armed forces. D is thus the best answer, while Wilson's decisive stance

and call for action can be used to eliminate C. A and B also neglect Wilson's practical purpose: the war has already begun and America's position is already morally valid, so that action is now needed.

2) CORRECT ANSWER: A
The word "state" refers to the "defense" (line 10) of the country, which must be enhanced or attended to through "immediate steps" (line 9). In other words, the defense condition or position of the country must be enhanced. A is the best answer, while B and C wrongly refer to the nation ITSELF and D indicates how the nation may seem, not how the nation will in fact ACT.

3) CORRECT ANSWER: B
In lines 25-29, Wilson supports the idea of increasing "the armed forces of the United States" by "at least five hundred thousand men". This information supports B and can be used to eliminate A, since it is never made clear how many men (if any) will be directed to the navy. C and D both focus on interaction with Germany, while Wilson's proposals mainly address the need to strengthen America and win the war, making these answers inaccurate.

4) CORRECT ANSWER: D
See above for the explanation of the correct answer. A indicates Wilson's determination to defeat Germany and end the war (but does not align with a specific answer to the previous question), B indicates Wilson's desire to cooperate with Germany's other enemies, and C indicates the need to equip the navy to deal with German submarines. Do not wrongly take C as evidence for Question 3 A, since only navy equipment (NOT manpower) is considered in the passage.

5) CORRECT ANSWER: C
While Wilson in Passage 1 acknowledges the "solemn and even tragical character" (lines 1-2) of entering into war, La Follette in Passage 2 argues that matters of war involve the destiny of the United States "and of the civilized world as well" (lines 57-58). This information supports C, while neither passage argues that the declaration of war is unprecedented (eliminating A), only Passage 2 considers the role of the press at length (eliminating B), and only Passage 1 analyzes America's allies at length (eliminating D).

6) CORRECT ANSWER: A
While Wilson argues that his support for war is motivated by "constitutional duty" (line 4), La Follette argues that his own opposition to Wilson's measures is motivated by "the duty of senators and representatives in Congress" (line 33). This information supports A (even though the two passages disagree about the proper response in terms of war), while B is contradicted by Passage 2 (which considers the will of the voters), C is absent from Passage 1 (which mainly considers international affairs), and D is also absent from Passage 1 (which mostly URGES a majority to approve wartime efforts).

7) CORRECT ANSWER: B
The information in lines 13-31 is presented to "the Congress" in an effort to show what a war effort will entail: the author of Passage 2 is a member of Congress and would thus have access to this information, but is still determined to "oppose, regretfully but not the less firmly, the demands of the Executive" (lines 61-63). This information supports B and can be used to eliminate A, since the author of Passage 2 is decisive in his opposition to the war. Because the information in Passage 1 is directed to Congress, it is impossible to

tell how such information would affect constituents (who are never mentioned in Passage 1, thus eliminating C and D).

8) CORRECT ANSWER: A
The word "assorted" refers to "letters and telegrams" (line 67), which have been divided up "according to whether they speak in criticism or commendation" (lines 69-70). The documents have thus been classified or organized in specific manner: A is an effective choice, while B wrongly indicates that some of messages are BETTER or WORSE (not simply that they are different). C and D, in context, would wrongly indicate that the task of assorting MINIMIZES regularity or ELIMINATES order.

9) CORRECT ANSWER: B
In lines 58-63, La Follette notes that even after "patient research and conscientious consideration", he must "firmly" oppose the demands of the Executive (or President). B is the best answer, while A wrongly applies a negative ("cynical") to the forthright and principled La Follette. C and D both wrongly assume that La Follette is indecisive and should thus be eliminated.

10) CORRECT ANSWER: C
See above for the explanation of the correct answer. A describes a new doctrine that involves consent to the president, B explains that legislators should not be afraid to voice their opinions, and D indicates that constituents agree with La Follette's decisive stance (but does not depict La Follette himself as thoughtful). Only in the correct answer, C, is La Follette the main focus of the given line reference.

3.03 | Carrie Chapman Catt

1) CORRECT ANSWER: C
Early in the passage, Catt argues that "The time for woman suffrage has come" (lines 11-12) and argues that "the party which opposes it" (line 15) may perish: this theme of women's progress, and negative results for those who oppose such progress, is returned to later in the passage (for example, in lines 72-74). This information supports C and can be used to eliminate A and D, which indicate greater uncertainty about the fate of women's suffrage. B is a trap answer: although this answer is rightly positive about women's suffrage, it focuses on an issue (the workforce) that is not clearly related to Catt's main focus on political rights.

2) CORRECT ANSWER: D
In lines 38-41, Catt explains that her speech "is not meant" for those who already support women's suffrage: rather, her intention is to engage those who are not necessarily loyal to the cause. D is thus the best answer, while the same information can be used to eliminate C. Although Catt characterizes women's suffrage as inevitable and refers to foreign countries, her AIM is to persuade a somewhat inhospitable audience: A and B must thus be eliminated as tangential to the question.

3) CORRECT ANSWER: B
See above for the explanation of the correct answer. A indicates the practical power of ideas, C acknowledges the progress that has been made in women's rights, and D rejects ideas that impede progress. Although C refers to Catt's central topic of women and their political powers, it does not directly state the AIM of the passage in the manner of B.

4) CORRECT ANSWER: C

The word "cause" refers to something that has been supported by the "Senate and House" (lines 38-39) and that has thus been the subject of attention by politicians: in this context, a cause would be a political initiative or effort. C is thus the best answer, while A (meaning a ploy or excuse) and D introduce faulty negatives. B introduces a literal meaning of the word "cause" that is not fully appropriate to the context of politicians and reformers working together.

5) CORRECT ANSWER: D

The word "indifferent" refers to people who have been unable "to give more than casual attention to this question [women's rights and suffrage]" (lines 47-48). Thus, these people have not been invested in or involved in the issue, so that D is the best answer. A and C, in context, would wrongly indicate that the people are too expected or dull to warrant Catt's attention (when in fact she is making an effort to appeal to them), while B is a faulty positive.

6) CORRECT ANSWER: A

While Catt may be quoting slogans or documents in the first and second paragraphs, she does not actually name sources for her quotations; in contrast, the quotations that begin the third paragraph are attributed to "Vance Thompson" (lines 23-24) and "Treitschke" (line 26). This information supports A and can be used to eliminate D, since there is no way of COMPARING the sources of the quotations if the earlier quotations remain unsourced. In both segments, quotations are used to support or clearly explain Catt's position: B and C assume the opposite function (weakening or questioning) and must thus be eliminated.

7) CORRECT ANSWER: C

In lines 1-4, Catt argues that even though party platforms "have pledged women suffrage", the Congressmen do not adopt the policy "in reality". This information supports C, while the declared acceptance of women's suffrage by the Congressmen can be used to eliminate A and D (which wrongly assume very strong negatives about women). B is problematic because the contrast between ideas and action, not between two DIFFERENT types of issues, is central to Catt's critique.

8) CORRECT ANSWER: A

See above for the explanation of the correct answer. B condemns maneuvers that are designed to deny women their rights, C calls attention to groups that are not fully participating in Catt's vision of progress, and D indicates that nations abroad have embraced women's rights. Make sure not to wrongly align B with Question 7 D, C with Question 7 A, or D with Question 7 B.

9) CORRECT ANSWER: C

Earlier, Catt notes that "liberty" (line 32) does not "pause to heed the plaint of men and women with a grouch" (lines 32-33): the "She" similarly does not "wait for those who have a special interest to serve" (line 34) and may thus be understood as a personification of "liberty". C is the best answer, while A and B wrongly refer to actual women and D refers a type of woman at odds with liberty, not to "liberty" herself.

10) CORRECT ANSWER: B

In arguing for women's suffrage, Catt argues that the issue has been approvingly considered by "our allies in wartime" (line 50) and urges the United States not to fall behind "the trend of world progress" (line 63). B is thus the best answer, while the comparison to other nations (as opposed to the consideration of the United States alone) eliminates A and C. D is a trap answer: although the United States may be a great economic power, Catt compares nations in humanitarian or political terms (not economic terms) to make her points.

3.04 | Woodrow Wilson and Warren G. Harding

1) CORRECT ANSWER: B
While Wilson in Passage 1 is mainly concerned with advocating for the League of Nations, which will include "All the nations that have power that can be mobilized" (lines 26-27), Harding in Passage 2 focuses on internal improvements to America, declaring that "My best judgment of America's needs is to steady down, to get squarely on our feet, to make sure of the right path" (lines 68-70). This information supports B and can be used to eliminate A (since to both passages involve practical proposals) and C (since both passages urge unity and conciliation). D is a trap answer that involves negative judgments: though an uninterested student may find one passage "simplistic" and the other "complicated", there are no context clues that directly support these adjectives.

2) CORRECT ANSWER: D
In lines 5-8, Wilson explains that the League of Nations will enable people from different perspectives to "contribute their part to the settlement of the great questions" that his era faces. This information supports D. The United Nations, as a deliberative body that resolves conflicts, is not strongly aggressive (eliminating B) but is also portrayed as having a role confined mainly to debate and negotiation (eliminating A and C, which attribute much greater powers to the United Nations).

3) CORRECT ANSWER: A
See above for the explanation of the correct answer. B indicates that the United Nations will fail without broad-based cooperation, C states that Germany (for a time) will not be included in the United Nations, and D indicates that the United Nations is designed to prevent aggression. Make sure not to wrongly align C with Question 2 B (which is much more negative) or D with Question 2 C (which mentions much more extreme measures).

4) CORRECT ANSWER: B
In Passage 2, Harding explains that America needs "not heroics, but healing" (line 44), and goes on to explain how other moderate values are needed; he then contrasts the idea of vigorous international efforts with the values of "tranquillity at home" (line 73) and "the normal forward stride of all the American people" (lines 75-76). This information supports B. Despite the context of the passage, war heroes are never mentioned (eliminating A) and the events of the First World War are only mentioned in passing (not in an orderly chronology, eliminating D). C is a trap answer: although Harding does have some broad ideas about politics and economics, it is not clear whether these ideas are in fact NEW or are simply re-emerging for the sake of his political goals.

5) CORRECT ANSWER: D
In Passage 1, Wilson refers to "all the questions which have eaten into the confidence of men toward their governments" (lines 2-3); similarly, in Passage 2, Harding notes that the fever of war has "rendered men irrational" (line 40) and has at times urged them to replace sound government with "barbarity" (line 41). D is thus the best answer, while

Passage 1 generally focuses on diplomatic instead of economic questions (eliminating A and B). For its part, Passage 2 argues that America can spread democracy, not that democracy HAS spread as the result of war, making C a problematic answer.

6) CORRECT ANSWER: C
In lines 50-52, the author of Passage 2 argues that the United States must set a positive example to end "false economics" and become a "commanding example of world leadership": this proactive approach contrasts with the idea in Passage 1 that large populations are "entitled to determine their own destiny" (line 35). C is thus the best answer, while positive answers A and B should be readily eliminated. D misstates the argument of Passage 1, which is that international stability will give "foreign governments" the stability that they need to ensure their own destinies.

7) CORRECT ANSWER: C
See above for the explanation of the correct answer. A indicates that recent warfare has created a negative and distorted view of world civilization, B indicates that America needs a moderate or balanced approach, and D indicates that government intervention cannot effectively replace the initiative of citizens. Only B directly refers to America's role in the world, but does not directly align with an answer to the previous question.

8) CORRECT ANSWER: B
The word "integrity" refers to a territorial property of a nation, which its neighbors agree "that they will never impair" (line 31). In other words, these neighbors will allow the nation to exist on its own or will respect its sovereignty. B is the best answer, while A and C refer to personality or morality and C is contradicted by the context, since a country with "neighbors" could not logically be isolated.

9) CORRECT ANSWER: C
While Passage 1 is designed to promote "the Covenant of the League of Nations" (line 14) and thus focuses on international affairs, Passage 2 argues against the "enactment and excess of government" (line 60). Neither author wishes to see the government take a larger role in the daily lives of citizens, so that C is the best answer. A is strongly recommended by Passage 1, B is strongly recommended by Passage 2, and D is at times put forward as a reasonable approach in Passage 2.

10) CORRECT ANSWER: C
The phrase "substitute for" is used to explain how "enactment and excess of government" (line 60) is not a satisfying replacement for another influence, "quality of citizenship" (line 61). C is thus the best answer, while A refers to depiction or similarity (not the act of REPLACEMENT), B is too strongly negative, and D refers to the actions of individuals.

3.05 | Elizabeth Morris

1) CORRECT ANSWER: B
The word "survey" refers to an action performed as Morris walks "through the shops" (line 1) and takes in a "depressing spectacle" (line 3). She would thus be taking an overview of the "contents" (line 2) of these shops, so that B is an excellent answer. A and D wrongly assume that Morris is observing PEOPLE, not things, while C wrongly takes her activity ("record") as more precise and formal than it actually is.

2) CORRECT ANSWER: A

Morris begins the passage by noting that "It is an age of things" (line 1) and that "there seems little hope" (lines 13-14) of escaping this condition; later in the passage, she shifts to a description of a time when "I chanced to go away to a little house by the sea" (lines 21-22) and thus for a time avoided being overwhelmed by material objects. A is the best answer, while B ("catastrophe") overstates the negative tone of the early part of the passage. C wrongly indicates that the author's main anecdote begins the passage (and again overstates the passage's negatives by describing an "intense conflict"), while D misstates the purpose of the example of the house: this example PROVES how overbearing things can be, since their absence is refreshing, rather than CONTRADICTING the author's main argument.

3) CORRECT ANSWER: D

Morris explains that the little house was empty of the objects that overwhelmed her elsewhere, a fact that gave her "a great peace, a sense of freedom, of infinite leisure" (lines 30-31). This information supports D and can be used to eliminate negative answers A and C, since the house offered an actual, pleasing condition. B is a trap answer: although Morris's prose may strike some readers as artistic, there is no direct indication that the house inspired her to CREATE art, or that it was even the main motivation for this passage.

4) CORRECT ANSWER: A

The words "clear of" describe a state in which an individual does not have "things" (line 19) and can "make at least a fresh start" (line 19). This information indicates that to be clear of is to be without the burden of things, or to be unencumbered by things. A is the best answer, while other choices raise topics that are not clearly related to physical BURDENS, such as clarity (B), forgiveness (C), and depiction or expression (D).

5) CORRECT ANSWER: D

In lines 61-64, Morris explains that she allows herself "to be overwhelmed by the invading host of things" and is not resolute in her opposition to this influence, even though her essay strongly criticizes such "things". D is thus the best answer, while Morris has attempted to free herself from things by going to the house by the sea (eliminating A) and finds this house peaceful and refreshing (eliminating B). C is out of scope: Morris never argues that she has profited from materialism at all, only that she is well acquainted with the materialism around her.

6) CORRECT ANSWER: D

See above for the explanation of the correct answer. A indicates that Morris is overwhelmed by things (but does not indicate why this situation is ironic), B describes Morris's pleasant conditions at the seaside dwelling, and C indicates that Morris is not truly secure in even the most isolated refuge from things. Although C does present something of an irony, it does not align with an answer to the previous question.

7) CORRECT ANSWER: B

Morris describes her friend as a person with a "soul serene" (line 49) who achieves peace by eliminating things that she does "not imperatively need" (line 51). The monks are described as similar in their uncomplicated lifestyle and "spiritual force" (line 59). This information supports B, since both the friend and the monks successfully live without things. A and D are irrelevant to the friend, who interacts with Morris and is aware of Morris's opinions, while C wrongly assumes that the strict lifestyles of the monks and of the friend are "well-known", when in fact Morris gives no context in terms of REPUTATION.

8) CORRECT ANSWER: D
In lines 4-6, Morris explains that people will accumulate things "for every event", even for an event as common as meeting friends for a luncheon. This information supports D and can be used to argue against A, B, and C, which all tie "things" to important factors, not to the mostly insignificant uses that Morris highlights.

9) CORRECT ANSWER: A
See above for the explanation of the correct answer. B indicates that people are burdened by things (but does not indicate WHY), C describes an older time when things were believed to follow an individual into the afterlife, and D provides testimony from Morris's friend, who often disregards unnecessary things. None of these answers provides a general reason for accumulating things in the manner of A.

10) CORRECT ANSWER: A
The word "bare" refers to the floors, walls, and tables of the "little house by the sea" (line 22), which Morris finds to be a refreshing and complete antidote to an everyday preoccupation with things. A is the best answer, since the house is thoroughly without distracting things, while B and C wrongly express negatives towards the house. D is a trap answer, since Morris has reasons for staying in the house beyond its bare state: she initially notes that she "was very tired" (line 21) in explaining the motives for her journey.

3.06 | Henry Ford

1) CORRECT ANSWER: D
In the passage, Ford explains that "machines and their use" (line 19) should not overwhelm humans, but should give people "time to enjoy" (line 21) nature and leisure; later, he argues that "Power and machinery, money and goods, are useful only as they set us free to live" (lines 28-29). This temperate spirit and willingness to reconcile, or balance, opposing principles justifies D and eliminates B (since Ford believes that materialism can be destructive on its own). A is contradicted by Ford's emphasis on people working together in business, while C, though potentially important as a business principle, is not a device that structures Ford's ARGUMENT.

2) CORRECT ANSWER: C
The word "establishments" refers to an "industrial" (line 7) aspect of the country that uses less power than Americans do "merely in ploughing the soil" (line 7): in the context of such work and capabilities, Ford is discussing industrial centers of work or facilities. C is thus the best answer, while A and B do not clearly refer to the issue of work and D indicates a comparison involving time, not a comparison involving work or power.

3) CORRECT ANSWER: B
The word "return" indicates a positive good that could be obtained from "service" (line 48), since it is contrasted with the idea of "every kind of waste" (line 47). B, "benefit", is an appropriately positive answer, while A refers to time or travel, C refers to a return to strength (not an EXISTING form of strength), and D is both out of context and somewhat negative.

4) CORRECT ANSWER: A

In lines 28-29, Ford explains that power, money, and other resources "are useful only as they set us free to live". This information supports A and can be used to eliminate C (which wrongly assumes that power and authority do not serve a further, PRACTICAL purpose). B and D are both out of scope: although these answers are rightly positive, neither education nor Ford's own life before attaining money is discussed prominently in the passage.

5) CORRECT ANSWER: C

See above for the explanation of the correct answer. A indicates the need to reflect on the course of human life in a time of turmoil, B speaks of a drawback of machinery and industry (not of a benefit, as demanded by the previous question), and D both criticizes the current system and notes that Ford has not been diminished by it. Make sure not to take D as evidence for Question 4 D, which raises the very different issue of poverty.

6) CORRECT ANSWER: C

While the first paragraph raises the topic of Americans' vigorous "development of our country" (lines 1-2), the second paragraph argues that increasing "power, machinery, and industry" (lines 13-14) should not diminish the enjoyment of life or nature. This information supports C, while the first paragraph in fact notes the strength of American agriculture (eliminating A), the second paragraph only praises an attitude of appreciation and reflection that MAY NOT actually be popular (eliminating B), and both paragraphs consider domestic and international issues alongside each other (eliminating D).

7) CORRECT ANSWER: A

In this passage's discussion of industry and business, Ford criticizes the "present system" (line 45) as encouraging "every kind of waste" (line 47) and advocates constructive changes. This information supports A and can be used to eliminate B and D, even though Ford admits that the present system is sometimes profitable. C distorts Ford's argument: although Ford emphasizes spirituality and enjoyment of life, he does not tie these qualities to his discussion of production systems (which he considers mostly in terms of commitment and efficiency).

8) CORRECT ANSWER: D

Ford explains that he has developed a machine-based "theory of business" (line 33) and further explains that the successes of the Ford Motor Company demonstrate "that the theory is right to date" (lines 38-39). This information supports D, while A discusses a topic (service in business) that is only a focus somewhat later in the passage. B (Ford's investments) and C (the automotive industry as a whole) raise topics that are at best tangentially related to Ford's THEORY, and must thus be deleted.

9) CORRECT ANSWER: B

In lines 53-55, Ford praises skepticism as "the balance wheel of civilization", since carefully investigating leads people to make the best possible decisions about broad ideas. B is the best answer, while A introduces a negative, C refers to how skepticism is perceived (not to its EFFECTS in helping civilization), and D wrongly assumes that skepticism cannot have practical benefits (when in fact it is an asset to "civilization").

10) CORRECT ANSWER: B

See above for the explanation of the correct answer. A indicates Ford's willingness to object to new ideas, C indicates that ideas should be evaluated in terms of practicality (not age), and D indicates that ideas are valuable in some respects. None of these answers directly characterize "skepticism" as demanded by the previous question.

3.07 | William Osler

1) CORRECT ANSWER: A

In explaining the best relationship between a teacher and students, Osler endorses "A fraternal attitude" (line 21) and compares a good teacher not to an imposing authority, but to "a senior student anxious to help his juniors" (line 29). This information supports A, while B understates the amount of effort ("anxious") that can go into such a relationship, C is wrongly negative, and D is problematic in context: sympathy between teachers and students is a new attitude, while the "tradition" of unapproachable teachers is criticized by Osler.

2) CORRECT ANSWER: B

The word "senior" refer to a student who is "anxious to help his juniors" (line 29) and would thus be a guide to a younger group: thus, B rightly designates such a student as older. A and D both refer to issues of merit, not age (and wrongly make the senior "student" seem unapproachable), while C is strongly negative.

3) CORRECT ANSWER: C

In describing a sympathetic method of education, Osler tells the members of his audience that "You have all become brothers in a great society" (line 16); he later indicates to the same audience that "you can all become good students" (line 43). This information supports C and can be used to eliminate A (academics) and B (professionals who might help Osler and who are, most likely, not students). D is a trap answer: although Osler does describe an ideal education system, he addresses actual, not ideal, students as "you".

4) CORRECT ANSWER: D

In lines 47-48, Osler explains that "the hurry and bustle of a business world" make it difficult to produce first-class students. This information supports D, while the other answers do not necessarily bear out Osler's argument. A student who successfully rejects commerce and distraction may nonetheless study only a few subjects (eliminating A), may accept institutions such as the education system that Osler ENDORSES (eliminating B), and may learn largely through his or her own efforts (eliminating C).

5) CORRECT ANSWER: C

See above for the explanation of the correct answer. A notes the importance of a fraternal or cooperative attitude, B calls attention to the benefits of cooperation, and D notes the DRAWBACKS of studying many subjects. While D can eliminate Question 4 A, A and B refer to a quality of outstanding students (a spirit of fellowship) that is not directly referenced in any answer to the previous question.

6) CORRECT ANSWER: D

In the first paragraph, Osler criticizes a student temperament that is "given to judgment, not mercy" (lines 7-8) and instead advocates "generous, friendly rivalry untinged by the green peril, jealousy" (lines 11-12). This information supports D. Note that Osler is concerned with two different study mentalities (not with contrasting study and leisure, eliminating A), that he recommends a way of acting (not a broader social initiative, eliminating B), and that he is in fact contrasting two different practical approaches (eliminating C).

7) CORRECT ANSWER: A
The word "badly" refers to how some tasks are performed, and is contrasted with the idea of doing such tasks "easily and well" (line 45). Thus, the tasks are performed without competence or ineptly, so that A is the best answer. B refers to hatred, C refers to defiance, and D refers to death: all of these topics are out of context in a discussion of how well a task may be performed.

8) CORRECT ANSWER: D
Although Osler recommends study habits that involve focus and fellowship, he admits that "Under present conditions it is hard to get the needful seclusion" (line 49) to produce a large number of outstanding students. This information supports D, while Osler in fact expresses agreement with Ferriar in line 46 (eliminating A). Osler's ideas are meant both to be understandable to students and to bring in the cooperation of students themselves: both B and C, which indicate that the ideas are alienating and hostile, should be eliminated as inaccurate.

9) CORRECT ANSWER: D
In lines 36-39, Osler argues that education is a "life course" that simply begins with a student's formal studies. This information supports D, while Osler's focus on education as a pursuit that involves the commitment of students as a large group disqualifies A. B and C both misstate some of Osler's actual ideas: he argues that society and business at present actually IMPEDE education, not that education has an enormously strong effect on either society or business.

10) CORRECT ANSWER: B
See above for the explanation of the correct answer. A indicates that students can meet the world effectively if they have the right mentality, C indicates that concentration and success are incompatible, and D indicates that thoroughness is a difficult quality to maintain. Make sure not to take A as evidence for Question 9 B: the lines in question indicate that a student may ADAPT to the world, but do not clearly deal with the issue of REFORM.

3.08 | Calvin Coolidge

1) CORRECT ANSWER: C
The word "speedy" refers to a "solution" (line 11) which is possible because the people of America have "ample powers with which to meet our problems" (lines 10-11). In other words, the problems can be solved well or with efficiency, so that C is the best answer. A is wrongly negative, B refers to EMOTIONS (not to practical RESULTS), and D is illogical in context. Even though the problems may be solved easily due to the "ample powers", some "effort" will still be necessary to address these problems at all.

2) CORRECT ANSWER: D
In the course of lines 18-21, Coolidge begins three separate sentences with the phrase "We have": he also uses collective voice ("we") at several other points in the paragraph,

so that D is the best answer. Although the figures cited in the paragraph are large, they are not meant to seem exaggerated (eliminating A) or humorous (eliminating B): instead, they simply serve as evidence. Nor is Coolidge referencing distant history: instead, he wants to call attention to recent domestic problems that the country must face (eliminating C).

3) CORRECT ANSWER: A
In lines 52-55, Coolidge notes that at present no American citizen can "escape being affected by the cost of our government": this information supports A. While Coolidge does criticize the sheer amount of government expenditure, he does not in fact argue that the government is irresponsible (eliminating B) or explain that reforms are underway (even though he may WANT reforms, eliminating D). C is similarly out of scope: the focus of the passage is economics as it relates to government policy, not "education".

4) CORRECT ANSWER: D
See above for the explanation of the correct answer. A praises America's resources and capabilities, B indicates that America may be able to ensure peace and prosperity, and C indicates the cost (per person) for various aspects of the American government. Do not wrongly take A or B as justification for a positive answer to the previous question, and make sure not to mistake C as justification for Question 3 B.

5) CORRECT ANSWER: C
Coolidge explains that Economy "reaches everywhere. It carries a blessing to everybody" (lines 48-49): in context, this Economy is a means of reducing taxes and expenditures in a way that will help the entire country. C is thus the best answer, while neither A nor B accurately describes the POLICIES that Coolidge recommends, even though these answers are positive. D is a trap answer, since Coolidge's ideas are not in fact used to explain "historical patterns" but are intended to address a set of current conditions.

6) CORRECT ANSWER: C
In the final paragraph, Coolidge addresses the "fallacy of the claim" (line 50) that the rich are mostly burdened by the costs of government, claiming instead that the expenses of government are supported by "the work of the people" (lines 63-64). C is thus the best answer, while the often negative emphasis of this paragraph can be used to eliminate positive answers B and D. A is a trap answer, since Coolidge does in fact propose a spirit of sound management, but does so EARLIER in the passage.

7) CORRECT ANSWER: D
Coolidge notes that America "holds a position unsurpassed in all former human experience" (line 5); even though he acknowledges that there are problems, he is convinced that the government can "remedy the economic ills of the people" (lines 28-29). This information supports D and can be used to readily eliminate A and B (which assume that the passage is thoroughly negative towards America) and C (which assumes that Coolidge is not taking a strong position regarding the country's future).

8) CORRECT ANSWER: A
The word "work" refers to an action performed by "the people" (line 64) in order to meet "The continuing costs of public administration" (lines 62-63). If the work is used to pay a cost, the work naturally involves money or earnings itself: A is the best answer,

while B and C wrongly praise the work and D wrongly criticizes the work. Instead, the work should be understood in a manner that relates it directly to the idea of money and expenditure, rather than linking it to positive or negative personality traits.

9) CORRECT ANSWER: B
In lines 42-48, Coolidge argues that "The establishment of a system of drastic economy" has aided Americans in "reestablishing a prosperity": since prosperity has been successfully re-established, America has (logically) recently left behind a period of hardship. B is thus the best answer, while A and C (by targeting specific segments of the country) misstate Coolidge's argument that the burden of government should be lowered OVERALL. D attributes the wrong effect to Coolidge's proposals, which would lead to prosperity and confidence (not necessarily patriotic sentiment) if adopted.

10) CORRECT ANSWER: B
See above for the explanation of the correct answer. A states a fact about government expenditures, C indicates that the costs of government are not sustained by the rich alone, and D indicates that lower government costs will enable the people to thrive. Make sure not to align A with Question 9 A, C with Question 9 C, or D with Question 9 D.

3.09 | Franklin Roosevelt and Huey Long

1) CORRECT ANSWER: C
While Passage 1 calls attention to the necessity of "relief from over-work" (lines 16-17), Passage 2 argues that it has become necessary to "limit hours of work" (line 69) and rein in excessively long schedules. C is the best answer, while only Passage 1 discusses child labor (eliminating A), neither passage discusses tax loopholes (eliminating B), and only Passage 2 argues that new pension programs are needed, or raises the issue of pensions at all (eliminating D).

2) CORRECT ANSWER: D
Passage 1 explains how the National Recovery Administration has enabled "fair competition" (line 5) and has imparted benefits "not only to labor" (line 16) but also "to the owners and managers of industry" (lines 17-18). This information supports D and can be used to eliminate B and C, since the passage emphasizes positive effects that have ALREADY been observed. A introduces a faulty topic ("private acts of charity"), when in fact Passage 1 focuses mainly on work conditions and the national economy.

3) CORRECT ANSWER: D
While Passage 1 states a series of facts about improved conditions in the United States (and does so while remaining entirely third-person), Passage 2 frequently refers to the people who will participate in the author's projects as "We". This information supports D. Passage 1 introduces an employment statistic in lines 11-12 (eliminating A), explains overall how the National Recovery Administration has improved American job conditions (eliminating B), and indicates in line 24 that Americans may not be "completely satisfied" with the results of new initiatives (eliminating C).

4) CORRECT ANSWER: C
In lines 23-26, the author of Passage 1 acknowledges dissatisfaction with recent economic progress and notes that even employed workers have not entirely "enjoyed a return to the earnings of prosperous times". Passage 2 responds to the idea that people

are dissatisfied with their basic earnings and living conditions, so it is likely that the discontent cited in Passage 1 contributed to the popularity of more radical ideas. C is the best answer. A (major class divisions) and D (workers taking ownership) refer to topics that are not analyzed at any length in Passage 1, while B contradicts one of the passage's own arguments. Passage 1 indicates that government CAN address economic problems, but may not do so to the complete satisfaction of all employees.

5) CORRECT ANSWER: B
In lines 49-51, the author of Passage 2 argues in favor of making specific material goods available to even the most disadvantaged Americas, so that "there will be no such thing as a family living in poverty and distress". B is the best answer, while A wrongly focuses on political power (not economics), C is contradicted by the author's own statement in line 39, and D wrongly focuses on further KNOWLEDGE instead of practical ACTION.

6) CORRECT ANSWER: B
See above for the explanation of the correct answer. A describes how the measures proposed in Passage 2 will limit the wealth of some members of society, C indicates that most people and their families cannot manage to spend large amounts of money in their lifetimes, and D indicates that hours of work should be subject to limitations. Make sure not to wrongly align A with Question 5 A or D with question 5 D.

7) CORRECT ANSWER: D
The word "codes" refers to items that enable "fair competition" (line 5) and which have been "approved by the President" (line 6). If these codes are sanctioned by the government and result in fairness, they are measures or standards that ensure positive conditions. D is the best answer. A and C both refer to basic communication (as in sending a signal or a sequence of letters), while B indicates (in contradiction of the context of the passage) that the codes are unknown.

8) CORRECT ANSWER: D
The word "piled up" refers to "wealth" (line 62) which, because of how it is distributed in society, stays with the wealthy and cannot be used to help the poor. Such wealth is concentrated or accumulated among the wealthy, so that D is the best answer. A and B refer to physical objects (while wealth, as represented by statistics, can be NON-PHYSICAL); C introduces a faulty positive, since the author is criticizing the situation with regard to wealth.

9) CORRECT ANSWER: A
While Passage 1 promotes policies that will clearly benefit "owners and managers of industry" (lines 17-18), Passage 2 promotes policies that will "limit the wealth of big men in the country" (lines 36-37) but does not cite any direct benefits for the wealthy themselves. A is thus the best answer, while B neglects the argument in Passage 1 that the wealthy are not "completely satisfied with present conditions" (lines 24-25). Both passages are based on the moral principle of helping the public at large (eliminating C), while both discuss recent developments and neither cites earlier traditions (eliminating D).

10) CORRECT ANSWER: C
See above for the explanation of the correct answer. A indicates that new and widespread standards of fair competition have been adopted, B lists a few specific reforms in terms of work days and wages, and D notes that many workers have experienced improvements in pay. Make sure not to wrongly align one of these positive answers with Question 9 C,

which is ALSO relevant to Passage 2.

3.10 | Franklin Roosevelt

1) CORRECT ANSWER: D
In lines 56-58, Roosevelt explains that the vision embodied in the freedoms is "attainable in our own time and generation". These principles are practical and realistic, thus supporting D and eliminating B. A is illogical because it is the duty of Congress to MAINTAIN the principles (which Roosevelt has ALREADY formulated), while C is illogical because it applies a negative tone to principles that Roosevelt strongly advocates.

2) CORRECT ANSWER: B
See above for the explanation of the correct answer. A calls on Congress to maintain the four basic freedoms, C indicates that a world that adheres to the freedoms is sharply opposed to a world that allows tyranny, and D reiterates the contrast between the morality of the freedoms and the presence of tyranny. Make sure not to wrongly take A as a justification for Question 1 A.

3) CORRECT ANSWER: D
Roosevelt argues that the "basic things" are tied to "The inner and abiding strength of our economic and political systems" (lines 17-18): in other words, the basic things have positive results in real life, so that D is the best answer and C must be eliminated. A and B are both too narrow: while Roosevelt is a clear supporter of the general "basic things", he does not in fact tie them to any specific stage of his career.

4) CORRECT ANSWER: D
The word "rising" refers to a "standard of living" (line 14) which is related to "scientific progress" (line 13): naturally, progress would be related to a positive and improving standard of living. D is the best choice, while A and C both refer literally to physical things that could "rise" and B would only refer to a human or an animal which could "awaken".

5) CORRECT ANSWER: A
Roosevelt links the third freedom to healthy peacetime life "everywhere in the world" (line 50); somewhat similarly, he links the fourth freedom to another large objective in international policy, the "world-wide reduction of armaments" (line 52). This information supports A, while the fact that Roosevelt does not analyze any specific nations (as opposed to explaining broad goals associated with the freedoms) can be used to eliminate B. Note that the first two freedoms are never mentioned in the paragraphs that introduce the second two freedoms: thus, C and D introduce comparisons that a reader may make independently but that are not in any way contained in the passage itself.

6) CORRECT ANSWER: B
Roosevelt describes social change in America as "a perpetual, peaceful revolution" (line 65), contrasting such change with the brutal and inhumane conditions that other countries may adopt. This information supports B and can be used to eliminate A, since Roosevelt sees change in America as happening "steadily" (line 66), and C, since a peaceful change may still involve much debate. If change is peaceful and steady, it would naturally occur at times when the country is not at war: thus, D is also contradicted by the passage.

7) CORRECT ANSWER: B

The word "supremacy" refers to a condition of "human rights everywhere" (line 74) that Roosevelt clearly promotes. B is thus the best answer, because such rights should be emphasized or prioritized. A and D both introduce negatives, while C is a trap answer: in context, "abundance" would refer to wealth or multiplicity, while Roosevelt simply wants a FEW major and fundamental rights and freedoms to be widespread.

8) CORRECT ANSWER: B

In the relevant lines, Roosevelt explains what "Freedom means" (line 73), thus offering a definition of this concept. B is the best answer, while Roosevelt is mostly concerned with expressing support for measures to ensure freedoms that are broad (not based on defined or precise policies, eliminating A) and positive (not problematic or deserving objection, eliminating C). A "paradox" is an apparent incompatibility or oddity that reveals a truth; however, in this paragraph, Roosevelt simply supports valid ideas WITHOUT resorting to such contradiction (eliminating D).

9) CORRECT ANSWER: C

In lines 33-36, Roosevelt argues that "No person should try, or be allowed to get rich" by manipulating a newly-proposed tax payment program. This information supports C, while other answers distort Roosevelt's actual ideas. In this passage, Roosevelt discusses old-age programs (but also promotes opportunities for young people, eliminating A), argues for improving medical care opportunity (but does not argue that anyone is trying to prevent other people from obtaining medical care, eliminating B), and criticizes hostile and oppressive nations (but does not raise the possibility that free nations might be mistaken for these nations, eliminating D).

10) CORRECT ANSWER: C

See above for the explanation of the correct answer. A describes a few basic economic and political opportunities that Roosevelt promotes, B expresses Roosevelt's support for vulnerable citizens, and D indicates Roosevelt's enthusiasm for cooperation among free countries. Make sure not to wrongly align A with Question 9 A, B with Question 9 B, or D with Question 9 D.

CHAPTER 4
Post-Colonial Era

The Post-Colonial Era
1945-1989

The international landscape, in the years following World War II, was dramatically reshaped by two forces. First, the world powers of earlier eras—such as Britain and France—definitively lost control of the areas that they had once dominated in Africa and Asia. Second, the United States and the Soviet Union—both victors in the recent conflict—cemented their status as the world's competing superpowers. From the 1940s to the end of the 1980s, a clash of ideas would take place between the democratic U.S. and the communistic U.S.S.R.—a clash that would play out both in proxy altercations such as the Vietnam War and, at times, on American soil.

With the end of hostilities against Germany and Japan, diplomats such as Eleanor Roosevelt and John Foster Dulles put forward a vision of America as a globally engaged proponent of democracy. But this was also an era of anxiety about the communist threat—some justified, some completely overblown. In the 1950s, Senator Joseph McCarthy led an effort to root out communist sympathizers in the U.S. Government; his initiative was attacked by his fellow legislators, such as Margaret Chase Smith, as little more than an unfounded "witch hunt." President Eisenhower, who led America through the prosperous 1950s, was also critical of McCarthy's efforts—and of other troubling possibilities that a newly empowered country faced. A hero of World War II, Eisenhower warned that excessive military buildup could have dire consequences for society.

The 1960s would begin on a hopeful note with the election of John F. Kennedy, a youthful and optimistic president who was nonetheless convinced that power and prestige could have negative consequences. As the decade progressed, Americans would demand fundamental alterations to their society, new protections of racial, gender, and economic rights. Kennedy (who was assassinated in 1963) would not live to ensure these changes, but leaders in civil rights such as Reverend Martin Luther King, President Lyndon Johnson, Congresswoman Shirley Chisholm, and Supreme Court Justice Thurgood Marshall would see them through. But even as the Civil Rights and Second Wave Feminism movements modernized America, presidents such as Johnson and Richard Nixon grappled with the Vietnam War—a campaign against the communist Vietcong government, and still one of the most controversial episodes in American foreign policy.

After the celebrated Democratic presidencies of Kennedy and Johnson, America's political parties began a major realignment. Nixon, a Republican, began to break up the mammoth coalition of Northern and Southern voters that the Democrats had inherited from Franklin Roosevelt. And even though Nixon's own presidency ended in scandal, the Republican Party had begun to create a durable national alliance in the South, West, and industrial Midwest. For its part, the Democratic Party was weakened by a landslide loss in the 1972 Presidential Election and, later in the decade, by the principled yet embattled presidency of Jimmy Carter. In 1980, Ronald Reagan won election over Carter on a platform of reduced government spending, assertive foreign policy, and general optimism. His presidency was defined for many Americans by a hard line towards the Soviet Union, even though Reagan—like his predecessors—was aware of the virtues of moderation and diplomacy.

Questions 1-10 are based on the following passage.
4.01
Adapted from "The Struggle for Human Rights," a speech delivered by Eleanor Roosevelt in 1948. Roosevelt had served as First Lady of the United States and was named as a Delegate to the United Nations by President Harry S. Truman in 1945.

I have come this evening to talk with you on one of the greatest issues of our time—that is the preservation of human freedom. I have chosen to discuss it here in France,
Line at the Sorbonne, because here in this soil the roots of human
5 freedom have long ago struck deep and here they have been richly nourished. It was here the Declaration of the Rights of Man was proclaimed, and the great slogans of the French Revolution—liberty, equality, fraternity—fired the imagination of men. I have chosen to discuss this issue in Europe because
10 this has been the scene of the greatest historic battles between freedom and tyranny. I have chosen to discuss it in the early days of the General Assembly because the issue of human liberty is decisive for the settlement of outstanding political differences and for the future of the United Nations.
15   The decisive importance of this issue was fully recognized by the founders of the United Nations at San Francisco. Concern for the preservation and promotion of human rights and fundamental freedoms stands at the heart of the United Nations. Its Charter is distinguished by its preoccupation
20 with the rights and welfare of individual men and women. The United Nations has made it clear that it intends to uphold human rights and to protect the dignity of the human personality. In the preamble to the Charter the keynote is set when it declares: "We the people of the United Nations
25 determined . . . to reaffirm faith in fundamental human rights, in the dignity and worth of the human person, in the equal rights of men and women and of nations large and small, and . . . to promote social progress and better standards of life in larger freedom." This reflects the basic premise of the Charter
30 that the peace and security of mankind are dependent on mutual respect for the rights and freedoms of all.
    One of the purposes of the United Nations is declared in Article 1 to be: "to achieve international cooperation in solving international problems of an economic, social, cultural, or
35 humanitarian character, and in promoting and encouraging respect for human rights and for fundamental freedoms for all without distinction as to race, sex, language, or religion."
    . . . In the United States we are old enough not to claim perfection. We recognize that we have some problems of
40 discrimination but we find steady progress being made in the solution of these problems. Through normal democratic processes we are coming to understand our needs and how we can attain full equality for all our people. Free discussion on the subject is permitted. Our Supreme Court has recently
45 rendered decisions to clarify a number of our laws to guarantee the rights of all.
    The U.S.S.R. claims it has reached a point where all races within her borders are officially considered equal and have equal rights and they insist they have no discrimination
50 where minorities are concerned.
    This is a laudable objective but there are other aspects of the development of freedom for the individual which are essential before the mere absence of discrimination is worth much, and these are lacking in the Soviet Union. Unless
55 they are being denied freedoms which they want and which they see other people have, people do not usually complain of discrimination. It is these other freedoms—the basic freedoms of speech, of the press, of religion and conscience, of assembly, of fair trial and freedom from arbitrary arrest
60 and punishment, which a totalitarian government cannot safely give its people and which give meaning to freedom from discrimination.
    It is my belief, and I am sure it is also yours, that the struggle for democracy and freedom is a critical struggle,
65 for their preservation is essential to the great objective of the United Nations to maintain international peace and security.
    Among free men the end cannot justify the means. We know the patterns of totalitarianism—the single political party, the control of schools, press, radio, the arts, the
70 sciences, and the church to support autocratic authority; these are the age-old patterns against which men have struggled for three thousand years. These are the signs of reaction, retreat, and retrogression.
    The United Nations must hold fast to the heritage of
75 freedom won by the struggle of its peoples; it must help us to pass it on to generations to come.

1

Roosevelt's main purpose in delivering this speech is to

A) explain why the United Nations must deal harshly with the Soviet Union.

B) connect the activities of the United Nations to broad humanitarian principles.

C) recapitulate early debates over the need for the United Nations.

D) urge the United Nations to take a more assertive stance in world politics.

CONTINUE

2

In lines 51-62 ("This is . . . discrimination"), Roosevelt argues that

A) the political system in the Soviet Union will eventually collapse.

B) the Soviet Union is completely indifferent to the efforts of the United Nations to promote human rights.

C) the Soviet Union has wildly exaggerated its success in eliminating discrimination.

D) the Soviet Union has aggressively promoted some civil rights while clearly undermining others.

3

As used in line 8, "fired" most nearly means

A) stimulated.

B) damaged.

C) toughened.

D) ejected.

4

In this speech, Roosevelt addresses an audience that she assumes to be

A) highly knowledgeable about American history.

B) active in political protests.

C) unaware of the realities of totalitarianism.

D) sympathetic to democratic principles.

5

In presenting her ideas, Roosevelt acknowledges that

A) the aims of the United Nations may strike some observers as hopelessly idealistic.

B) the Soviet Union has improved its economy by restricting some civic freedoms.

C) the United States has not developed an optimal system for protecting individual rights.

D) the United Nations is incapable of providing short-term solutions to international problems.

6

Which choice provides the best evidence for the answer to the previous question?

A) Lines 29-31 ("This reflects . . . of all")

B) Lines 39-41 ("We recognize . . . problems")

C) Lines 67-72 ("We know . . . years")

D) Lines 74-76 ("The United . . . come")

7

As used in line 70, "authority" most nearly means

A) rule.

B) experience.

C) wisdom.

D) truth.

8

Roosevelt's speech is premised on the idea that

A) institutions such as the United Nations were once a source of controversy.

B) the basic principles of the United Nations charter have not been effectively publicized.

C) the recent efforts of the United Nations are widely supported by citizens of the United States.

D) there is a firm link between her overall topic and the context of her speech.

9

Which choice provides the best evidence for the answer to the previous question?

A) Lines 9-11 ("I have chosen . . . tyranny")

B) Lines 15-16 ("The decisive . . . San Francisco")

C) Lines 23-26 ("In the preamble . . . person")

D) Lines 44-46 ("Our Supreme . . . of all")

10

According to Roosevelt, the Soviet Union's system of government is problematic because this system does not promote

A) freedom from discrimination.

B) freedom of expression.

C) international trade.

D) international diplomacy.

152

CONTINUE

Questions 1-10 are based on the following passages.
4.02
In the early 1950s, Senator Joseph McCarthy led a campaign to root out "Communists and Communist sympathizers" in the State Department and other branches of the United States government. Widely condemned in the decades since, McCarthy's actions were also opposed by his contemporaries, including Senator Margaret Chase Smith. Passage 1 is from a speech delivered by McCarthy; Passage 2 is from Smith's "Declaration of Conscience," which vigorously criticized McCarthy and his tactics.

Passage 1

At war's end we were physically the strongest nation on Earth and, at least potentially, the most powerful intellectually and morally. Ours could have been the honor of being a
Line beacon in the desert of destruction, a shining, living proof that
5 civilization was not yet ready to destroy itself. Unfortunately, we have failed miserably and tragically to arise to the opportunity.

The reason why we find ourselves in a position of impotency is not because our only powerful, potential enemy
10 has sent men to invade our shores, but rather because of the traitorous actions of those who have been treated so well by this nation. It has not been the less fortunate or members of minority groups who have been selling this nation out, but rather those who have had all the benefits that the wealthiest
15 nation on earth has had to offer—the finest homes, the finest college education, and the finest jobs in government we can give . . .

I have in my hand 57 cases of individuals who would appear to be either card-carrying members or certainly loyal to
20 the Communist Party, but who nevertheless are still helping to shape our foreign policy.

One thing to remember in discussing the communists in our government is that we are not dealing with spies who get 30 pieces of silver to steal the blueprints of new weapons. We
25 are dealing with a far more sinister type of activity because it permits the enemy to guide and shape our policy . . .

I know that you are saying to yourself, "Well, why doesn't the Congress do something about it?" Actually, ladies and gentlemen, one of the important reasons for the graft, the
30 corruption, the dishonesty, the disloyalty, the treason in high government positions—one of the most important reasons why this continues—is a lack of moral uprising on the part of the 140 million American people. In the light of history, however, this is not hard to explain.
35 It is the result of an emotional hangover and a temporary moral lapse which follows every war. It is the apathy to evil which people who have been subjected to the tremendous evils of war feel. As the people of the world see mass murder, the destruction of defenseless and innocent people, and all of the
40 crime and lack of morals which go with war, they become numb and apathetic. It has always been thus after war. However, the morals of our people have not been destroyed. They still exist. This cloak of numbness and apathy has only needed a spark to rekindle them. Happily, this spark has
45 finally been supplied.

Passage 2

As a woman, I wonder how the mothers, wives, sisters, and daughters feel about the way in which members of their families have been politically mangled in Senate debate— and I use the word "debate" advisedly.
50 As a United States senator, I am not proud of the way in which the Senate has been made a publicity platform for irresponsible sensationalism. I am not proud of the reckless abandon in which unproved charges have been hurled from this side of the aisle. I am not proud of the obviously staged,
55 undignified countercharges which have been attempted in retaliation from the other side of the aisle.

I do not like the way the Senate has been made a rendezvous for vilification, for selfish political gain at the sacrifice of individual reputations and national unity. I am
60 not proud of the way we smear outsiders from the floor of the Senate and hide behind the cloak of congressional immunity and still place ourselves beyond criticism on the floor of the Senate.

As an American, I am shocked at the way Republicans
65 and Democrats alike are playing directly into the Communist design of "confuse, divide, and conquer." As an American, I do not want a Democratic administration "whitewash" or "coverup" any more than I want a Republican smear or witch hunt.
70 It is high time that we stopped thinking politically as Republicans and Democrats about elections and started thinking patriotically as Americans about national security based on individual freedom. It is high time that we all stopped being tools and victims of totalitarian techniques—
75 techniques that, if continued here unchecked, will surely end what we have come to cherish as the American way of life.

According to Passage 1, America is threatened by people who are members of

A) the economic elite.

B) a foreign intelligence agency.

C) the military.

D) a new political party.

CONTINUE

2

Which choice provides the best evidence for the answer to the previous question?

A) Lines 1-3 ("At war's . . . morally")

B) Lines 12-15 ("It has not . . . offer")

C) Lines 18-20 ("I have . . . Party")

D) Lines 22-24 ("One thing . . . weapons")

3

As used in line 23, "dealing with" most nearly means

A) negotiating with.

B) suffering through.

C) considering.

D) promoting.

4

One of the rhetorical tactics used by McCarthy is

A) a paraphrase of an expected response.

B) a quotation from a statistical study.

C) an extended metaphor that explains a problem.

D) a satiric depiction of his ideological opponents.

5

Unlike McCarthy in Passage 1, Smith in Passage 2 argues that

A) Democrats and Republicans should not follow two distinct ideologies.

B) the American people have for too long neglected the opinions of women.

C) the American people have the necessary resolve to overcome their present difficulties.

D) seemingly dissimilar ideologies are contributing to a common problem.

6

The "position of impotency" (lines 8-9) in Passage 1 resembles the "irresponsible sensationalism" (line 52) in Passage 2 in that both problems

A) are explained by the immediate outcome of World War II.

B) are directly linked to immorality at the high levels of government.

C) suggest the need for improved security and surveillance measures.

D) have been vocally criticized by the American public.

7

The tone that Passage 2 uses when describing the Senate's conduct can best be described as one of

A) disdain.

B) confusion.

C) melancholy.

D) vindictiveness.

8

Which choice provides the best evidence for the answer to the previous question?

A) Lines 46-47 ("As a woman . . . feel")

B) Lines 52-54 ("I am not . . . aisle")

C) Lines 66-69 ("As an American . . . hunt")

D) Lines 70-73 ("It is high . . . freedom")

9

Both Passage 1 and Passage 2 encourage Americans to embrace a principle of

A) cooperation.

B) debate.

C) vigilance.

D) self-sacrifice.

10

As used in line 60, "smear" most nearly means

A) warp.

B) obscure.

C) slander.

D) spread.

CONTINUE

Questions 1-10 are based on the following passages.
4.03

These two readings deal with principles of American military policy. In Passage 1, John Foster Dulles, who served as Secretary of State under President Dwight D. Eisenhower, outlines an foreign policy for dealing with possible aggression by the Soviet Union. In Passage 2, Eisenhower himself explains the growth of the American armed forces in the years after World War II. The speeches from which these passages are excerpted were delivered in 1954 and 1960, respectively.

Passage 1

The Soviet Communists are planning for what they call "an entire historical era," and we should do the same. They seek, through many types of maneuvers, gradually to divide
Line and weaken the free nations by overextending them in efforts
5 which, as Lenin put it, are "beyond their strength, so that they come to practical bankruptcy." Then, said Lenin, "our victory is assured." Then, said Stalin, will be "the moment for the decisive blow."

In the face of this strategy, measures cannot be judged
10 adequate merely because they ward off an immediate danger. It is essential to do this, but it is also essential to do so without exhausting ourselves.

When the Eisenhower administration applied this test, we felt that some transformations were needed.
15 It is not sound military strategy permanently to commit U.S. land forces to Asia to a degree that leaves us no strategic reserves.

It is not sound economics, or good foreign policy, to support permanently other countries; for in the long run, that
20 creates as much ill will as good will . . .

We need allies and collective security. Our purpose is to make these relations more effective, less costly. This can be done by placing more reliance on deterrent power and less dependence on local defensive power.
25 This is accepted practice so far as local communities are concerned. We keep locks on our doors, but we do not have an armed guard in every home. We rely principally on a community security system so well equipped to punish any who break in and steal that, in fact, would be aggressors
30 are generally deterred. That is the modern way of getting maximum protection at a bearable cost.

What the Eisenhower administration seeks is a similar international security system. We want, for ourselves and the other free nations, a maximum deterrent at a bearable cost.
35 Local defense will always be important. But there is no local defense which alone will contain the mighty landpower of the Communist world. Local defenses must be reinforced by the further deterrent of massive retaliatory power. A potential aggressor must know that he cannot always prescribe battle

40 conditions that suit him. Otherwise, for example, a potential aggressor, who is glutted with manpower, might be tempted to attack in confidence that resistance would be confined to manpower. He might be tempted to attack in places where his superiority was decisive.
45 The way to deter aggression is for the free community to be willing and able to respond vigorously at places and with means of its own choosing.

Passage 2

A vital element in keeping the peace is our military establishment. Our arms must be mighty, ready for instant
50 action, so that no potential aggressor may be tempted to risk his own destruction.

Our military organization today bears little relation to that known by any of my predecessors in peacetime, or indeed by the fighting men of World War II or Korea.
55 Until the latest of our world conflicts, the United States had no armaments industry. American makers of plowshares could, with time and as required, make swords as well. But now we can no longer risk emergency improvisation of national defense; we have been compelled to create a
60 permanent armaments industry of vast proportions. Added to this, three and a half million men and women are directly engaged in the defense establishment. We annually spend on military security more than the net income of all United States corporations.
65 This conjunction of an immense military establishment and a large arms industry is new in the American experience. The total influence—economic, political, even spiritual—is felt in every city, every State house, every office of the Federal government. We recognize the imperative need for
70 this development. Yet we must not fail to comprehend its grave implications. Our toil, resources and livelihood are all involved; so is the very structure of our society.

In the councils of government, we must guard against the acquisition of unwarranted influence, whether sought or
75 unsought, by the military-industrial complex. The potential for the disastrous rise of misplaced power exists and will persist.

We must never let the weight of this combination endanger our liberties or democratic processes. We should
80 take nothing for granted. Only an alert and knowledgeable citizenry can compel the proper meshing of the huge industrial and military machinery of defense with our peaceful methods and goals, so that security and liberty may prosper together.

CONTINUE

1

As used in line 6, "practical" most nearly means

A) resourceful.

B) effectual.

C) viable.

D) businesslike.

2

The method of national defense that Dulles envisions in Passage 1 can best be described as

A) modeled on the Russian military system.

B) large in scope and popular among civilians.

C) reliant on advanced technology.

D) nimble and relatively inexpensive.

3

Which choice best describes the developmental pattern of lines 9-24 ("In the face . . . power")?

A) The principles of Communism are mentioned, the need to fight Communism is emphasized, and a practical measure is outlined.

B) A recent law is explained, its effectiveness is assessed, and the need for new ideas is invoked.

C) A crisis is described, an initiative is praised, and slight modifications are recommended.

D) Criteria are introduced, shortcomings are noted, and a specific course of action is endorsed.

4

Unlike Passage 2, Passage 1 addresses which of the following topics?

A) The possibility that America will be attacked

B) The civic duties of individual Americans

C) The role of nations sympathetic to America

D) The founding principles of American democracy

5

Which choice provides the best evidence for the answer to the previous question?

A) Lines 9-12 ("In the face . . . ourselves")

B) Lines 25-27 ("This is accepted . . . home")

C) Lines 32-34 ("What the Eisenhower . . . cost")

D) Lines 40-43 ("Otherwise . . . manpower")

6

Eisenhower in Passage 2 characterizes the American armed forces as a whole as

A) needlessly expensive.

B) surprisingly corrupt.

C) unprecedented in nature.

D) vigilant and spiritually noble.

7

Which choice provides the best evidence for the answer to the previous question?

A) Lines 52-54 ("Our military . . . Korea")

B) Lines 62-64 ("We annually . . . corporations")

C) Lines 73-75 ("In the councils . . . complex")

D) Lines 78-80 ("We must never . . . granted")

8

As used in line 76, "misplaced" most nearly means

A) ill-used.

B) forgotten.

C) discarded.

D) haphazard.

CONTINUE

9

Which statement best describes how the two passages differ in their assessments of increased national security measures?

A) Passage 1 is concerned entirely with land-based military maneuvers; Passage 2 discusses a variety of combat settings.

B) Passage 1 argues that newly-adopted measures have been uniquely cost-effective; Passage 2 implies that national security spending can increase poverty among civilians.

C) Passage 1 links particular measures to items of common sense already present in society; Passage 2 suggests that current measures could transform society.

D) Passage 1 sees American military buildup as a very recent development; Passage 2 sees such buildup as a time-honored American practice.

10

According to both Passage 1 and Passage 2, an effective way to keep a hostile nation from attacking is to

A) garner a large number of allies and force the belligerent nation to negotiate.

B) take an aggressive yet pragmatic stance in local and regional conflicts.

C) combine military measures with arrangements that will slowly weaken the hostile nation's economy.

D) accumulate enough power to pose the threat of a devastating counter-attack.

CONTINUE

Questions 1-10 are based on the following passage.
4.04

In the fall of 1963, President John F. Kennedy visited Amherst College and delivered a speech in honor of American poet Robert Frost. Kennedy's elegy for Frost has since been known as "Poetry and Power": the following is an excerpt from this address.

     This day, devoted to the memory of Robert Frost, offers an opportunity for reflection which is prized by politicians as well as by others and even by poets. For Robert Frost was one of the
Line granite figures of our time in America. He was supremely two
5 things: an artist and an American. A nation reveals itself not only by the men it produces but also by the men it honors, the men it remembers.

     In America our heroes have customarily been men of large accomplishments. But today this college and country honor a
10 man whose contribution was not to our size but to our spirit; not to our political beliefs but to our insight; not to our self-esteem but to our self-comprehension.

     In honoring Robert Frost we therefore can pay honor to the deepest sources of our national strength. That strength takes
15 many forms, and the most obvious forms are not always the most significant.

     The men who create power make an indispensable contribution to the nation's greatness, but the men who question power make a contribution just as indispensable, especially
20 when that questioning is disinterested, for they determine whether we use power or power uses us. Our national strength matters; but the spirit which informs and controls our strength matters just as much. This was the special significance of Robert Frost.

25   He brought an unsparing instinct for reality to bear on the platitudes and pieties of society. His sense of the human tragedy fortified him against self-deception and easy consolation.

     "I have been," he wrote, "one acquainted with the night." And because he knew the midnight as well as the high noon,
30 because he understood the ordeal as well as the triumph of the human spirit, he gave his age strength with which to overcome despair.

     At bottom he held a deep faith in the spirit of man. And it is hardly an accident that Robert Frost coupled poetry and
35 power, for he saw poetry as the means of saving power from itself.

     When power leads man towards arrogance, poetry reminds him of his limitations. When power narrows the areas of man's concern, poetry reminds him of the richness and diversity of
40 his existence. When power corrupts, poetry cleanses, for art establishes the basic human truths which must serve as the touchstones of our judgment. The artist, however faithful to his personal vision of reality, becomes the last champion of the individual mind and sensibility against an intrusive society

45 and an officious state. The great artist is thus a solitary figure. He has, as Frost said, "a lover's quarrel with the world." In pursuing his perceptions of reality he must often sail against the currents of his time. This is not a popular role. If Robert Frost was much honored during his lifetime, it was because
50 a good many preferred to ignore his darker truths. Yet, in retrospect, we see how the artist's fidelity has strengthened the fiber of our national life.

     If sometimes our great artists have been the most critical of our society, it is because their sensitivity and their concern
55 for justice, which must motivate any true artist, make them aware that our nation falls short of its highest potential.

     I see little of more importance to the future of our country and our civilization than full recognition of the place of the artist. If art is to nourish the roots of our culture, society must
60 set the artist free to follow his vision wherever it takes him.

1

The main purpose of this passage is to

A) relate the poetry of Robert Frost to values essential to American society.

B) connect the poetry of Robert Frost to a new initiative in American politics.

C) summarize the content of Robert Frost's most important poems.

D) explain how Robert Frost became a popular poet.

2

Robert Frost's life and poetry were informed by his

A) stern personality.

B) wealth of experience.

C) knowledge of politics.

D) moments of despair.

3

Which choice provides the best evidence for the answer to the previous question?

A) Lines 3-4 ("For Robert . . . America")

B) Lines 13-14 ("In honoring . . . national strength")

C) Lines 21-24 ("Our national . . . Frost")

D) Lines 29-32 ("And because . . . despair")

CONTINUE

4

As used in line 20, "questioning" most nearly means

A) cynicism.

B) analysis.

C) confusion.

D) pessimism.

5

As used in line 43, "personal" most nearly means

A) domestic.

B) touchy.

C) peculiar.

D) individualized.

6

In the course of lines 17-32 ("The men . . . despair"), the focus of the passage shifts from

A) outlining broad principles to relating those principles directly to Robert Frost.

B) criticizing the use of power to praising the role of poetry.

C) paraphrasing a public opinion to outlining Kennedy's personal opinion.

D) portraying Robert Frost in a heroic manner to emphasizing a few of Frost's flaws.

7

In lines 37-42 ("When power . . . judgment"), Kennedy explains that "power" and "poetry" are

A) seldom both present within a single society.

B) understood as working in direct opposition.

C) purely abstract or theoretical principles.

D) two inspirations that artists must choose between.

8

Which of the following statements would most clearly contradict Kennedy's arguments about the nature of poetry?

A) Robert Frost was similar to other poets of his era.

B) Robert Frost was most influential during his lifetime.

C) Great artists have often been indifferent to social issues.

D) Great artists have sometimes celebrated the society to which they belong.

9

Kennedy characterizes the relationship between artists and society as

A) completely unpredictable.

B) mutually destructive.

C) consistently cooperative.

D) potentially antagonistic.

10

Which choice provides the best evidence for the answer to the previous question?

A) Lines 8-9 ("In America . . . accomplishments")

B) Lines 17-19 ("The men . . . indispensable")

C) Lines 45-48 ("The great . . . time")

D) Lines 57-59 ("I see little . . . artist")

159

CONTINUE

Questions 1-10 are based on the following passage.
4.05
This reading is an excerpt from a televised address delivered by president Lyndon B. Johnson in 1965. In this speech, Johnson explained and advocated recent voting rights legislation that would protect the civil rights of African Americans: his address is most famous for its often-quoted call to action against injustice, "We shall overcome."

Our fathers believed that if this noble view of the rights of man was to flourish, it must be rooted in democracy. The most basic right of all was the right to choose your own leaders. The
Line history of this country, in large measure, is the history of the
5 expansion of that right to all of our people. Many of the issues of civil rights are very complex and most difficult. But about this there can and should be no argument.

Every American citizen must have an equal right to vote. There is no reason which can excuse the denial of that
10 right. There is no duty which weighs more heavily on us than the duty we have to ensure that right.

Yet the harsh fact is that in many places in this country men and women are kept from voting simply because they are Negroes. Every device of which human ingenuity is capable
15 has been used to deny this right. The Negro citizen may go to register only to be told that the day is wrong, or the hour is late, or the official in charge is absent. And if he persists, and if he manages to present himself to the registrar, he may be disqualified because he did not spell out his middle name
20 or because he abbreviated a word on the application. And if he manages to fill out an application, he is given a test. The registrar is the sole judge of whether he passes this test. He may be asked to recite the entire Constitution, or explain the most complex provisions of State law. And even a college degree
25 cannot be used to prove that he can read and write.

For the fact is that the only way to pass these barriers is to show a white skin. Experience has clearly shown that the existing process of law cannot overcome systematic and ingenious discrimination. No law that we now have on the
30 books—and I have helped to put three of them there—can ensure the right to vote when local officials are determined to deny it. In such a case our duty must be clear to all of us. The Constitution says that no person shall be kept from voting because of his race or his color. We have all sworn an oath
35 before God to support and to defend that Constitution. We must now act in obedience to that oath.

Wednesday, I will send to Congress a law designed to eliminate illegal barriers to the right to vote.

The broad principles of that bill will be in the hands of the
40 Democratic and Republican leaders tomorrow. After they have reviewed it, it will come here formally as a bill. I am grateful for this opportunity to come here tonight at the invitation of the

leadership to reason with my friends, to give them my views, and to visit with my former colleagues. I've had prepared a
45 more comprehensive analysis of the legislation which I had intended to transmit to the clerk tomorrow, but which I will submit to the clerks tonight. But I want to really discuss with you now, briefly, the main proposals of this legislation.

This bill will strike down restrictions to voting in all
50 elections—Federal, State, and local—which have been used to deny Negroes the right to vote. This bill will establish a simple, uniform standard which cannot be used, however ingenious the effort, to flout our Constitution. It will provide for citizens to be registered by officials of the United States Government, if the
55 State officials refuse to register them. It will eliminate tedious, unnecessary lawsuits which delay the right to vote. Finally, this legislation will ensure that properly registered individuals are not prohibited from voting.

I will welcome the suggestions from all of the Members
60 of Congress—I have no doubt that I will get some—on ways and means to strengthen this law and to make it effective. But experience has plainly shown that this is the only path to carry out the command of the Constitution.

To those who seek to avoid action by their National
65 Government in their own communities, who want to and who seek to maintain purely local control over elections, the answer is simple: open your polling places to all your people.

1

The main purpose of the passage is to

A) recapitulate the history of voting rights abuses.

B) encourage an end to partisan politics.

C) explain and justify a new government measure.

D) determine how to eliminate racial prejudice entirely.

2

Johnson refers to racial discrimination as "systematic and ingenious" (lines 28-29) in order to

A) demonstrate how better education can eliminate discrimination.

B) show why the government must be restructured.

C) concede that many Americans will probably disagree with his proposals.

D) underscore the difficulty involved in fighting discrimination.

CONTINUE

3

As used in line 9, "denial of" most nearly means

A) restriction of.

B) incomprehension of.

C) disbelief in.

D) discipline of.

4

In order to eliminate discrimination in voting, the bill presented by Johnson will

A) clarify ambiguous portions of the Constitution.

B) establish a new federal agency that will monitor local elections.

C) create a standardized method for proper voter registration.

D) disenfranchise those who continue to discriminate against African Americans.

5

Johnson claims that African Americans have often been kept from voting on account of

A) political propaganda.

B) amendments to the Constitution.

C) an inefficient federal government.

D) minor technicalities.

6

Which choice provides the best evidence for the answer to the previous question?

A) Lines 10-11 ("There is no . . . that right")

B) Lines 17-20 ("And if he . . . application")

C) Lines 24-25 ("And even . . . and write")

D) Lines 37-38 ("Wednesday . . . to vote")

7

According to Johnson, opponents of voting rights have responded to the Constitution and its principles with

A) irreverence.

B) confusion.

C) hatred.

D) disbelief.

8

Which choice provides the best evidence for the answer to the previous question?

A) Lines 22-24 ("He may . . . law")

B) Lines 33-34 ("The Constitution . . . color")

C) Lines 34-36 ("We have all . . . that oath")

D) Lines 51-53 ("This bill . . . Constitution")

9

Johnson concludes his discussion by both

A) inviting feedback and issuing a warning.

B) praising his allies and countering his critics.

C) recapitulating recent history and describing a future initiative.

D) condemning racism and listing specific reformers.

10

As used in line 62, "plainly" most nearly means

A) without beauty.

B) without wordiness.

C) without question.

D) without adornment.

CONTINUE

Questions 1-10 are based on the following passage.
4.06
Adopted from a 1969 speech delivered by Shirley Chisholm, who represented New York in the House of Representatives and was a prominent advocate of women's rights and civil rights generally.

Mr. Speaker, when a young woman graduates from college and starts looking for a job, she is likely to have a frustrating and even demeaning experience ahead of her. If she
Line walks into an office for an interview, the first question she will
5 be asked is, "Do you type?"

There is a calculated system of prejudice that lies unspoken behind that question. Why is it acceptable for women to be secretaries, librarians, and teachers, but totally unacceptable for them to be managers, administrators, doctors,
10 lawyers, and Members of Congress?

The unspoken assumption is that women are different. They do not have executive ability, orderly minds, stability, leadership skills, and they are too emotional . . .

As a black person, I am no stranger to race prejudice. But
15 the truth is that in the political world I have been far oftener discriminated against because I am a woman than because I am black.

Prejudice against blacks is becoming unacceptable although it will take years to eliminate it. But it is doomed
20 because, slowly, white America is beginning to admit that it exists. Prejudice against women is still acceptable. There is very little understanding yet of the immorality involved in double pay scales and the classification of most of the better jobs as "for men only."

25 More than half of the population of the United States is female. But women occupy only 2 percent of the managerial positions. They have not even reached the level of tokenism yet. No women sit on the AFL-CIO council or Supreme Court There have been only two women who have held Cabinet
30 rank, and at present there are none. Only two women now hold ambassadorial rank in the diplomatic corps. In Congress, we are down to one Senator and 10 Representatives.

Considering that there are about 3 1/2 million more women in the United States than men, this situation is
35 outrageous.

It is true that part of the problem has been that women have not been aggressive in demanding their rights. This was also true of the black population for many years. They submitted to oppression and even cooperated with it. Women
40 have done the same thing. But now there is an awareness of this situation particularly among the younger segment of the population.

As in the field of equal rights for blacks, Spanish-Americans, the Indians, and other groups, laws will not change
45 such deep-seated problems overnight. But they can be used

to provide protection for those who are most abused, and to begin the process of evolutionary change by compelling the insensitive majority to reexamine its unconscious attitudes.

It is for this reason that I wish to introduce today a
50 proposal that has been before every Congress for the last 40 years and that sooner or later must become part of the basic law of the land—the equal rights amendment.

Let me note and try to refute the commonest arguments that are offered against this amendment. One is that women
55 are already protected under the law and do not need legislation. Existing laws are not adequate to secure equal rights for women. Sufficient proof of this is the concentration of women in lower paying, menial, unrewarding jobs and their incredible scarcity in the upper level jobs. If women are
60 already equal, why is it such an event whenever one happens to be elected to Congress?

It is obvious that discrimination exists. Women do not have the opportunities that men do. And women that do not conform to the system, who try to break with the accepted
65 patterns, are stigmatized as "odd" and "unfeminine." The fact is that a woman who aspires to be chairman of the board, or a Member of the House, does so for exactly the same reasons as any man. Basically, these are that she thinks she can do the job and she wants to try. . .

70 Women need no protection that men do not need. What we need are laws to protect working people, to guarantee them fair pay, safe working conditions, protection against sickness and layoffs, and provision for dignified, comfortable retirement. Men and women need these things
75 equally. That one sex needs protection more than the other is a male supremacist myth as ridiculous and unworthy of respect as the white supremacist myths that society is trying to cure itself of at this time.

1

The main purpose of this passage is to

A) encourage women to become more involved in electoral politics.

B) summarize conditions that make new legislation necessary.

C) provide a detailed history of injustices against American women.

D) urge greater solidarity between African Americans and women.

CONTINUE

2

Chisholm believes that the improvement of women's lives will most likely come about

A) unexpectedly.

B) chaotically.

C) inadvertently.

D) gradually.

3

The third paragraph (lines 11-13) serves to

A) present a broad viewpoint that Chisholm finds massively flawed.

B) summarize arguments made by Chisholm's political opponents.

C) expose stereotypes that afflict both women and African Americans.

D) urge women to understand how they differ from men.

4

According to the passage, Chisholm herself has most often been discriminated against on account of her

A) race.

B) class.

C) gender.

D) intellect.

5

As used in line 35, "outrageous" most nearly means

A) flamboyant.

B) debatable.

C) unacceptable.

D) fascinating.

6

Chisholm describes it as an "event" (line 60) for a woman to be elected to Congress because

A) women are most interested in high-powered careers unrelated to government.

B) women's reasons for seeking out positions of authority are not well understood.

C) few women have developed the job skills that would qualify them to take on such great responsibilities.

D) the relatively small number of women in the national government makes such an election seem extraordinary.

7

Which choice provides the best evidence for the answer to the previous question?

A) Lines 3-5 ("If she walks . . . type?")

B) Lines 7-10 ("Why is it . . . Congress?)

C) Lines 29-32 ("There have . . . Representatives")

D) Lines 65-68 ("The fact . . . man")

8

As used in line 59, "incredible" most nearly means

A) doubtful.

B) fanciful.

C) stunning.

D) unconvincing.

9

In the passage, Chisholm criticizes women for

A) ignoring basic economic facts about their position.

B) praising existing laws that are actually problematic.

C) believing that men do not need legal protections.

D) being complacent about the inequalities they face.

10

Which choice provides the best evidence for the answer to the previous question?

A) Lines 21-24 ("There is . . . only")

B) Lines 36-37 ("It is true . . . rights")

C) Lines 54-56 ("One is . . . legislation")

D) Lines 75-78 ("That one . . . time")

CONTINUE

Questions 1-10 are based on the following passage.
4.07
Adapted from "President Richard Nixon's Address to the Nation on the War in Vietnam" (1969), more popularly known as Nixon's "The Silent Majority" speech.

My fellow Americans, I am sure you can recognize from what I have said that we really only have two choices open to us if we want to end this war.

Line
5 – I can order an immediate, precipitate withdrawal of all Americans from Vietnam without regard to the effects of that action.

– Or we can persist in our search for a just peace through a negotiated settlement if possible, or through continued implementation of our plan for Vietnamization if necessary—a
10 plan in which we will withdraw all of our forces from Vietnam on a schedule in accordance with our program, as the South Vietnamese become strong enough to defend their own freedom.

I have chosen this second course.
15 It is not the easy way.
It is the right way.
It is a plan which will end the war and serve the cause of peace—not just in Vietnam but in the Pacific and in the world.

In speaking of the consequences of a precipitate
20 withdrawal, I mentioned that our allies would lose confidence in America.

Far more dangerous, we would lose confidence in ourselves. Oh, the immediate reaction would be a sense of relief that our men were coming home. But as we saw the
25 consequences of what we had done, inevitable remorse and divisive recrimination would scar our spirit as a people.

We have faced other crises in our history and have become stronger by rejecting the easy way out and taking the right way in meeting our challenges. Our greatness as a nation has been
30 our capacity to do what had to be done when we knew our course was right.

I recognize that some of my fellow citizens disagree with the plan for peace I have chosen. Honest and patriotic Americans have reached different conclusions as to how peace
35 should be achieved.

In San Francisco a few weeks ago, I saw demonstrators carrying signs reading: "Lose in Vietnam, bring the boys home."

Well, one of the strengths of our free society is that any
40 American has a right to reach that conclusion and to advocate that point of view. But as President of the United States, I would be untrue to my oath of office if I allowed the policy of this Nation to be dictated by the minority who hold that point of view and who try to impose it on the Nation by mounting
45 demonstrations in the street.

For almost 200 years, the policy of this Nation has been

made under our Constitution by those leaders in the Congress and the White House elected by all of the people. If a vocal minority, however fervent its cause, prevails over reason and
50 the will of the majority, this Nation has no future as a free society.

And now I would like to address a word, if I may, to the young people of this Nation who are particularly concerned, and I understand why they are concerned, about this war.
55 I respect your idealism.
I share your concern for peace.
I want peace as much as you do.
There are powerful personal reasons I want to end this war. This week I will have to sign 83 letters to mothers, fathers,
60 wives, and loved ones of men who have given their lives for America in Vietnam. It is very little satisfaction to me that this is only one-third as many letters as I signed the first week in office. There is nothing I want more than to see the day come when I do not have to write any of those letters.
65 – I want to end the war to save the lives of those brave young men in Vietnam.

– But I want to end it in a way which will increase the chance that their younger brothers and their sons will not have to fight in some future Vietnam someplace in the world.

1

Why does Nixon oppose immediate withdrawal from Vietnam?

A) Because a coherent strategy has not been developed for removing all forces from Vietnam.

B) Because partisan divisions in American politics would be worsened as a result.

C) Because there are no precedents for the proposed withdrawal in American history.

D) Because short-term rewards would be outweighed by long-term repercussions.

2

Which choice provides the best evidence for the answer to the previous question?

A) Lines 4-6 ("I can order . . . action")

B) Lines 23-26 ("Oh, the immediate . . . people")

C) Lines 32-35 ("I recognize . . . achieved")

D) Lines 46-48 ("For almost . . . people")

CONTINUE

3

In lines 27-35, Nixon transitions from

A) praising the efforts of his supporters to attacking the ideas of his enemies.

B) justifying a proposal to acknowledging that proposal's opponents.

C) highlighting an American tradition to showing why that tradition has been discarded.

D) warning against an ill-advised proposal to predicting a broad consensus.

4

As used in line 28, "taking" most nearly means

A) acquiring.

B) pursuing.

C) estimating.

D) conveying.

5

As used in line 45, "demonstrations" most nearly means

A) lectures.

B) portrayals.

C) protests.

D) scenarios.

6

Which of the following values does Nixon explicitly praise in this speech?

A) Freedom of expression and dissent

B) Freedom to form new political parties

C) Expansion of the armed forces

D) Education for young people

7

Which choice provides the best evidence for the answer to the previous question?

A) Lines 7-9 ("Or we can . . . necessary")

B) Lines 27-29 ("We have faced . . . challenges")

C) Lines 39-41 ("Well, one of . . . view")

D) Lines 67-69 ("But I want . . . world")

8

According to Nixon, sound government decisions should be based on

A) "confidence in ourselves" (lines 22-23).

B) "different conclusions" (line 34).

C) "the will of the majority" (line 50).

D) "idealism" (line 55).

9

Why does Nixon receive "very little satisfaction" from the duty he describes in lines 58-64 ("There are . . . letters")?

A) He finds that he is distracted from other presidential obligations.

B) His motives for continuing the war are not appreciated by the public.

C) He is troubled by the number of casualties in Vietnam.

D) He has no real authority to end the war in Vietnam.

10

Nixon addresses the "young people" mentioned in line 53 in a manner that can best be described as

A) condescending.

B) lighthearted.

C) reserved.

D) sympathetic.

CONTINUE

Questions 1-10 are based on the following passage.
4.08
Adapted from the speech "Energy and the National Goals: A Crisis of Confidence" by Jimmy Carter (1979).

I know, of course, being President, that government actions and legislation can be very important. That's why I've worked hard to put my campaign promises into law—and I
Line have to admit, with just mixed success. But after listening to
5 the American people I have been reminded again that all the legislation in the world can't fix what's wrong with America. So, I want to speak to you first tonight about a subject even more serious than energy or inflation. . .

This threat is nearly invisible in ordinary ways. It is a
10 crisis of confidence. It is a crisis that strikes at the very heart and soul and spirit of our national will. We can see this crisis in the growing doubt about the meaning of our own lives and in the loss of a unity of purpose for our Nation.

The erosion of our confidence in the future is threatening
15 to destroy the social and the political fabric of America.

The confidence that we have always had as a people is not simply some romantic dream or a proverb in a dusty book that we read just on the Fourth of July. It is the idea which founded our Nation and has guided our development as a people.
20 Confidence in the future has supported everything else—public institutions and private enterprise, our own families, and the very Constitution of the United States. Confidence has defined our course and has served as a link between generations. We've always believed in something called progress. We've
25 always had a faith that the days of our children would be better than our own.

Our people are losing that faith, not only in government itself but in the ability as citizens to serve as the ultimate rulers and shapers of our democracy. As a people we know our past
30 and we are proud of it. Our progress has been part of the living history of America, even the world. We always believed that we were part of a great movement of humanity itself called democracy, involved in the search for freedom, and that belief has always strengthened us in our purpose. But just as we are
35 losing our confidence in the future, we are also beginning to close the door on our past.

In a nation that was proud of hard work, strong families, close-knit communities, and our faith in God, too many of us now tend to worship self-indulgence and consumption.
40 Human identity is no longer defined by what one does, but by what one owns. But we've discovered that owning things and consuming things does not satisfy our longing for meaning. We've learned that piling up material goods cannot fill the emptiness of lives which have no confidence or purpose.
45 The symptoms of this crisis of the American spirit are all around us. For the first time in the history of our country a majority of our people believe that the next 5 years will be

worse than the past 5 years. Two-thirds of our people do not even vote. The productivity of American workers is actually
50 dropping, and the willingness of Americans to save for the future has fallen below that of all other people in the Western world.

As you know, there is a growing disrespect for government and for churches and for schools, the news
55 media, and other institutions. This is not a message of happiness or reassurance, but it is the truth and it is a warning.

These changes did not happen overnight. They've come upon us gradually over the last generation, years that were
60 filled with shocks and tragedy.

We were sure that ours was a nation of the ballot, not the bullet, until the murders of John Kennedy and Robert Kennedy and Martin Luther King, Jr. We were taught that our armies were always invincible and our causes
65 were always just, only to suffer the agony of Vietnam. We respected the Presidency as a place of honor until the shock of Watergate. . .

Looking for a way out of this crisis, our people have turned to the Federal Government and found it isolated from
70 the mainstream of our Nation's life. Washington, D.C., has become an island. The gap between our citizens and our Government has never been so wide. The people are looking for honest answers, not easy answers; clear leadership, not false claims and evasiveness and politics as usual.

1

The crisis of confidence in America is described by Carter as having impacted

A) legislative reform and political leadership.
B) voter apathy and economic output.
C) education levels and personal wealth.
D) patriotic sentiment and willingness to fight wars.

2

Which choice provides the best evidence for the answer to the previous question?

A) Lines 16-18 ("The confidence . . . July")
B) Lines 48-52 ("Two-thirds . . . world")
C) Lines 58-60 ("These changes . . . tragedy")
D) Lines 71-72 ("The gap . . . wide")

CONTINUE ➡

3

In this speech, Carter describes "confidence" as a virtue that

A) is being widely confused with wealth and ambition.

B) is most threatened during times of war and hardship.

C) is easiest to foster in small countries with patriotic citizens.

D) is related to the founding principles of the United States.

4

As used in line 9, "invisible" most nearly means

A) transparent.

B) negligible.

C) imperceptible.

D) hidden.

5

Which of the following would most clearly indicate that the "crisis of confidence" analyzed in the passage has come to an end?

A) Dramatically decreased crime rates

B) Dramatically increased voter participation

C) The elimination of failing schools

D) The disappearance of the most biased media outlets

6

In the course of his argument, Carter establishes a contrast that involves

A) popularity and honesty.

B) religion and politics.

C) education and pragmatism.

D) materialism and fulfillment.

7

In lines 53-60 ("As you . . . tragedy"), Carter transitions from

A) describing some manifestations of a negative trend to explaining the origins of that trend.

B) explaining widespread discontent to explaining how his political opponents created that discontent.

C) mentioning specific tragedies to indicating that similar tragedies will take place in the future.

D) criticizing apathy on social issues to calling for immediate and productive action.

8

As used in line 32, "movement" most nearly means

A) displacement.

B) motion.

C) advancement.

D) activity.

9

Carter would most likely agree with which of the following criticisms of his own leadership?

A) He has prioritized economic problems that appear to be more severe than they really are.

B) He has increased the size of the federal government with poor results.

C) He has not effectively fulfilled some of his stated political goals.

D) He has created policies that were popular yet increased partisanship.

10

Which choice provides the best evidence for the answer to the previous question?

A) Lines 2-4 ("That's . . . success")

B) Lines 7-8 ("So . . . inflation")

C) Lines 65-67 ("We . . . Watergate")

D) Lines 68-70 ("Looking . . . life")

CONTINUE

Questions 1-10 are based on the following passage.
4.09

Adapted from Ronald Reagan, "Address to the Nation on the Soviet-United States Summit Meeting" (1987). Mikhail Gorbachev, referred to in this speech, was the head of state of the Soviet Union for much of Reagan's presidency.

As I am speaking to you now, General Secretary Gorbachev is leaving on his return trip to the Soviet Union. His departure marks the end of three historic days here in
Line Washington in which Mr. Gorbachev and I continued to build
5 a foundation for better relations between our governments and our peoples. During these three days we took a step—only a first step, but still a critical one—toward building a more durable peace, indeed, a step that may be the most important taken since World War II to slow down the arms buildup.
10 I'm referring to the treaty that we signed Tuesday afternoon in the East Room of the White House. I believe this treaty represents a landmark in postwar history, because it is not just an arms control but an arms reduction agreement. Unlike treaties of the past, this agreement does not simply establish
15 ceilings for new weapons: It actually reduces the number of such weapons. In fact, it altogether abolishes an entire class of U.S. and Soviet nuclear missiles.
The verification measures in this treaty are also something new with far-reaching implications. On-site inspections and
20 short-notice inspections will be permitted within the Soviet Union. Again, this is a first-time event, a breakthrough, and that's why I believe this treaty will not only lessen the threat of war, it can also speed along a process that may someday remove that threat entirely.
25 Indeed, this treaty, and all that we've achieved during this summit, signals a broader understanding between the United States and the Soviet Union. It is an understanding that will help keep the peace as we work toward the ultimate goal of our foreign policy: a world where the people of every land can
30 decide for themselves their form of government and way of life.
Yet as important as the newly signed Intermediate-Range Nuclear Forces treaty is, there is a further and even more crucial point about the last three days and the entire summit process: Soviet-American relations are no longer focused only
35 on arms control issues. They now cover a far broader agenda, one that has, at its root, realism and candor. Let me explain this with a saying I've often repeated: Nations do not distrust each other because they're armed; they are armed because they distrust each other. And just as real peace means the presence
40 of freedom and justice as well as the absence of war, so, too, summits must be discussions not just about arms but about the fundamental differences that cause nations to be armed.
Dealing then with the deeper sources of conflict between nations and systems of government is a practical and moral

45 imperative. And that's why it was vital to establish a broader summit agenda, one that dealt not only with arms reductions but also people-to-people contacts between our nations and, most important, the issues of human rights and regional conflicts.
50 This is the summit agenda we've adopted. By doing so, we've dealt not just with arms control issues but also with fundamental problems such as Soviet expansionism, human rights violations, as well as our own moral opposition to the ideology that justifies such practices. In this way, we have put
55 Soviet-American relations on a far more candid and far more realistic footing. It also means that, while there's movement—indeed, dramatic movement—in the arms reduction area, much remains to be done in that area as well as in these other critical areas that I've mentioned, especially—and this goes
60 without saying—in advancing our goal of a world open to the expansion of human freedom and the growth of democratic government.
So, much work lies ahead. Let me explain: On the matter of regional conflicts, I spoke candidly with Mr. Gorbachev on
65 the issues of Afghanistan, Iran-Iraq, Cambodia, Angola, and Nicaragua. I continue to have high hopes—and he assured me that he did too—that we can have real cooperation in resolving regional conflicts on terms that promote peace and freedom. This is essential to a lasting improvement in our relations.

1

Throughout the passage, Reagan's tone regarding the future of U.S.-Soviet relations is one of

A) penitence.

B) relief.

C) disillusionment.

D) optimism.

2

As used in line 3, "historic" most nearly means

A) widely commemorated.

B) ancient.

C) pivotal.

D) clearly precedented.

CONTINUE

3

In this speech, Reagan suggests that he views Mr. Gorbachev as

A) a valued collaborator.

B) a potential aggressor.

C) a personal friend.

D) a superior authority.

4

The "verification measures" mentioned in line 18 are significant because they

A) were initially opposed by the public but proved to be a wise policy.

B) are a first step towards the adoption of democratic principles in the Soviet Union.

C) are a completely novel development that may promote international peace.

D) are gradually being adopted by countries other than the Soviet Union and the United States.

5

With which of the following statements would Reagan most likely agree?

A) Earlier American politicians have been oblivious to the political and ideological differences between the United States and the Soviet Union.

B) New arms reduction efforts will soon be unnecessary on account of the progress that has recently been made in this area.

C) Negotiation with the Soviet Union is necessary, even though the Soviet Union's past conduct has been objectionable.

D) The Soviet Union has created a new alliance with the United States in order to improve conditions in smaller nations.

6

Which choice provides the best evidence for the answer to the previous question?

A) Lines 43-45 ("Dealing then . . . imperative")

B) Lines 51-56 ("we've dealt . . . footing")

C) Lines 56-59 ("It also means . . . mentioned")

D) Lines 64-66 ("I spoke candidly . . . Nicaragua")

7

As used in lines 56 and 57, "movement" most nearly means

A) turmoil.

B) progress.

C) rearrangement.

D) liveliness.

8

It can be inferred from the speech that diplomacy between the United States and the Soviet Union was at one point

A) based entirely on fighting common enemies.

B) premised on the idea that the two nations would always be hostile.

C) limited to a small set of military concerns.

D) hampered by restrictions on trade and travel.

9

Which choice provides the best evidence for the answer to the previous question?

A) Lines 6-9 ("During these . . . buildup")

B) Lines 15-17 ("It actually . . . missiles")

C) Lines 19-21 ("On-site . . . Union")

D) Lines 31-35 ("Yet as . . . issues")

10

Which of the following scenarios would most strongly contradict the principle that Reagan lays out in lines 37-39 ("Nations do not . . . other")?

A) A nation doubles the size of its armed forces in response to military buildup in neighboring nations.

B) A nation uses both diplomacy and military pressure to resolve a conflict.

C) A nation with no foreign enemies steadily increases investment in its military.

D) A nation reduces its armed forces in response to pressure from an international coalition.

CONTINUE

Questions 1-10 are based on the following passages.
4.10

Passage 1 is adapted from a speech delivered by John F. Kennedy in 1963; Passage 2 is adapted from a speech delivered by Ronald Reagan in 1987. Both of these readings address the situation in Germany, which had been divided into sections supervised by democratic nations (West Germany) and the Soviet Union (East Germany) since the end of World War II. The German city of Berlin had been similarly partitioned.

Passage 1

What is true of this city is true of Germany: real, lasting peace in Europe can never be assured as long as one German out of four is denied the elementary right of free men, and that
Line is to make a free choice. In 18 years of peace and good faith,
5 this generation of Germans has earned the right to be free, including the right to unite their families and their nation in lasting peace, with good will to all people.

You live in a defended island of freedom, but your life is part of the main. So let me ask you, as I close, to lift your eyes
10 beyond the dangers of today, to the hopes of tomorrow, beyond the freedom merely of this city of Berlin, or your country of Germany, to the advance of freedom everywhere, beyond the wall to the day of peace with justice, beyond yourselves and ourselves to all mankind.
15 Freedom is indivisible, and when one man is enslaved, all are not free. When all are free, then we look—can look forward to that day when this city will be joined as one and this country and this great Continent of Europe in a peaceful and hopeful globe. When that day finally comes, as it will, the people of
20 West Berlin can take sober satisfaction in the fact that they were in the front lines for almost two decades.

All—All free men, wherever they may live, are citizens of Berlin.

And, therefore, as a free man, I take pride in the words "*Ich*
25 *bin ein Berliner.*"[1]

Passage 2

Where four decades ago there was rubble, today in West Berlin there is the greatest industrial output of any city in Germany: busy office blocks, fine homes and apartments, proud avenues, and the spreading lawns of parkland. Where
30 a city's culture seemed to have been destroyed, today there are two great universities, orchestras and an opera, countless theaters, and museums. Where there was want, today there's abundance—food, clothing, automobiles. . . From devastation, from utter ruin, you Berliners have, in freedom, rebuilt a city
35 that once again ranks as one of the greatest on earth. Now the Soviets may have had other plans. . .

In the 1950s—In the 1950s Khrushchev[2] predicted: "We will bury you."

But in the West today, we see a free world that has
40 achieved a level of prosperity and well-being unprecedented in all human history. In the Communist world, we see failure, technological backwardness, declining standards of health, even want of the most basic kind—too little food. Even today, the Soviet Union still cannot feed itself. After these four
45 decades, then, there stands before the entire world one great and inescapable conclusion: Freedom leads to prosperity. Freedom replaces the ancient hatreds among the nations with comity and peace. Freedom is the victor.

And now—now the Soviets themselves may, in a limited
50 way, be coming to understand the importance of freedom. We hear much from Moscow about a new policy of reform and openness. Some political prisoners have been released. Certain foreign news broadcasts are no longer being jammed. Some economic enterprises have been permitted to operate with
55 greater freedom from state control.

Are these the beginnings of profound changes in the Soviet state? Or are they token gestures intended to raise false hopes in the West, or to strengthen the Soviet system without changing it? We welcome change and openness; for we
60 believe that freedom and security go together, that the advance of human liberty—the advance of human liberty can only strengthen the cause of world peace.

There is one sign the Soviets can make that would be unmistakable, that would advance dramatically the cause of
65 freedom and peace.

General Secretary Gorbachev, if you seek peace, if you seek prosperity for the Soviet Union and Eastern Europe, if you seek liberalization: Come here to this gate.

Mr. Gorbachev, open this gate.
70 Mr. Gorbachev—Mr. Gorbachev, tear down this wall!

1: A German sentence that translates to "I am a Berliner"
2: A former Soviet head of state, most influential during the 1950s and 1960s

Both Kennedy and Reagan characterize freedom as a quality that

A) is closely linked to international harmony.

B) has never been found in a Communist economy.

C) will eventually be embraced by the Soviet Union.

D) has guided German politics for centuries.

CONTINUE

2

As used in line 12, "advance" most nearly means

A) compensation.

B) progress.

C) aggression.

D) motion.

3

Passage 1 differs from Passage 2 in that Passage 1 does not involve

A) an analysis of human and political rights.

B) allusions to recent hardships.

C) a direct address to the residents of Berlin.

D) direct references to the Soviet Union.

4

The author of Passage 2 would most likely argue that the cause of advancing "freedom everywhere" (line 12)

A) has made no progress in the Soviet Union.

B) will quickly bring about the collapse of the Soviet Union.

C) has made limited progress in the Soviet Union.

D) is turning the Soviet Union into an economic superpower.

5

In Passage 2, Reagan responds to the new Soviet initiatives by

A) demanding further reforms.

B) delivering an ultimatum.

C) expressing his trust.

D) outlining a new political ideology.

6

In Passage 1, Kennedy appeals to his audience by

A) offering inspiring anecdotes from recent German history.

B) envisioning a prosperous future.

C) renouncing mistaken beliefs.

D) describing virtues unique to German citizens.

7

Which choice provides the best evidence for the answer to the previous question?

A) Lines 4-7 ("In 18 years . . . all people")

B) Lines 8-9 ("You live in . . . the main"

C) Lines 16-19 ("When all . . . globe")

D) Lines 22-25 ("All—All . . . *Berliner*")

8

As used in line 53, "jammed" most nearly means

A) obstructed.

B) overcrowded.

C) warped.

D) pushed together.

9

Reagan harshly criticizes the Soviet Union for its

A) unwillingness to interact with West Berlin.

B) economic and humanitarian shortcomings.

C) belligerent foreign policy.

D) misguided infrastructure projects.

10

Which choice provides the best evidence for the answer to the previous question?

A) Lines 32-36 ("Where there . . . other plans")

B) Lines 37-38 ("In the 1950s . . . bury you")

C) Lines 41-44 ("In the Communist . . . itself")

D) Lines 66-70 ("General secretary . . . this wall!")

Answer Key on Next Page

Answer Key: CHAPTER FOUR

SAT

4.01	4.02	4.03	4.04	4.05
1. B	1. A	1. B	1. A	1. C
2. D	2. B	2. D	2. B	2. D
3. A	3. C	3. D	3. D	3. A
4. D	4. A	4. C	4. B	4. C
5. C	5. D	5. C	5. D	5. D
6. B	6. B	6. C	6. A	6. B
7. A	7. A	7. A	7. B	7. A
8. D	8. B	8. A	8. C	8. D
9. A	9. A	9. C	9. D	9. A
10. B	10. C	10. D	10. C	10. C

4.06	4.07	4.08	4.09	4.10
1. B	1. D	1. B	1. D	1. A
2. D	2. B	2. B	2. C	2. B
3. A	3. B	3. D	3. A	3. D
4. C	4. B	4. C	4. C	4. C
5. C	5. C	5. B	5. C	5. B
6. D	6. A	6. D	6. B	6. B
7. C	7. C	7. A	7. B	7. C
8. C	8. C	8. C	8. C	8. A
9. D	9. C	9. C	9. D	9. B
10. B	10. D	10. A	10. C	10. C

Answer Explanations
Chapter 04 | Colonial Era

4.01 | Eleanor Roosevelt

1) CORRECT ANSWER: B
In this passage, Roosevelt argues that "the issue of human liberty" (lines 12-13) is strongly linked to "the future of the United Nations" (line 14); she then goes on to examine the efforts of the United Nations to "maintain international peace and security" (line 66). This information supports B and can be used to eliminate C (since Roosevelt focuses on the PRESENT tasks of the United Nations) and D (since Roosevelt approves of the course that the United Nations is taking). A is a trap answer: while Roosevelt does in fact criticize the Soviet Union, she does not explicitly argue that the United Nations must intervene in a harsh manner.

2) CORRECT ANSWER: D
In the relevant lines, Roosevelt acknowledges the Soviet Union's "laudable objective" (line 51) of protecting minorities, but also notes that in many other respects people in the Soviet Union "are being denied freedoms which they want and which they see other people have" (lines 55-56). This information supports D and can be used to eliminate C (since Roosevelt states that the Soviet Union has successfully eliminated discrimination). A wrongly focuses on future events (not on the present conditions that concern Roosevelt), while B introduces the topic of the United Nations, which is not actually raised in the relevant lines.

3) CORRECT ANSWER: A
The word "fired" refers to the effect that ideals such as "liberty, equality, [and] fraternity" (line 8) had on "the imagination of men" (lines 8-9). Roosevelt approves of these qualities, which energized or stimulated people in the pursuit of social justice, so that this information supports A and can be used to eliminate negative answers B and D. C refers to a physical action (or to the act of becoming personally insensitive) and thus does not correctly fit the context.

4) CORRECT ANSWER: D
Early in the speech, Roosevelt tells her audience that the preservation of human freedom is "one of the greatest issues of our time" (lines 1-2): later on, she notes that "It is my belief, and I am sure it is also yours, that the struggle for democracy and freedom is a critical struggle" (lines 63-64). Roosevelt thus is speaking to an audience that is assumed to embrace her own democratic principles: D is thus correct, while Roosevelt refers to American history and totalitarianism in order to build her ARGUMENT (not to indicate the extent of her audience's KNOWLEDGE, eliminating A and C). B is out of scope: although members of the audience might be willing to protest unjust governments, protests are never analyzed at length in the passage.

5) CORRECT ANSWER: C

In lines 38-41, Roosevelt admits that the United States are "not old enough to claim perfection" in humanitarian progress and still "have problems of discrimination". This information supports C, while Roosevelt describes the United Nations in a primarily positive and optimistic manner (eliminating A and D) and criticizes the Soviet Union in almost all respects EXCEPT its efforts against discrimination (eliminating B).

6) CORRECT ANSWER: B

See above for the explanation of the correct answer. A indicates that the United Nations Charter is premised on upholding essential human rights, C argues that totalitarian governments are recognizable and destructive, and D argues that the United Nations must engage in a long-term project to uphold freedom. Note that the lines referenced in the false answers can be used to ELIMINATE the false answers to Question 5.

7) CORRECT ANSWER: A

The word "authority" refers to a feature of totalitarianism that closely-controlled institutions "support" (line 70): by controlling these institutions, totalitarian governments would maintain autocratic power or rule. A is the best answer, while B refers to a more likely trait of INDIVIDUALS and C and D both introduce inappropriate positives.

8) CORRECT ANSWER: D

In lines 9-11, Roosevelt declares that she is discussing rights and freedom "in Europe" because the continent "has been the scene of the greatest historic battles between freedom and tyranny". Thus, the setting and topic of her speech are firmly related, making D the best answer. Roosevelt's primarily positive tone towards the United Nations can be used to eliminate A and B (which are both clearly negative), while the United States is mainly referenced in terms of the issue of DISCRIMINATION: how popular the United Nations is within the United States is never considered (eliminating C).

9) CORRECT ANSWER: A

See above for the explanation of the correct answer. B indicates that the United Nations was created in San Francisco (but not necessarily that the United Nations is POPULAR in the United States), C approvingly quotes the Charter of the United Nations, and D indicates that the United States Supreme Court is attempting to clarify laws related to citizens' rights.

10) CORRECT ANSWER: B

In line 58, Roosevelt explains that the Soviet Union does not permit "freedoms of speech, of the press, of religion and conscience": together, these freedoms involve forms of expression, so that B is the best answer. The Soviet Union has, in fact, eliminated discrimination against minorities (eliminating A). Roosevelt's discussion also confines itself to conditions WITHIN the Soviet Union: international considerations such as trade (C) and diplomacy (D) are never her focus.

4.02 | Joseph McCarthy and Margaret Chase Smith

1) CORRECT ANSWER: A

In lines 12-15, the author of Passage 1 claims that the individuals who have been "selling this nation out" are the people who have most thoroughly enjoyed "all the benefits that the wealthiest nation on earth has had to offer". This information supports A and eliminates B, since the people who threaten America are themselves Americans. Elsewhere in the passage, the author states that these enemies are involved in government policy (but not necessarily in the military, eliminating C) and claims that they are communists (but not that communism is itself new, eliminating D).

2) CORRECT ANSWER: B
See above for the explanation of the correct answer. A describes America's state after the end of World War II, C states that McCarthy has identified communists who are shaping foreign policy, and D notes that the communists are in the government and have more than a few objectives. Make sure not to mistake C as justification for Question 1 C or Question 1 D, or D as justification for Question 1 B.

3) CORRECT ANSWER: C
The phrase "dealing with" refers to the "communists in our government" (lines 22-23) whom McCarthy is "discussing" (line 22) in a negative fashion. He is thus analyzing or considering the communists, so that C is the best answer, while A and D both introduce faulty positives. B would best refer to a difficult or painful process, not to a topic that is simply being considered.

4) CORRECT ANSWER: A
In lines 27-28, McCarthy addresses his audience, claiming that he knows what "you are saying to yourself", and then offers a hypothetical question from the audience in quotations. This expected response to his claims about the presence of communists supports A and can be used to eliminate B, since this is the only quotation in the passage (and since McCarthy never sources any statistics as coming from a "study"). McCarthy does use metaphors, as with the "cloak" (line 43) and the "spark" (line 44) in the final paragraph, but does not return to a single metaphor in an EXTENDED fashion (eliminating C). He also depicts communism as a strong threat, rather than subjecting it to humorous exaggeration or SATIRE (eliminating D).

5) CORRECT ANSWER: D
While McCarthy in Passage 1 attacks only communists, Smith in Passage 2 argues that "Republicans and Democrats alike are playing directly into the Communist design" (lines 64-66), thus arguing that three different ideologies are causing a single problem. D is the best answer, while B refers to a topic (women) unrelated to each passage's emphasis on discord and foreign affairs and C is relevant to BOTH passages. A is a trap answer: although Republicans and Democrats are distinct, the course recommended in Passage 2 is for them to cease vilifying innocent Americans, not for them to stop functioning as different parties.

6) CORRECT ANSWER: B
While the position of impotency mentioned in Passage 1 involves the "traitorous actions" (line 11) of individuals in America who "are still helping to shape our foreign policy" (lines 20-21), the irresponsible sensationalism mentioned in Passage 2 has emerged in "the Senate" (line 51) as a source of ill repute. This information supports B, while only Passage 1 mentions World War II (eliminating A) or suggests that new security measures will be taken (eliminating C). D applies to neither passage, since the authors are citing threats that DESERVE criticism, not that already HAVE been criticized at large.

7) CORRECT ANSWER: A

In lines 52-54, Smith declares that she is "not proud" of the way that the Senate has exhibited "reckless abandon" and relied on "unproved charges". She has strong dislike, contempt, or disdain for this conduct, so that A is the best answer. B is inaccurate because Smith's beliefs are very strong and are not confused at all, C indicates moody sadness (not assertive dislike), and D indicates that Smith seeks vengeance, when in fact she only wants to CHANGE bad practices.

8) CORRECT ANSWER: B

See above for the explanation of the correct answer. A calls attention to the perspective of female Americans (not the Senate), C refers to problems involving political parties (but does not specifically mention the Senate), and D urges Republicans and Democrats to unite. Although all important to Smith's argument, these answers do not characterize the Senate as demanded by the previous question.

9) CORRECT ANSWER: A

While Passage 1 criticizes the "lack of moral uprising" (line 32) in American society and indicates that an inspiration for such uprising "has finally been supplied" (lines 44-45), Passage 2 urges Americans to set aside partisan divisions and start "thinking patriotically as Americans" (line 72). This shared emphasis on unity or cooperation supports A and can be used to eliminate B. C is mostly relevant to Passage 1 (which warns Americans to be alert to a new threat), while D is relevant to neither passage (since the authors focus on the benefits, not the COSTS, of working together).

10) CORRECT ANSWER: C

The word "smear" refers to how members of the Senate discuss "outsiders" (line 60) while hiding "behind the cloak of congressional immunity" (liens 61-62): unlike Senators, the outsiders are harmed or slandered by Senate discussions. C is the best answer. A and B refer to acts of distortion (not acts involving harming or attacking), while D is a neutral term that would refer to popularity or prevalence (not inflicted harm).

4.03 | John Foster Dulles and Dwight D. Eisenhower

1) CORRECT ANSWER: B

The word "practical" refers to "bankruptcy" (line 6), a state which free nations would supposedly fall into if they engage in efforts which are "beyond their strength" (line 5). The bankruptcy would thus be a real cause of such negatives, or an effectual (meaning actual) state: B is the best answer, while A, C, and D would all function to PRAISE the negative bankruptcy and are thus incorrect in context.

2) CORRECT ANSWER: D

Passage 1 endorses a military approach that United States officials can implement "without exhausting ourselves" (lines 11-12) and that can respond to local threats in a manner that is "more effective, less costly" (line 22). D is thus the best answer, while the focus on a streamlined yet effective military structure can be used to eliminate B. Note that the United States forces are never compared to the Russian military forces, and that the passage is most preoccupied with military size and expenses (not necessarily technology): on these accounts, eliminate A and C as out of scope.

3) CORRECT ANSWER: D

In the relevant lines, the author of Passage 1 explains the need to fight immediate dangers without exhausting American forces, calls attention to measures that are "not sound economics, or good foreign policy" (line 18), and speaks in favor of "placing more reliance on deterrent power and less dependence on local defensive power" (lines 23-24). This information supports D, while A ("principles of Communism") and B ("law") introduce false topics. C is problematic because it assumes that the middle portions of the discussion are positive, and because it assumes "slight" (rather than significant) modifications.

4) CORRECT ANSWER: C

In lines 32-34, the author of Passage 1 discusses the security measures that Americans want "for ourselves and the other free nations; the author of Passage 2 focuses entirely on the "military organization" (line 52) of the United States as it relates to domestic life, and indicates that the role of this expanded organization may affect American citizens negatively. C is the best answer, while B is addressed in Passage 2. Both passages indicate that there are security threats to America (eliminating A), while neither discusses America's founding principles (eliminating D).

5) CORRECT ANSWER: C

See above for the explanation of the correct answer. A indicates that both security and efficiency are necessary, B uses a comparison to explain how geopolitical security measures work, and D notes how a potential aggressor might act under certain conditions. Make sure not to take B as a justification for Question 4 A or Question 4 B.

6) CORRECT ANSWER: C

In lines 52-54, Eisenhower indicates that the current military organization in America "bears little relation to that known by any of my predecessors in peacetime". C is thus the best answer, while Eisenhower spends other portions of the passage criticizing the size and scope of the armed forces, not citing wasteful expenses (eliminating A) or calling attention to corruption (eliminating B). D is a trap answer: although the armed forces have played a valuable role in world affairs, they (unlike American civilians) are nowhere directly characterized in terms of spirituality.

7) CORRECT ANSWER: A

See above for the explanation of the correct answer. B indicates the extent of current military expenditures, C cautions that the military may come to exert too much influence, and D urges Americans (not the military) to be vigilant. Do not mistake B as evidence for Question 6 A, C as evidence for Question 6 B, or D as evidence for Question 6 D.

8) CORRECT ANSWER: A

The word "misplaced" refers to "power" (line 76), and occurs in the context of Eisenhower's warnings against "unwarranted influence" (line 74) and the "disastrous rise" (line 76) of such power. The power would thus be used for destructive ends, so that A is the best answer. B and C wrongly assume that the power is NOT being used, while D is out of context: the power may be used for clear (though destructive) objectives, and thus would not be used in a "haphazard" fashion.

9) CORRECT ANSWER: C

While Passage 1 explains its recommendations for the use of American power by creating a comparison with "accepted practice so far as local communities are concerned" (lines 25-26), Passage 2 describes a national security situation that is "new in the American experience" (line 66) and that influences society in ways that are "economic, political, even spiritual" (line 67). This information supports C. Other answers misstate the functions of Passage 2, which considers American society at large (not combat settings, eliminating A), avoids the issue of poverty (eliminating B), and argues that recent military buildup is unprecedented (eliminating D).

10) CORRECT ANSWER: D

The author of Passage 1 recommends the "deterrent of massive retaliatory power" (line 38) as a means of preventing aggression; similarly, the author of Passage 2 notes that, in the presence of sufficiently large United States armed forces, "no potential aggressor may be tempted to risk his own destruction" (lines 50-51). This information supports D. Only Passage 1 discusses allies at length (eliminating A) or calls attention to local conflicts (eliminating B), while Passage 2 discusses the link between the United States military and economy (NOT between the United States military and the economies of hostile nations, eliminating C).

4.04 | John F. Kennedy

1) CORRECT ANSWER: A

In lines 13-14, Kennedy notes that "In honoring Robert Frost we therefore can pay honor to the deepest sources of our national strength": this idea is related to arguments elsewhere in the passage that Frost's critical poetry is socially important. A is thus an effective answer, while the fact that Kennedy relates Frost to long-held American virtues can be used to eliminate B ("new initiative"). C and D both shift the focus from Frost's broad significance in society to the details of Frost's writing, and should be eliminated as raising the wrong primary topic.

2) CORRECT ANSWER: B

In lines 29-32, Kennedy argues that Frost was aware of different aspects of human nature, "midnight as well as the high noon" and "the ordeal as well as the triumph of the human spirit". This range of human emotion and experience was central to Frost's work, so that B is the best answer. A and D both introduce negatives (yet Kennedy has words of strong praise for Frost overall), while C refers to a theme of the passage ("politics") that is never defined as one of Frost's own areas of expertise.

3) CORRECT ANSWER: D

See above for the explanation of the correct answer. A praises Robert Frost as a strong and prominent figure, B notes that Frost's virtues are related to America's own virtues, and C indicates that Frost's valuable contribution was to control power within America. Make sure not to wrongly take A as evidence for Question 2 A: the term "granite" is used to praise Frost's virtue and prominence, not to critique his personality as "stern".

4) CORRECT ANSWER: B

The word "questioning" refers to a "disinterested" (line 20) process performed by Americans who determine "whether we use power or power uses us" (line 21). These individuals thus inspect or analyze an issue to determine the best results: B is an effective answer. A, C, and D all introduce negatives, which are incorrect in context because Kennedy clearly ADMIRES the individuals who perform the "questioning".

5) CORRECT ANSWER: D

The word "personal" refers to an artist's "vision of reality" (line 43), which is related to how the artist "becomes the last champion of the individual mind and sensibility" (lines 43-44) against overbearing social concerns. The artist's vision is thus specific to the artist or is highly individualized, making D the best answer. A refers to household duties (and introduces a different context), and B and C both introduce faulty negatives, since Kennedy sees the artist's "personal" activity as valuable.

6) CORRECT ANSWER: A

The relevant portion of the passage begins with a general consideration of the "men who create power" (line 17) and "the men who question power" (lines 18-19); it is then argued that Frost, as a man who questioned power, examined the "platitudes and pieties of society" (line 26). This information supports A and can be used to eliminate B, since poetry and power are contrasted THROUGHOUT the discussion. Note also that the relevant lines are devoted throughout to Kennedy's opinions (eliminating C) and to praise of Frost (eliminating D).

7) CORRECT ANSWER: B

In the relevant lines, Kennedy argues that power is associated with arrogance, narrowness, and corruption, while poetry indicates humility, richness, and cleansing influence. By casting one force as negative and the other as positive, he places these forces in opposition. B is the best answer, while A is directly contradicted by the earlier idea that a "nation's greatness" (line 18) involves both poetry and power. C must be eliminated because both poetry and power are practical, while D must be eliminated because the role of artists, according to Kennedy, is to QUESTION power (not to treat it as an option).

8) CORRECT ANSWER: C

In this passage, Kennedy argues that an important function of art is to rein in excesses of power and explains that "great artists have been the most critical of our society" (lines 53-54). The idea that great art and social consciousness are not related would contradict Kennedy's ideas: C is the best answer, while D is actually one of Kennedy's ideas, since an artist may "nourish the roots" (line 59) of his or her culture by celebrating what that culture does well. A and B both refer to biographical issues related to Frost, which are at best tangential to the passage: Kennedy is most interested in Frost's role in society, not his impact on other poets or the timeline of his life.

9) CORRECT ANSWER: D

In lines 45-48, Kennedy argues that a "great artist is a solitary figure" and "must often sail against the currents of his time". Such an artist thus opposes what is socially common or expected, so that D is the best answer. A wrongly assumes that the relationship CANNOT be determined, B overstates the effect of the relationship (antagonism or conflict, but not necessarily destruction), and C introduces a positive when a negative would be most logical.

10) CORRECT ANSWER: C

See above for the explanation of the correct answer. A indicates a standard of American heroism, B compares men who create power to men who question power, and D notes that the place of the artist is important. A and B do not explicitly mention artists, while D mentions an idea about artists (their high worth) that does not align with an answer to the previous question.

4.05 | Lyndon B. Johnson

1) CORRECT ANSWER: C

In this passage, Johnson considers problems in race relations and makes the argument that "Every American citizen must have an equal right to vote" (line 8); he then declares that he "will send to Congress a law designed to eliminate illegal barriers to the right to vote" (lines 37-38). This information supports C, while B and D state goals that are much broader than Johnson's aim of removing voting restrictions that work against African Americans. A is a trap answer: while Johnson uses a discussion of the history of voting rights abuses to SUPPORT his argument, his main PURPOSE is to end these abuses.

2) CORRECT ANSWER: D

In the relevant portion of the passage, Johnson argues that it is difficult to ensure the right to vote when "local officials are determined to deny it" (lines 31-32); his description of discrimination as "systematic and ingenious" is meant to show that such discrimination is difficult to successfully combat. D is the best answer, while A (education) and B (government restructuring, which is NOT the same as creating new laws) introduce irrelevant topics. C is a problematic answer because, while the people who perpetuate racial discrimination would disagree with Johnson, there is no indication that MANY Americans would.

3) CORRECT ANSWER: A

The phrase "denial of" refers to "an equal right to vote" (line 8); in context, Johnson is explaining why measures that restrict this right based on ethnicity must be opposed. A is thus the best answer, while B and C indicate that people do not understand the right in question (when in fact the right is understood, yet is also wrongly limited). In context, D would either be a positive (as in "self-discipline") or would refer to punishment (making it off-topic) and must thus be eliminated.

4) CORRECT ANSWER: C

In lines 52-53, Johnson explains that the intended bill will create a "uniform standard which cannot be used, however ingenious the effort, to flout [insult] the Constitution". The bill will thus create regular and well-controlled procedures, so that C is the best answer. A must be eliminated because Johnson's bill is based on ideas ALREADY made clear in the Constitution, while the measures in B (a new agency) and D (punishment) are never explicitly linked to Johnson's bill, which will simply use existing resources to ensure justice.

5) CORRECT ANSWER: D

In lines 17-20, Johnson explains that an African American may be disqualified from voting "because he did not spell out his middle name or because he abbreviated a word on the application": these are minor and insignificant factors for Johnson, so that D is the best answer. Johnson never mentions political propaganda (as opposed to direct oppression at polling places, eliminating A), uses the Constitution to SUPPORT his ideas about voting rights (eliminating B), and mostly attacks local governments as sources of voter suppression (eliminating C).

6) CORRECT ANSWER: B
See above for the explanation of the correct answer. A indicates the importance of ensuring the right to vote, C records one of the ways that African Americans have been denied the right to vote, and D indicates that Johnson is taking action to protect voting rights. Only C refers to a problem with voting, yet this answer does not align with an answer to the previous question.

7) CORRECT ANSWER: A
In lines 51-53, Johnson accuses his political opponents of making "ingenious" efforts "to flout [insult] our Constitution". These opponents are thus disrespectful or irreverent towards the Constitution in Johnson's view, so that A is the best answer. B and D both imply that the opponents of voting rights do not know what to think of the Constitution (when in fact they consciously disobey it), while C overstates their opposition. They may disobey or degrade certain parts of the Constitution, but are not moved to hatred, anger, and open opposition to it.

8) CORRECT ANSWER: D
See above for the explanation of the correct answer. A indicates how the Constitution is used to disqualify African Americans from voting, B summarizes a principle of the Constitution, and C indicates the duty that Americans have towards the Constitution. Only B describes Johnson's opponents, but simply describes a procedure they follow and does not define a clear attitude in the manner of the correct answer.

9) CORRECT ANSWER: A
In his final two paragraphs, Johnson both notes that he welcomes suggestions "to strengthen this law and to make it effective" (line 61) and indicates that "purely local control over elections" (line 66) can only be ensured by following the law. A is thus the best answer. Other answers distort Johnson's actual strategies: he invites his allies to offer suggestions (rather than offering praise, eliminating B), describes a present government initiative (not a future one, eliminating C), and addresses broad groups (not specific reformers, eliminating D).

10) CORRECT ANSWER: C
The word "plainly" refers to the "only path" (line 62) that will enable Johnson's proposal to be put into action, a path that has been clearly shown by "experience" (line 62). It is thus impossible to dispute or question such a sure path, so that C is the best answer. A and D both introduce criticisms (and are thus out of context), while B introduces an issue ("wordiness") that is not directly related to how EVIDENT or VALID a particular approach is.

4.06 | Shirley Chisholm

1) CORRECT ANSWER: B
In this passage, Chisholm calls attention to an "outrageous" (line 35) situation that has

resulted from inequalities and barriers faced by women; this situation moves Chisholm to introduce a Congressional proposal "that sooner or later must become part of the basic law of the land—the equal rights amendment" (lines 51-52). This information supports B and can be used to eliminate A, since Chisholm urges Congress (not women) to take action. C (women) and D (African Americans) refer to topics that Chisholm raises, but neglect the practical PURPOSE of her speech, which is to propose an amendment to help women.

2) CORRECT ANSWER: D
Chisholm argues that laws cannot change "deep-seated problems overnight" (line 45) and refers to improvement for women as a process of "evolutionary change" (line 47). This information supports D and can be used to eliminate A and B, since Chisholm envisions a process that is steady, predictable, and somewhat time-consuming. C is inaccurate because laws are needed to improve women's lives, so that such improvements must happen intentionally, not accidentally or inadvertently.

3) CORRECT ANSWER: A
The relevant paragraph describes an "unspoken assumption" (line 11) that indicates negatives about women's capabilities; however, Chisholm argues elsewhere in the passage that women lack yet deserve "the opportunities that men do" (line 63). She thus uses the third paragraph to present a viewpoint on women that she rejects, justifying A and eliminating C (since African Americans are not mentioned directly) and D (which does not account for the negative tone). B is a trap answer: although Chisholm rejects the ideas in the paragraph, it is not clear exactly which people promote these ideas, making the idea that they come from Chisholm's "political opponents" a faulty inference.

4) CORRECT ANSWER: C
Chisholm notes that "I have been far oftener discriminated against because I am a woman than because I am black" (lines 15-17), thus justifying C and eliminating A. Although Chisholm discusses the issues of class (or at least leadership positions) and intellect as they relate to women at large, she does not specifically relate these issues to her OWN life. Thus, B and D are out of scope.

5) CORRECT ANSWER: C
The word "outrageous" refers to the "situation" (line 34) that Chisholm is describing: women significantly outnumber men in the United States, while men significantly outnumber women in United States leadership positions. As an advocate for women, Chisholm would find this situation objectionable or unacceptable: C is the best answer. A refers to showy appearances (and is thus out of context), while B and D do not introduce appropriately strong negatives and should thus be eliminated.

6) CORRECT ANSWER: D
In lines 29-32, Chisholm criticizes the United States government because women have few leadership positions: Congress, for instance, is "down to one Senator and 10 Representatives". Electing a woman to Congress would be "extraordinary" because women are normally so scarce in the government. D is thus the best answer. A is problematic because Chisholm also notes that women are scarce in high-powered careers, B is problematic because Chisholm notes that women's motives in seeking authority are the same as men's (and are thus well understood), and C is wrongly critical of women (whose situation Chisholm is attempting to improve).

7) CORRECT ANSWER: C

See above for the explanation of the correct answer. A records a negative gender stereotype about women, B calls attention to the negative assumption that women are unsuited for high-powered careers, and D indicates that women have the SAME motives as men in seeking positions of authority. Note that D can be used to disqualify Question 6 B.

8) CORRECT ANSWER: C

The word "incredible" refers to the "scarcity" (line 59) of women in upper level jobs: such scarcity is contrasted with "the concentration of women in lower paying, menial, unrewarding jobs" (line 57). The scarcity is incredible because it is apparent and is clearly or stunningly negative, making C the best answer. In context, A, B, and D all serve to diminish the significance of the "scarcity" or to make it seem uncertain, and must thus be eliminated.

9) CORRECT ANSWER: D

In lines 36-37, Chisholm argues that women "have not been aggressive enough in demanding their rights": this information supports D, while other answers distort Chisholm's actual arguments. Women face economic and workplace problems (but are not oblivious to economics, eliminating A) and face problematic conditions (but do not PRAISE the laws that make those conditions possible, eliminating B). Moreover, while Chisholm supports clear rights for both men and women, she does not ever define women as OPPOSING this position (eliminating C).

10) CORRECT ANSWER: B

See above for the explanation of the correct answer. A indicates widespread incomprehension of the true injustice of gender inequality, C indicates that some people wrongly believe that existing laws sufficiently protect women, and D indicates that the sexes need similar protections. Make sure not to take A as evidence for Question 9 A, C as evidence for Question 9 B, or D as evidence for Question 9 C.

4.07 | Richard Nixon

1) CORRECT ANSWER: D

In lines 23-26, Nixon contrasts the positive "immediate" reaction to withdrawal, "a sense of relief", with the negative longer-term consequences, "inevitable remorse and divisive recrimination". This evidence supports D. A is incorrect because Nixon argues that withdrawal IS possible (but not advisable), B is incorrect because Nixon does not argue at length that the "divisive" effects of withdrawal are "partisan" or based on political allegiance, and C is incorrect because Nixon is most concerned with practical consequences, not historical "precedents".

2) CORRECT ANSWER: B

See above for the explanation of the correct answer. A indicates that Nixon could immediately withdraw American forces from Vietnam, C indicates that some well-meaning citizens do not agree with Nixon's decision, and D explains the decision-making process traditionally followed by the United States government. None of these answers directly responds to the topic raised in the previous question, Nixon's opposition to "immediate withdrawal", so that each one must be eliminated.

3) CORRECT ANSWER: B
In the relevant lines, Nixon refers to his earlier decision regarding Vietnam and endorses "rejecting the easy way out and taking the right way" (line 28) as a source of strength; he then goes on to explain that "some of my fellow citizens disagree with the plan for peace I have chosen" (lines 32-33). This information supports B and can be used to eliminate D, which wrongly indicates consensus. A and C are much too negative towards the individuals who disagree with Nixon, whom Nixon places in a tradition of reasonable disagreement among "Honest and patriotic Americans" (lines 33-34).

4) CORRECT ANSWER: B
The word "taking" refers to the "right way" (line 28) that Nixon endorses: he also creates a contrast with the idea of "rejecting the easy way out" (line 28). Thus, the right way in these circumstances would be accepted or pursued. B is the best answer, while A (which would refer to an object), C (which would refer to a measurement), and D (which would refer to messages or transportation) are all inappropriate to the context of choosing and pursuing a course of action.

5) CORRECT ANSWER: C
The word "demonstrations" refers to events staged by a minority: this minority wants to impose its views "on the Nation" (line 44) by holding demonstrations "in the street" (line 45). This minority is thus speaking out or protesting against the majority position: C is the best answer, while A, B, and D are more neutral terms that do not raise the topic of CONFLICT, which is essential to Nixon's remarks at this point.

6) CORRECT ANSWER: A
In lines 39-41, Nixon notes that "one of the strengths of our free society" is that people may reach conclusions and viewpoints that do not agree with his own. A is the best answer, while political parties (B) and education (D) are not closely related to Nixon's discussion of foreign policy and civil liberties. C is off topic in a different way: while increased commitment may be necessary in Vietnam, Nixon never praises such military commitment as an American VALUE.

7) CORRECT ANSWER: C
See above for the explanation of the correct answer. A indicates a strategy that might be followed regarding Vietnam, B indicates that rejecting easy alternatives has enabled Americans to respond effectively to crises, and D indicates that Nixon wants to bring a secure and conclusive end to the Vietnam conflict. While some of these answers may indicate values (weighing alternatives, accepting challenges, and avoiding future crises), none of these answers aligns with an answer to the previous question.

8) CORRECT ANSWER: C
In the passage, Nixon explains that "this Nation has no future as a free society" (lines 50-51) if the ideas of a minority prevail over the will of the majority. This information supports C, while a system that wrongly values the minority could STILL be informed by confidence (eliminating A), premised on debate (eliminating B), or based on idealism (eliminating D).

9) CORRECT ANSWER: C

Nixon explains that he has had to send letters to the contacts of "men who have given their lives for America in Vietnam" (lines 60-61); because of the loss of human life involved, he hopes that he will not "have to write any of those letters" (line 64) in the future. This negative tone towards the loss of life justifies C, while A (other obligations) and B (public appreciation) raise topics that distract from (and are less significant than) the loss of life in Vietnam. D is problematic in relation to the rest of the passage, because Nixon does cite immediate withdrawal from Vietnam as a valid option.

10) CORRECT ANSWER: D

In addressing the "young people", Nixon states that "I respect your idealism" (line 55) and declares that "I share your concern for peace" (line 56). Nixon thus understands and sympathizes with their goals, justifying D and eliminating A (which is negative and would indicate disrespect). B and C are both incorrect in context, since Nixon is discussing important issues (not taking a lighthearted approach) and is taking a clear (not reserved) stance.

4.08 | Jimmy Carter

1) CORRECT ANSWER: B

In lines 48-52, Carter explains that a large number of Americans "do not even vote" and that "the productivity of American workers is actually dropping": these are the negative electoral and economic effects of the crisis of confidence, so that B is the best answer. Although the crisis of confidence does result in a general spirit of pessimism and apathy, it is not EXPLICITLY argued that the crisis relates to areas such as reform (eliminating A) and education (eliminating C). D is a trap answer: although Vietnam (line 65) shook America's confidence, it is never explained how Vietnam impacted America's willingness to fight OTHER wars.

2) CORRECT ANSWER: B

See above for the explanation of the correct answer. A addresses a possible misconception about American confidence, C explains that the changes associated with the crisis of confidence were part of a historical process, and D explains that there is a considerable gap between government and citizens. While A and C do not refer to SPECIFIC effects of the crisis, D should not be wrongly taken as evidence for Question 1 A, since the line reference does not raise the topic of "reform".

3) CORRECT ANSWER: D

Carter argues that "confidence" (line 16) is "the idea which founded our Nation and has guided our development as a people" (lines 18-19). This information supports D and can be used to eliminate C, since America is the only country that this passage considers. Carter argues that wealth and ambition are clearly not the same as confidence (eliminating A) and indicates that American confidence HAS been threatened by war and hardship, but not that confidence is ALWAYS most threatened by such circumstances (eliminating B).

4) CORRECT ANSWER: C

The word "invisible" refers to a "threat" (line 9) that may not be apparent in "ordinary ways" (line 9) but still attacks the "soul and spirit" (line 11) of America's national will. This insidious threat is thus difficult to detect or perceive, or is nearly imperceptible. C is the best answer while A and D both refer to things or substances, not moral threats. B is a trap answer: in context, a "negligible" threat would be powerless, while Carter is describing a threat that is powerful but hard to notice.

5) CORRECT ANSWER: B

In describing "The symptoms of this crisis of the American spirit" (line 45), Carter critically notes that "Two thirds of our people do not even vote" (lines 48-49): dramatically increased voter participation would indicate that a symptom of the crisis has been eliminated. B is the best answer, while crime rates are never mentioned in the passage (eliminating A). Both C and D refer to the wrong kind of actions: the crisis involves loss of faith in institutions, and ELIMINATING institutions would not necessarily RESTORE Americans' faith in their institutions. It would be possible to eliminate schools and media outlets, and for Americans to stay cynical about the institutions that remain.

6) CORRECT ANSWER: D

In explaining the crisis of confidence in America, Carter argues that "owning things and consuming things does not satisfy our longing for meaning" (lines 41-42). This information supports D. Honesty is not a major topic of the passage (and would, on the basis of the final paragraph, in fact LEAD to popularity, eliminating A), while religion is not a topic of the passage at all (eliminating B). C is a trap answer: Carter criticizes educational institutions, but does so because they inspire little confidence, NOT because they are impractical.

7) CORRECT ANSWER: A

In the relevant lines, Carter explains that there is "a growing disrespect for government" (lines 53-54) and for other institutions, then explains that recent "years that were filled with shocks and tragedy" (lines 59-60) caused this widespread disrespect. This information supports A, while Carter never mentions his political opponents (despite his negative tone, eliminating B) and never calls for action at this point (even though the situation may require action in order to be addressed, eliminating D). C is a trap answer: Carter's discussion of "specific tragedies" occurs primarily in the section of the passage that FOLLOWS the relevant lines, and never involves the idea that these tragedies will be replicated. Rather, a more general spirit of low confidence persists.

8) CORRECT ANSWER: C

The word "movement" refers to the historical action of "democracy" (line 33), which involves a strengthening influence. Carter thus believes that the "movement" is a positive force for progress or advancement: C is the best answer, while A is wrongly negative and B and D are both neutral (and would best refer to physical objects, not to a historical principle).

9) CORRECT ANSWER: C

In lines 2-4, Carter explains that he has attempted to fulfill his "campaign promises", but has only experienced "mixed success" in attempting to do so. This information supports C: note that Carter's exact policy objectives are not defined at any other point in the

188

passage, so that B (size of government) and D (increased partisanship) introduce possible failures that are completely out of scope. A is a trap answer: in his discussion of society, Carter does not exaggerate problems, but instead ACKNOWLEDGES problems that are truly extreme in his view.

10) CORRECT ANSWER: A
See above for the explanation of the correct answer. B indicates that energy and inflation are not America's worst problems, C indicates that Watergate caused the presidency to lose respect, and D indicates that the federal government appears to be isolated from American citizens. Make sure not to wrongly take B as evidence for Question 9 A or D as evidence for Question 9 B.

4.09 | Ronald Reagan

1) CORRECT ANSWER: D
Early in the passage, Reagan argues that he and Gorbachev have taken measures that could ensure "a foundation for better relations between our governments and our peoples" (lines 5-6); later, he indicates that he has "high hopes" (line 66) for his diplomatic work with the Soviet Union. This information supports D and eliminates A and C as much too negative. B is problematic because it involves a slight negative and indicates that a crisis has passed, when in fact Reagan is most focused on a FUTURE that looks promising.

2) CORRECT ANSWER: C
The word "historic" refers to three days in which Reagan and Gorbachev "continued to build a foundation for better relations between our governments" (lines 4-5): the days were thus "historic" because they involved important issues, or were pivotal in U.S.-Soviet relations. C is thus the best answer while B (which wrongly refers to an earlier time period) and D (which wrongly indicates that new breakthroughs did not take place) are contradicted by the context. A is also problematic in context: because the days were recent, it is unlikely that they would be commemorated or officially celebrated in any meaningful way.

3) CORRECT ANSWER: A
In the course of his speech, Reagan states that he and Gorbachev are building "a foundation for better relations between our governments" (line 5) and that he "spoke candidly with Mr. Gorbachev" (line 64). Such positive comments indicate cooperation and justify A, but also eliminate B (since the relationship with Gorbachev is not negative) and D (since Reagan and Gorbachev are working on the same level). C is out of context: while Gorbachev is viewed positively by Reagan, he is considered in a political and professional (not personal) context.

4) CORRECT ANSWER: C
In describing the verification measures, Reagan notes that they have "far-reaching implications" (line 19) and represent "a first-time event, a breakthrough" (line 21) in reducing the threat of war. This information supports C and can be used to eliminate the negative answer A. B (politics WITHIN the Soviet Union) and D (OTHER countries) introduce topics irrelevant to Reagan's consideration of foreign affairs involving the United States and Soviet Union at this point in the passage, and must thus be eliminated.

5) CORRECT ANSWER: C

In lines 51-56, Reagan cites problems with the Soviet Union and notes his "moral opposition to the ideology that justifies such practices"; however, he advocates putting relations with the Soviet Union "on a far more candid and far more realistic footing". This balance of negatives and positives supports C. A (earlier politicians) and D (an alliance targeting smaller nations) introduce topics that are not among Reagan's primary considerations, while B misstates Reagan's argument: progress has been made, but further progress may STILL be needed.

6) CORRECT ANSWER: B

See above for the explanation of the correct answer. A indicates the need to investigate how government structures relate to conflict, C indicates that much progress remains to be made in foreign affairs, and D indicates that Reagan and Gorbachev have discussed various issues in foreign affairs. Make sure not to take A as a justification for Question 5 A, C as a justification for Question 5 B, or D as a justification for Question 5 D.

7) CORRECT ANSWER: B

The word "movement" refers to what has been accomplished "in the arms reduction area" (line 57), even though more can still be done. In other words, some successes have been achieved or progress has been made, making B the best answer and eliminating negative answer A. C is a neutral term that would best refer to physical objects (not foreign policy goals), while D indicates a personality trait.

8) CORRECT ANSWER: C

In lines 31-35, Reagan notes that "Soviet-American relations are no longer focused only on arms control issues", indicating that the scope of Soviet-American diplomacy has been expanded. C is the best answer, while A assumes much closer cooperation than Reagan indicates anywhere in his description of the United States and the Soviet Union, which had been rivals. B and D, however, overstate the extent of rivalry or hostility between the two nations (a rivalry largely based on IDEOLOGY according to the passage) and should thus be eliminated.

9) CORRECT ANSWER: D

See above for the explanation of the correct answer. A notes that an important step has been taken towards reducing arms buildup, B indicates that certain weapons are being eliminated, and C indicates that the Soviet Union is allowing inspections. All of these answers describe positive developments, so that negative answers such as Question 8 B and Question 8 D become extremely problematic.

10) CORRECT ANSWER: C

In the relevant lines, Reagan explains that military buildup is a product of distrust: a situation in which military buildup occurs WITHOUT clear distrust would contradict his idea. C describes such a situation, while A and B describe uses of force that MAY be motivated in part by distrust and thus cannot be taken as valid answers. D describes a REDUCTION in military force, not an increase, and thus does not relate directly to Reagan's scenario.

4.10 | John F. Kennedy and Ronald Reagan

1) CORRECT ANSWER: A
In relating freedom in Germany to international affairs at large, Kennedy in Passage 1 notes that "when one man is enslaved, all are not free" (lines 15-16); somewhat similarly, Reagan in Passage 2 argues that "Freedom replaces the ancient hatreds among the nations with comity and peace" (lines 47-48). This shared emphasis on freedom as a way of maintaining international peace supports A. While Kennedy does not explicitly address Communism (eliminating B) or the Soviet Union (eliminating C), Reagan does not address Germany beyond its recent history (eliminating D).

2) CORRECT ANSWER: B
The word "advance" refers to the action of "freedom everywhere" (line 12), an action that Kennedy sees spreading "to all mankind" (line 14). This sense that freedom is a positive, spreading influence and thus making progress supports B and eliminates negative answer C. A refers to finances and D best refers to physical objects (and is not strongly positive), so that these answers must be eliminated as inappropriate to the context.

3) CORRECT ANSWER: D
While Passage 2 lists a series of problems in "the Soviet Union" (line 44), Passage 1 considers Berlin and Europe as its primary topics and does not contain explicit references to the Soviet Union. This information supports D, while BOTH passages analyze the human and political rights related to freedom, discuss the challenges faced in Berlin, and address the people of Berlin (lines 8 and 34) directly. Thus, A, B, and C must all be eliminated.

4) CORRECT ANSWER: C
Although Passage 2 praises the progress that has been made in Berlin, the Soviet Union is harshly criticized: freedom enables prosperity yet the Soviet Union experiences "failure, technological backwardness, declining standards of health" (lines 41-42), and other problems. Freedom has thus not made sufficient progress in the Soviet Union, so that this evidence justifies C and eliminates the positive answer D. Note that the Soviets, however, are beginning to understand "the importance of freedom" (line 50): this somewhat optimistic statement can be used to eliminate strongly negative answers A and B.

5) CORRECT ANSWER: B
In Passage 2, Reagan acknowledges that there is a new Soviet policy of "reform and openness" (lines 51-52) and challenges Gorbachev to take action in Berlin in order to "dramatically advance the cause of freedom and peace" (lines 64-65). This ultimatum supports B and eliminates C, since Gorbachev is being challenged to demonstrate that he DESERVES Reagan's trust. A (reform) and D (ideology) introduce false topics onto Reagan's discussion of a few practical actions and must thus be eliminated.

6) CORRECT ANSWER: B
In lines 16-19, Kennedy explains that "when all are free" humanity will enjoy "a peaceful and hopeful globe". This information supports B, while Kennedy focuses on broad principles (not anecdotes, eliminating A) and on valid beliefs (not mistaken ones, eliminating C). D is a trap answer: although Kennedy clearly admires the German citizens, he never argues that they do not SHARE their virtues with other groups of people that value freedom.

7) CORRECT ANSWER: C

See above for the explanation of the correct answer. A refers to the benefits that the Germans have earned through their virtues, B indicates that the Germans are connected to other populations, and D expresses Kennedy's sense of fellowship with his audience. Do not mistake A as a justification for Question 6 A, since Kennedy's passing reference to a time period does not amount to an "anecdote" or reported narrative.

8) CORRECT ANSWER: A

The word "jammed" refers to "foreign news broadcasts" (line 53): because the Soviet Union is exhibiting new "reform and openness" (lines 51-52), it would naturally no longer be restricting or obstructing outside influences. A is the best answer, while B would best refer to a group of people, C refers to whether something is understandable (NOT to whether it is available), and D refers to physical objects.

9) CORRECT ANSWER: B

In lines 41-44, Reagan criticizes the "declining standards of health" and food shortages in the Soviet Union, which "still cannot feed itself". The Soviet Union thus faces problems both in production (economic) and in quality of life (humanitarian), so that B is the best answer. Reagan primarily criticizes the domestic policies of the Soviet Union (not its foreign policy, eliminating C) but does not specifically target infrastructure flaws (eliminating D, since in fact infrastructure may be one of the improving "economic enterprises" mentioned in line 54). A is a trap answer: Reagan does not explicitly attack the relationship between the Soviet Union and West Berlin, but instead CHALLENGES the Soviet Union to take action in Berlin.

10) CORRECT ANSWER: C

See above for the explanation of the correct answer. A indicates a contrast between prosperity in Berlin and Soviet aims (but does not fully define the Soviet aims), B offers a statement from a Soviet leader critical of democratic nations, and D offers a challenge to a more recent Soviet leader. Make sure not to wrongly align A with Question 9 A or B with Question 9 C.

CHAPTER 5
The Age of Information

The Age of Information
1989-Present

The end of the 1980s also marked the end of the Soviet Union: the communist experiment had apparently failed, but another great historical experiment was already in the works. With the advent of the 1990s came the rise of information technology as a force in both the modern marketplace and the lives of everyday consumers. Older tech companies (Microsoft, Apple, Intel) thrived, while some of today's tech behemoths (Amazon, Google) got their starts. The era is remembered as yet another American decade of high innovation and relative calm, even though the rise of the Internet was, arguably, responsible for some of the political fractures that persist to this day.

Although Reagan's brand of conservatism would have a lasting impact, the Democrats held the presidency for most of the 1990s under Bill Clinton. Clinton was a moderate by his party's standards, but still faced the vigorous opposition of a Republican-held Congress; the fault lines between Democrats and Republicans would only widen with the breathtakingly unpopular George W. Bush administration and the more widely accepted Obama administration (another case of a relatively moderate Democrat and a firmly opposed Republican Congress). This state of polarization led to a 2016 presidential campaign that has astonished even seasoned media journalists. Candidates such as Republican Marco Rubio attempted to tap into old-fashioned American optimism, yet his party instead endorsed the economic nationalism (and sensational media manipulation) of Donald Trump. Many Democrats were swept up by the spectacular rallies and relentless social media presence of Bernie Sanders, perhaps the most radically liberal candidate ever to seek the party's nomination. Yet as of this writing, centrist candidate Hillary Clinton appears poised to face Trump in the general election.

Would the rise of Sanders and Trump have been remotely possible without the information technology currently at our fingertips? It's anyone's guess. But like all historical revolutions and convulsions, our age of information brings its own unique set of privileges and pitfalls. Social media has offered opportunities for political consciousness and social reform: from race relations and BlackLivesMatter, to the Arab Spring and documentary filmmaking, what we download, watch, read, and debate are now inextricable. Commentators such as Mignon Clyburn and Kamal Khashoggi are aware of these powers, but cautious of the possibilities of censorship and misunderstanding that could arise. We don't know how the Age of Information will end. Yet we can look back and understand the course of political history that led us here.

Questions 1-10 are based on the following passages.
5.01
The first of these readings is an excerpt from the First State of the Union Address (1993) delivered by President Bill Clinton, a moderate Democrat; the second is the opening of a document known as the "Contract with America" (1994), which was crafted and issued by a group of Republican Congressmen.

Passage 1

Our Nation needs a new direction. Tonight I present to you a comprehensive plan to set our Nation on that new course. I believe we will find our new direction in the basic
Line old values that brought us here over the last two centuries: a
5 commitment to opportunity, to individual responsibility, to community, to work, to family, and to faith. We must now break the habits of both political parties and say there can be no more something for nothing and admit frankly that we are all in this together.
10 The conditions which brought us as a nation to this point are well-known: two decades of low productivity, growth, and stagnant wages; persistent unemployment and underemployment; years of huge Government deficits and declining investment in our future; exploding health care
15 costs and lack of coverage for millions of Americans; legions of poor children; education and job training opportunities inadequate to the demands of this tough, global economy. For too long we have drifted without a strong sense of purpose or responsibility or community.
20 And our political system so often has seemed paralyzed by special interest groups, by partisan bickering, and by the sheer complexity of our problems. I believe we can do better because we remain the greatest nation on Earth, the world's strongest economy, the world's only military superpower. If
25 we have the vision, the will, and the heart to make the changes we must, we can still enter the 21st century with possibilities our parents could not even have imagined and enter it having secured the American dream for ourselves and for future generations.
30 I well remember 12 years ago President Reagan stood at this very podium and told you and the American people that if our national debt were stacked in thousand-dollar bills, the stack would reach 67 miles into space. Well, today that stack would reach 267 miles. I tell you this not to assign blame for
35 this problem. There is plenty of blame to go around in both branches of the Government and both parties. The time has come for the blame to end. I did not seek this office to place blame. I come here tonight to accept responsibility, and I want you to accept responsibility with me. And if we do right by this
40 country, I do not care who gets the credit for it.

Passage 2

As Republican Members of the House of Representatives and as citizens seeking to join that body we propose not just to change its policies, but even more important, to restore the bonds of trust between the people
45 and their elected representatives.
That is why, in this era of official evasion and posturing, we offer instead a detailed agenda for national renewal, a written commitment with no fine print.
This year's election offers the chance, after four decades
50 of one-party control, to bring to the House a new majority that will transform the way Congress works. That historic change would be the end of government that is too big, too intrusive, and too easy with the public's money. It can be the beginning of a Congress that respects the values and shares
55 the faith of the American family.
Like Lincoln, our first Republican president, we intend to act "with firmness in the right, as God gives us to see the right." To restore accountability to Congress. To end its cycle of scandal and disgrace. To make us all proud again of
60 the way free people govern themselves.
On the first day of the 104th Congress, the new Republican majority will immediately pass the following major reforms, aimed at restoring the faith and trust of the American people in their government:

65 FIRST, require all laws that apply to the rest of the country also apply equally to the Congress;
SECOND, select a major, independent auditing firm to conduct a comprehensive audit of Congress for waste, fraud or abuse;
70 THIRD, cut the number of House committees, and cut committee staff by one-third;
FOURTH, limit the terms of all committee chairs.

Which issue mentioned in Passage 1 also preoccupies the authors of Passage 2?

A) Decades of "low productivity" (line 11)
B) The "legions of poor children" (lines 15-16)
C) The responsibilities of being a "military superpower" (line 24)
D) The "problem" (line 35) of government spending

CONTINUE

2

As used in line 17, "tough" most nearly means

A) insensitive.
B) competitive.
C) durable.
D) forthright.

3

According to Passage 1, America can make progress if leaders and citizens focus on

A) domestic growth instead of on foreign intervention.
B) the ideals that motivated the settling of North America.
C) creating a new generation of leaders instead of celebrating past leaders.
D) practical measures instead of issues of perception and reputation.

4

Which choice provides the best evidence for the answer to the previous question?

A) Lines 10-13 ("The conditions . . . underemployment")
B) Lines 17-19 ("For too long . . . community")
C) Lines 30-33 ("I well remember . . . into space")
D) Lines 38-40 ("I come here . . . for it")

5

One purpose of lines 20-29 ("And our . . . generations") is to suggest that

A) America's prosperity has also led to many of its problems.
B) America enjoys a unique position despite its problems.
C) ending partisan politics will solve America's problems.
D) lack of investment in young people is the greatest of America's problems.

6

Both Passage 1 and Passage 2 attribute the problems facing America to

A) long-term patterns of inefficiency and wastefulness.
B) a succession of uninspiring and ultimately unpopular political leaders.
C) the intrusion of government into the personal lives of citizens.
D) increasingly corrupt generations of elected officials.

7

As used in line 59, "cycle of" most nearly means

A) rotation through.
B) series of.
C) progression from.
D) inclination towards.

8

It can be inferred that the authors of Passage 2 see their political adversaries as

A) too reliant on public opinion.
B) driven by financial gain.
C) ignorant of how the government works.
D) neither candid nor assertive.

9

Which choice provides the best evidence for the answer to the previous question?

A) Lines 46-48 ("in this era . . . fine print")
B) Lines 51-53 ("That historic . . . money")
C) Lines 56-58 ("Like Lincoln . . . right")
D) Lines 65-69 ("FIRST, require . . . abuse")

10

The authors of Passage 2 would most likely criticize the "new direction" (line 1) mentioned in Passage 1 for not involving

A) proposals designed to foster a spirit of unity in America.
B) significant reforms to the structure of the government.
C) ideas based on monitoring and reconfiguring government expenses.
D) an awareness of recent political developments.

CONTINUE

Questions 1-10 are based on the following passage.
5.02
Adapted from Barack Obama, Senate Floor Statement on the Death of Rosa Parks (2005).

Today the nation mourns a genuine American hero. Rosa Parks died yesterday in her home in Detroit. Through her courage and by her example, Rosa Parks helped lay the
Line foundation for a country that could begin to live up to its creed.
5   Her life, and her brave actions, reminded each and every one of us of our personal responsibilities to stand up for what is right and the central truth of the American experience that our greatness as a nation derives from seemingly ordinary people doing extraordinary things.
10   Rosa Parks' life was a lesson in perseverance. As a child, she grew up listening to the Ku Klux Klan ride by her house and lying in bed at night, fearing that her house would be burnt down. In her small hometown in Alabama, she attended a one-room school for African-American children that only went
15 through the sixth grade. When she moved to Montgomery, Alabama, to continue her schooling, she was forced to clean classrooms after school to pay her tuition. Although she attended the Alabama State Teachers College, Rosa Parks would later make her living as a seamstress and housekeeper.
20   But she didn't accept that her opportunities were limited to sewing clothes or cleaning houses. In her forties, Rosa Parks was appointed secretary of the Montgomery branch of the NAACP and was active in voter registration drives with the Montgomery Voters League. In the summer of 1955, she
25 attended the Highlander Folk School, where she took classes in workers' rights and racial equality. Well before she made headlines across the country, she was a highly respected member of the Montgomery community and a committed member of the civil rights effort.
30   Of course, her name became permanently etched in American history on December 1, 1955, when she was arrested for refusing to give up her seat to a white passenger on a Montgomery bus. It wasn't the first time Rosa Parks refused to acquiesce to the Jim Crow system. The same bus driver who
35 had her arrested had thrown her off a bus the year before for refusing to give up her seat.
      Some schoolchildren are taught that Rosa Parks refused to give up her seat because her feet were tired. Our nation's schoolbooks are only getting it half right. She once said: "The
40 only tired I was, was tired of giving in."
      This solitary act of civil disobedience became a call to action. Her arrest led a then relatively unknown pastor, Martin Luther King, Jr., to organize a boycott of the Montgomery bus system. That boycott lasted 381 days and culminated in
45 a landmark Supreme Court decision finding that the city's segregation policy was unconstitutional.
      This solitary act of civil disobedience was also the spark that ignited the beginning of the end for segregation and inspired millions around the country and ultimately around
50 the world to get involved in the fight for racial equality.
      Rosa Parks' persistence and determination did not end that day in Montgomery, nor did it end with the passage of the Civil Rights Act and Voting Rights Act years later. She stayed active in the NAACP and other civil rights groups for
55 years. From 1965 to 1988, Ms. Parks continued her public service by working for my good friend Congressman John Conyers. And in an example of her low-key demeanor, her job in Congressman Conyers' office did not involve appearances as a figurehead or celebrity; she helped
60 homeless folks find housing.
      At the age of 74, she opened the Rosa and Raymond Parks Institute for Self-Development, which offers education and job training programs for disadvantaged youth. And even into her 80s, Rosa Parks gave lectures and attended
65 meetings with civil rights groups.
      At the age of 86, Rosa Parks' courage and fortitude was recognized by President Bill Clinton, who awarded her the nation's highest honor for a civilian—the Congressional Gold Medal.
70   As we honor the life of Rosa Parks, we should not limit our commemorations to lofty eulogies. Instead, let us commit ourselves to carrying on her fight, one solitary act at a time, and ensure that her passion continues to inspire as it did a half-century ago. That, in my view, is how we can best
75 thank her for her immense contributions to our country.

1

In terms of developmental structure, the passage as a whole can best be described as

A) a refutation of historical misconceptions.

B) an explanation of a pivotal event.

C) a series of personal recollections.

D) a factual and appreciative biography.

2

As used in line 9, "extraordinary" most nearly means

A) artistic.

B) unrealistic.

C) heroic.

D) strange.

CONTINUE

3

As used in line 18, "attended" most nearly means

A) cared for.

B) waited for.

C) listened to.

D) enrolled in.

4

In this speech, Obama portrays Rosa Parks as

A) driven by results rather than by public recognition.

B) anguished by her humble employment prospects.

C) simultaneously idealistic and impractical.

D) most widely recognized for her most insignificant accomplishments.

5

Which choice provides the best evidence for the answer to the previous question?

A) Lines 15-17 ("When she moved . . . tuition")

B) Lines 33-36 ("It wasn't . . . seat")

C) Lines 57-60 ("And in an . . . housing")

D) Lines 70-71 ("As we honor . . . eulogies")

6

Obama characterizes the account of Parks that is taught to "schoolchildren" (line 37) as

A) simple yet incomplete.

B) humorous yet inspiring.

C) popular yet insulting.

D) heroic yet unreliable.

7

In the third and fourth paragraphs (lines 10-29) Obama shifts his emphasis from

A) problems common to many African Americans to conditions unique to Parks.

B) problems in the American education system to reforms championed by Parks.

C) the adversities Parks faced to the proactive role Parks assumed.

D) Parks' everyday activities to her system of political beliefs.

8

It can be inferred from the passage that Obama sees the social problems addressed by Parks as

A) requiring ongoing public attention and action.

B) recently subject to renewed and vigorous debate.

C) misunderstood by many politicians and civilians today.

D) largely resolved with the end of the Civil Rights Movement.

9

The passage indicates that Parks' involvement in the struggle for civil rights

A) extended beyond the events that made her famous.

B) can be explained by her childhood experiences of prejudice.

C) was inspired by the work of Martin Luther King.

D) led her to play a direct role in structuring new legislation.

10

Which choice provides the best evidence for the answer to the previous question?

A) Lines 10-13 ("As a child . . . down")

B) Lines 26-29 ("Well before . . . effort")

C) Lines 42-44 ("Her arrest . . . system")

D) Lines 51-53 ("Rosa Parks' . . . later")

CONTINUE

Questions 1-10 are based on the following passage.
5.03
Adapted from a series of comments delivered in February of 2015 by Commissioner Mignon Clyburn of the Federal Communications Commission (FCC). The FCC is responsible for supervising and regulating industries that control the public flow of information: its domain includes television, radio, telecommunications, and the Internet.

Following years of vigorous debate, the United States adopted the Bill of Rights in 1791. The Framers recognized that basic freedoms, as enshrined in the first ten amendments
Line to the Constitution, were fundamental to a free and open
5 democratic society. . .

I believe the Framers would be pleased to see these principles embodied in a platform that has become such an important part of our lives. I also believe that they never envisioned a government that would include the input and
10 leadership of women, people of color, and immigrants, or that there would be such an open process that would enable more than four million citizens to have a direct conversation with their government. They would be extremely amazed, I venture to say, because even we are amazed.

15 So here we are, 224 years later, at a pivotal fork in the road, poised to preserve those very same virtues of a democratic society—free speech, freedom of religion, a free press, freedom of assembly and a functioning free market.

As we look around the world we see foreign governments
20 blocking access to websites including social media—in sum, curtailing free speech. There are countries where it is routine for governments, not the consumer, to determine the type of websites and content that can be accessed by its citizens. I am proud to be able to say that we are not among them.

25 Absent the rules we adopt today, however, any Internet Service Provider (ISP) has the liberty to do just that. They would be free to block, throttle, favor or discriminate against traffic or extract tolls from any user for any reason or for no reason at all.

30 This is more than a theoretical exercise. Providers here in the United States have, in fact, blocked applications on mobile devices, which not only hampers free expression but also restricts competition and innovation by allowing companies, not the consumer, to pick winners and losers. . .

35 Today, we are here to answer a few simple questions:

- Who determines how you use the Internet?
- Who decides what content you can view and when?
- Should there be a single Internet or fast lanes and slow lanes?
40 - Should Internet service providers be left free to slow down or throttle certain applications or content as they see fit?

- Should your access to the Internet on your mobile device have the same protections as your fixed device at home?

45 These questions, for me, get to the essence of the Open Internet debate: How do we continue to ensure that consumers have the tools they need to decide based on their own user experience. The consumer . . . not me, not the government and not the industry, but you, the consumer,
50 makes these decisions.

Keeping in touch with your loved one overseas; interacting with your health care provider, even if you are miles away from the closest medical facility; enrolling in courses online to improve your educational, professional
55 or entrepreneurial potential without worrying whether the university paid for a fast lane to ensure that the lecture won't buffer for hours because the quality has been degraded or throttled; not wondering if that business affiliated with your Internet Service Provider is getting preferential treatment
60 over that start up you worked so hard to establish.

We are here so that teachers don't have to give a second thought about assigning homework that can only be researched online because they are sure that their students are free to access any lawful website, and that such websites
65 won't load at dial-up speed. And, today, we are answering the calls of more than four million commenters who raised their voices and made a difference through civic, and sometimes not so civil, discourse.

We are here to ensure that every American has the
70 ability to communicate by their preferred means over their chosen platform, because as one of our greatest civil rights pioneers, Representative John Lewis, said so eloquently: "If we had the Internet during the movement, we could have done more, much more, to bring people together from all
75 around the country, to organize and work together, to build the beloved community. That is why it is so important for us to protect the Internet. Every voice matters and we cannot let the interests of profit silence the voices of those pursuing human dignity."

In this passage, Clyburn presents herself as an advocate for

A) civilians who use electronic devices.
B) innovative technology companies.
C) politicians with strong moral principles.
D) commentators who take unpopular stances.

CONTINUE

2

Which choice provides the best evidence for the answer to the previous question?

A) Lines 15-17 ("So here we . . . society")

B) Lines 30-32 ("This is more . . . devices")

C) Lines 48-50 ("The consumer . . . decisions")

D) Lines 77-79 ("Every voice . . . dignity")

3

According to Clyburn, which of the following have behaved in similar ways?

A) "the Framers" (line 6) and "Representative John Lewis" (line 72)

B) "foreign governments" (line 19) and "Providers" (line 30)

C) the "loved one" (line 51) and the "teachers" (line 61)

D) the "university" (line 56) and the "commenters" (line 66)

4

As used in line 21, "routine" most nearly means

A) ritualized.

B) customary.

C) uninteresting.

D) repetitive.

5

It can reasonably be inferred that Clyburn describes the questions in lines 36-44 as "simple" (line 35) because

A) she believes that these questions have obvious answers.

B) she believes that consensus has been reached on these questions.

C) few people find these questions interesting.

D) few people are affected by the issues raised in the questions.

6

As used in line 43, "fixed" most nearly means

A) repaired.

B) loyal.

C) conservative.

D) stationary.

7

Clyburn argues that restrictions put in place by communications companies and Internet providers can be

A) racially divisive.

B) economically detrimental.

C) educationally useful.

D) necessary to national security.

8

Clyburn would most likely agree with which of the following statements?

A) The Internet has rendered racial prejudice widely unacceptable in America.

B) The expansion of the Internet has made teachers more willing to discuss controversial topics.

C) America should more vigorously oppose the curtailment of free speech in other countries.

D) Provocative and impolite forms of expression can serve valuable purposes on the Internet.

9

Which choice provides the best evidence for the answer to the previous question?

A) Lines 21-23 ("There are . . . citizens")

B) Lines 61-64 ("We are here . . . website")

C) Lines 65-68 ("And, today . . . discourse")

D) Lines 71-74 ("as one of . . . much more")

10

The second paragraph (lines 6-14) resembles the final paragraph (lines 69-79) in that both paragraphs involve

A) testimony from respected political leaders.

B) hypothetical scenarios featuring historical figures.

C) recommendations concerning future policies.

D) statements calling for national unity.

CONTINUE

Questions 1-10 are based on the following passages.
5.04
Passage 1 is adapted from a speech delivered in 2011 by Senator Bernie Sanders of Vermont; Passage 2 is adapted from a 2014 speech by Senator Marco Rubio. Both Sanders and Rubio were candidates in the 2016 Presidential Campaign, and returned to the ideas in the remarks below throughout the primary season.

Passage 1

There is a war going on in this country, and I am not referring to the wars in Iraq or Afghanistan. I am talking about a war being waged by some of the wealthiest and most
Line powerful people in this country against the working families
5 of the United States of America, against the disappearing and shrinking middle class of our country.

The reality is, many of the Nation's billionaires are on the warpath. They want more, more, more. Their greed has no end, and apparently there is very little concern for our country
10 or for the people of this country if it gets in the way of the accumulation of more and more wealth and more and more power . . .

Today, the Wall Street executives—the crooks on Wall Street whose actions resulted in the severe recession we are
15 in right now; the people whose illegal, reckless actions have resulted in millions of Americans losing their jobs, their homes, their savings—guess what? After we bailed them out, those CEOs today are now earning more money than they did before the bailout. And while the middle class of this country
20 collapses and the rich become much richer, the United States now has by far the most unequal distribution of income and wealth of any major country on Earth . . .

So I think that is where we are. We have to own up to it. There is a war going on. The middle class is struggling for
25 existence, and they are taking on some of the wealthiest and most powerful forces in the world whose greed has no end. And if we don't begin to stand together and start representing those families, there will not be a middle class in this country.

Passage 2

Let's understand what the problem is. I go back to my
30 own upbringing, where my parents were not highly educated, didn't have much of a formal education, came here as immigrants and were able to make it to the American middle class working service jobs. And the more important part of my childhood is that I grew up believing that I could go as far
35 as my talent and my work will take me. That I could have the same dreams and the same future as the son of a president, as the son of a millionaire.

Now you have a growing number of Americans that don't think that's true anymore. And today, I will highlight the story
40 of four separate groups of Americans. We have a young, single mother in Florida who is struggling to provide for her two daughters. She is stuck in a job that doesn't pay a lot of money. The only way she's ever going to be able to improve her prospects are to go back to school. But she can't because
45 we have a higher education cartel that does not allow innovation to enter the educational space and provide her cost-effective and time-effective ways to get that education.

We'll meet two young Americans living in Florida who did go to college and graduated, and neither one of them can
50 find a job in the field they graduated from. But one of them was about to start making payments on a student loan. And the other needs to go back to grad school, but is afraid to because she doesn't want to owe $50,000 or $60,000 when she finishes.

55 And the last is a family that runs a small business. They got hit hard by the recession. They were starting to climb out of it. Then they got hit by ObamaCare, and then they've gotten hit by just the general malaise in the economic growth. They don't know how they're going to save for
60 retirement.

For all these people, their dreams are not exotic. None of them are looking to be billionaires, or anything like that. They just want to be able to own a home, raise a family in a safe environment, have children with the opportunity to have
65 a life better than themselves. And we need to reclaim that.

The fundamental challenge that we face is that every single one of our institutions in this country— from government to higher education and everything in between—has completely failed to adjust to 21st century
70 reality. None of them are responsive to the new world that we now live in, where globalization and information technology have changed the nature of our economy.

1

Both Passage 1 and Passage 2 assign blame for the problems America faces. In what way do the two passages differ?

A) Passage 1 mostly blames government officials; Passage 2 mostly blames the business community.

B) Passage 1 blames wealthy Americans; Passage 2 blames working class Americans.

C) Passage 1 assigns blame to distant events; Passage 2 assigns blame to recent developments.

D) Passage 1 primarily blames a single group; Passage 2 blames a number of groups and factors.

CONTINUE

2

Which of the following rhetorical devices is used by the author of Passage 1?

A) Intentional exaggeration

B) Dark humor

C) An open-ended question

D) An extended analogy

3

In Passage 2, Rubio presents an ideal of American opportunity that

A) is based on individualism and treats all institutions with skepticism.

B) is based on saving and investing wealth rather than on spending it quickly.

C) is based on personal initiative rather than on personal background.

D) is based on everyday hard work and construes academics as secondary.

4

Which choice provides the best evidence for the answer to the previous question?

A) Lines 33-37 ("And the more . . . millionaire")

B) Lines 48-50 ("We'll meet . . . from")

C) Lines 61-62 ("For all these . . . that")

D) Lines 66-70 ("The fundamental . . . reality")

5

The individuals described in lines 40-60 of Passage 2 ("We have a . . . retirement") are important because they are

A) friends and acquaintances of the author of Passage 2.

B) political supporters of the author of Passage 2.

C) representative of the broad problems facing America.

D) representative of the spirit of paralysis common in America.

6

As used in line 55, "runs" most nearly means

A) quickens.

B) operates.

C) circulates.

D) departs from.

7

The author of Passage 1 would most likely respond to the remarks in lines 66-72 ("The fundamental . . . economy") by pointing out that the author of Passage 2

A) has failed to place America's problems in the context of foreign affairs.

B) has not defined a single and specific problem with life in America.

C) has neglected the extent to which unequal wealth distribution defines America.

D) has wrongly praised the wealthy businessmen who are undermining American society.

8

Which choice provides the best evidence for the answer to the previous question?

A) Lines 1-2 ("There is a . . . Afghanistan")

B) Lines 7-8 ("The reality . . . more, more")

C) Lines 17-19 ("After we bailed . . . bailout")

D) Lines 19-22 ("And while . . . Earth")

9

As used in line 61, "exotic" most nearly means

A) inspired.

B) noteworthy.

C) outlandish.

D) imported.

10

Unlike Passage 1, Passage 2 discuses the issue of

A) home ownership.

B) job opportunity.

C) warfare.

D) education.

CONTINUE

Questions 1-10 are based on the following passage.
5.05
Adapted from Kamal Khashoggi, "The Violent Owl of Minerva" (2016).

Philosophy is a violent activity. Of course, I am not speaking of a physical kind of violence—although the case could be made for those of us who have been up until four in
Line the morning, wrestling with Hegel. I am speaking of a violence
5 directed at our habitual patterns of thought, and at our ready-made answers. Thinking critically and coherently does not come easily to us.

René Descartes, often dubbed the father of modern philosophy, opens his *Meditations on First Philosophy*
10 with the following passage: "Some years ago I was struck by the large number of falsehoods that I had accepted as true in my childhood, and by the highly doubtful nature of the whole edifice that I had subsequently based on them. I realized that it was necessary, once in the course of my life,
15 to demolish everything and completely start again right from the foundations…" I know some don't see the power in this violent style of thinking. But every careful student of history knows the potency of abstract thought at its most incarnate. It is no surprise, after all, that Alexander the Great, the first
20 person to conquer the known world, had Aristotle for a teacher. It is no surprise that—for better or worse—if we examine the roots of every major political, scientific, religious, artistic or moral transformation in our history, we shall find there one if not a series of great philosophers and their ideas. Consider,
25 as examples, the genesis of the French Revolution in Locke, Rousseau, Hobbes and others. Consider, the rise of communist states during the twentieth century, inspired by the writings of Karl Marx. Or, consider the contributions of Descartes, Leibniz, Newton and others to mathematics and to scientific
30 methodology, which invigorated the scientific revolution.

This kind of power has never been more desirable, utile or important than today. For most of human history, our social institutions provided us with ready-made answers, which we could depend on whatever the questions that would arise.
35 That is, questions of morality, knowledge, religion, politics and so on, had fixed answers depending on our cultures. But this is no longer the case. Today, technological and cultural developments have burst open the floodgates of information, opinion, knowledge and even human migration. The result
40 is a world characterized by an accelerated clash of ideas and cultures occurring both at the global and the individual level. This is not just an abstract clash, either. With a Saudi father and an Iranian mother, I can tell you that my very flesh is an ideological flashpoint.
45 As some of you may have suspected, all that I have just said is not that we live in a world empty of philosophy, but exactly the opposite. In some sense, we have been condemned to philosophize from the beginning. The moment we have formed an opinion or made a judgment, we have
50 philosophized. There is no way out of it. The trouble is that we rarely philosophize well. Just consider the way news anchors and pundits on CNN or Fox News dangerously speculate on matters totally outside of their expertise, for an example of such bad philosophizing.
55 So in the absence of ready-made answers and right philosophy, we end up either with a more nefarious kind of ignorance—the bad philosophy I just mentioned—that is all the more dangerous for its conceit; or we end up with total paralysis in the face of competing ideas and choices. I
60 am not speaking, here, only of grand political or scientific problems. I am speaking of the responsibilities we hold to ourselves and to each other. How do our most mundane, little purchases at the supermarket affect people continents away? Which news programs shall inform us, and which
65 shall misinform us? How shall our traditions cohere with the rest of the world, now that the two have come to blows? The most concrete example of this crisis occurring presently is that of the refugee crisis in Europe. There, we find a symbol for every ideological, religious, economic, political, moral
70 and cultural clash which characterizes our age, and for which we have no ready-made answers.

Our old questions, too, should be revitalized by the new world. The nature of consciousness, for instance, is no longer a curiosity hidden away in the ivory tower, but of
75 central importance to how we shall make sense of and react to advances in artificial intelligence and bioengineering, which are on the horizon.

We must all, to a certain extent, become philosophers in the true sense, or else inherit a world of infinite conflict and
80 loss. It is no longer possible for us as individuals to navigate the world without the aid of philosophy.

CONTINUE

1

Over the course of the passage, the author's focus shifts from

A) an explanation of the origins of a particular viewpoint to an argument as to why that viewpoint is significant.

B) an overview of various philosophical principles to a promotion of the ideology that the author deems most practical.

C) a description of the role of philosophers throughout history to a discussion of the integration of philosophy into everyday life.

D) a summary of the significance of philosophy to a criticism of the lack of philosophical thinking in modern society.

2

As used in line 17, "careful" most nearly means

A) conscientious.

B) cautious.

C) conciliating.

D) clever.

3

Which of the following would Khashoggi most clearly define as an example of "bad philosophy"?

A) A televised news program that is clearly biased towards a single political ideology

B) A war strategy devised by a general who only spent the early years of his career in a direct combat role

C) A comprehensive plan to reduce unemployment created by a politician with little knowledge of economics

D) An attempt to stabilize a volatile nation that is endorsed by foreign policy experts but proves unsuccessful

4

Why does the author mention his parentage in lines 42-44?

A) To offer evidence of how the "clash of ideas" (line 40) plays out in real life

B) To establish that he is similar in background to "some of" (line 45) the individuals he is addressing

C) To explain exactly how and why he began "to philosophize" (line 48)

D) To indicate that his multicultural background has enabled him to "philosophize well" (line 51)

5

What does the passage suggest about philosophers from the past?

A) They have often been catalysts for important social and historical movements.

B) Their ideas have stood the test of time and are still being actively put into practice today.

C) They directly opposed those in power by writing about ideas that challenged the status quo.

D) Their ideas have contributed to the establishment of social norms in certain cultures.

6

Which choice provides the best evidence for the answer to the previous question?

A) Lines 4-6 ("I am . . . answers")

B) Lines 21-24 ("if . . . ideas")

C) Lines 33-36 ("Institutions . . . answers")

D) Lines 45-47 ("As . . .opposite")

7

According to the passage, which of the following is true of "violence directed at our habitual patterns of thought" (lines 4-5)?

A) It was most important in past centuries.

B) Its impact and significance are underestimated.

C) Its application in the twentieth century was ultimately destructive.

D) It is most important as applied to the realm of science.

8

Which choice provides the best evidence for the answer to the previous question?

A) Lines 6-7 ("Thinking . . . us")

B) Lines 16-17 ("I know . . . thinking")

C) Lines 26-28 ("Consider, . . . Marx")

D) Lines 28-30 ("Or, . . . revolution")

CONTINUE

9

As used in line 60, "grand" most nearly means

A) respectable.

B) overstated.

C) consequential.

D) elegant.

10

The fourth paragraph (lines 45-54) and the fifth paragraph (lines 55-71) are similar in that both paragraphs

A) elucidate philosophical concepts that the author acknowledges to be confusing to many readers.

B) encourage readers to understand the philosophical importance of seemingly insignificant activities.

C) move from statements of the author's own position to explanations of common counter-arguments.

D) move from broad statements about philosophy to specific evidence from current events.

Answer Key: CHAPTER FIVE

5.01	5.02	5.03	5.04	5.05
1. D	1. D	1. A	1. D	1. C
2. B	2. C	2. C	2. D	2. A
3. D	3. D	3. B	3. C	3. C
4. D	4. A	4. B	4. A	4. A
5. B	5. C	5. A	5. C	5. A
6. A	6. A	6. D	6. B	6. B
7. D	7. C	7. B	7. C	7. B
8. D	8. A	8. D	8. D	8. B
9. A	9. A	9. C	9. C	9. C
10. B	10. B	10. B	10. D	10. D

Answer Explanations

Chapter 05 | Age of Information

5.01 | Bill Clinton and the "Contract with America"

1) CORRECT ANSWER: D

The authors of Passage 2 advocate "the end of government that is too big, too intrusive, and too easy with the public's money" (lines 52-53): similarly, Passage 1 is critical of the problem of debt incurred by the government. D is thus the best answer. Note that Passage 2 focuses primarily on improving the functions of government and instituting new procedures: economic problems such as productivity (A) and poverty (B), and even foreign policy problems such as America's status as a military superpower (C), are not truly relevant to the discussion.

2) CORRECT ANSWER: B

The word "tough" refers to the "global economy" (line 17), which presents problems for America because of defective "education and job training opportunities" (line 16). If new skills are needed to match other parts of the world, the global economy is challenging or competitive. B is the best answer, while A and D both present human personality traits and C ("durable" or long-lasting) refers to time rather than to the extent of a challenge or difficulty.

3) CORRECT ANSWER: D

In lines 38-40, Clinton argues that he wants to "accept responsibility" and "do right" regardless of "who gets the credit for it". He thus values what is done over how those actions are perceived: D is the best answer. A is problematic because Clinton urges competition with other countries that can be achieved THROUGH a domestic focus on education and job training (and because he never calls for intervention of any other kind). And while Clinton does celebrate past values (line 4, eliminating C), he relates those values to America's general status as a nation, not to the specific act of "settling" America (eliminating B).

4) CORRECT ANSWER: D

See above for the explanation of the correct answer. A describes negative economic conditions that are present in America, B calls attention to a problematic mentality in America, and C presents an image used by an earlier president. None of these answers directly pinpoints a way that "America can make progress", so that all must be eliminated as irrelevant to the previous question.

5) CORRECT ANSWER: B

While the relevant lines call attention to a paralyzed "political system", they also suggest that America can successfully face its difficulties because it is "the greatest nation on Earth" (line 23). This information supports B, while "prosperity" (A) and "investment in young people" (D) are topics raised in the PREVIOUS paragraph. C is a trap answer:

while "partisan bickering" (line 21) is indeed an American problem, it is never argued that ending such partisanship will solve all of the OTHER problems.

6) CORRECT ANSWER: A
Passage 1 describes conditions of "low productivity, growth, and stagnant wages" (lines 11-12) and further points out that the government often appears to be "paralyzed" (line 20). Somewhat similarly, Passage 2 calls attention to ineffective "evasion and posturing" (line 46) and criticizes government for being "too big, too intrusive, and too easy with the public's money" (lines 52-53). This common focus on poor uses of resources makes A the best answer, while C is only relevant to Passage 2. Both B and D assume that the authors call attention to specific officials: instead, these passages criticize broad groups that are not, at times, fully defined.

7) CORRECT ANSWER: D
The phrase "cycle of" refers to the characteristics of "scandal and disgrace" (line 59) that are observed in the American government: "scandal and disgrace" would be tendencies or inclinations that the authors wish to combat. D is thus the best answer, while A and C both describe movement (not human traits) and B indicates a group of things or episodes, not a broad pattern or habit.

8) CORRECT ANSWER: D
In lines 46-48, the authors of Passage 2 contrast the "evasion and posturing" of their opponents with the "detailed agenda for national renewal" that they are offering. Unlike the authors of the passage, the opponents are thus not honest and specific, or are not "candid and assertive", making D the best answer. Neither public opinion (A) nor financial gain (B) are criticized as negative forces in the passage, while C is a trap answer: the authors' opponents MISUSE government, but might still UNDERSTAND its workings even if they use that knowledge to inappropriate ends.

9) CORRECT ANSWER: A
See above for the explanation of the correct answer. B criticizes the size and level of influence of government, C praises Lincoln and aligns him with the authors of the passage, and D presents some of the reforms that the authors have proposed. Only B criticizes the authors' opponents, yet presents qualities (large and invasive government) that do not align with the answer to the previous question.

10) CORRECT ANSWER: B
While Clinton in Passage 1 argues that the government must abandon gridlock and partisanship in order to facilitate social and economic progress, he does not actually argue that the government should be restructured. In contrast, the authors of Passage 2 want the government to "change its policies" (line 43) through major procedural reforms. B is the best answer, while A, C, and D all refer to ideas endorsed in BOTH passages and must be eliminated on this account.

5.02 | Barack Obama

1) CORRECT ANSWER: D
After explaining that Rosa Parks "helped lay the foundation for a country that could begin to live up to its creed" (lines 3-4), Obama goes on to record Parks' life events, from her childhood to her old age. This sense of a positive life story justifies D and can be used

to eliminate B (since many events are mentioned) and C (since Obama does not indicate that he personally knew Parks, even though he respects her). A is a trap answer: although Obama refers to a possible misconception in "schoolbooks" (line 39), he does so in order to offer a supporting point in his larger biographical and appreciative account of Parks.

2) CORRECT ANSWER: C
The word "extraordinary" refers to "things" (line 9) that are done by ordinary people and that nonetheless relate to America's "greatness as a nation" (line 8). The "things" are thus positive and (in contrast with "ordinary") exceptional or heroic: C is the best answer. A refers to a context (art) that is not raised in this political and social discussion, while B and D both introduce negatives.

3) CORRECT ANSWER: D
The word "attended" refers to Parks' activity regarding the "Alabama State Teachers College" (line 18): as a young person seeking to obtain an education, Parks would naturally become a student at or enroll in the college. D is the best answer while A, B, and D refer to how people would react to other PEOPLE or to specific EVENTS, not necessarily to how a student would approach a college.

4) CORRECT ANSWER: A
In lines 57-60, Obama notes that Parks was uninterested in "figurehead or celebrity" and instead "helped homeless folks find housing". She thus prioritized action over self-promoting publicity, making A the best answer and eliminating C (since Parks was practical) and D (since Parks was uninterested in recognition). B is problematic because, although Parks faced difficulties, "anguished" does not properly describe the spirit of courage and activity that Obama celebrates in describing her life.

5) CORRECT ANSWER: C
See above for the explanation of the correct answer. A describes how Parks earned money to pay for her schooling, B describes an action that is historically well known, and D indicates that honoring Rosa Parks should extend beyond verbal praise. Make sure not to wrongly align A with Question 4 B or B with Question 4 D.

6) CORRECT ANSWER: A
In describing the account of Rosa Parks that is commonly taught, and which indicates that Parks was simply tired, Obama notes that "Our nation's schoolbooks are only getting it half right" (lines 38-39). This sense that the account simplifies what Parks stood for justifies A, while the account (which simply records an action) does not clearly involve "humor" as related by Obama (eliminating B). C is too strongly negative about Parks, while D is too strongly positive.

7) CORRECT ANSWER: C
Obama begins the relevant lines by describing Parks' life as "a lesson in perseverance" (line 10) and by listing some of the hardships she faced; he then concludes by explaining how Parks took on roles that made her "a committed member of the civil rights effort" (lines 28-29). This information supports C and can be used to eliminate A and B, which wrongly indicate that the early lines are not primarily about Parks. D is a problematic answer, since the paragraphs involve a shift in TIME, not a shift in TYPE of topic, and describe Parks' everyday activities throughout.

8) CORRECT ANSWER: A

In the final paragraph of his consideration of Parks' activism, Obama indicates that Americans should "commit ourselves to carrying on her fight, one solitary act at a time" (lines 72-73). Such action would only be necessary if the problems Parks addressed are ongoing: A is the best answer, while the same information and logic can be used to eliminate D. B (debate) and C (misunderstanding) wrongly depict Parks as a source of disagreement and must be eliminated, since Obama argues that her example serves as a call to action and consensus.

9) CORRECT ANSWER: A

In lines 26-29, Obama argues that, before Parks made "headlines across the country" as a symbol of the civil rights struggle, she was "a committed member of the civil rights effort". This information supports A. Parks' difficult childhood is never directly linked to her civil rights work (eliminating B) and Parks herself inspired King (eliminating C as misstating the true relationship). D is a trap answer: while Parks did work with legislators, she chose to help groups such as "homeless folk" (line 60) through outreach instead of through drafting legislation.

10) CORRECT ANSWER: B

See above for the explanation of the correct answer. A describes the fear that Parks experienced as a child, C indicates Parks' influence on Martin Luther King, and D notes that Parks advocated civil rights legislation (but did not "structure" it). Make sure not to wrongly align A with Question 9 B, C with Question 9 C, or D with Question 9 D.

5.03 | Mignon Clyburn

1) CORRECT ANSWER: A

In lines 48-50, Clyburn argues that "not the government and not the industry" but "the consumer" should make pivotal decisions in terms of Internet access and usage issues. This information supports A and directly contradicts B and C. Although it is possible that Clyburn would advocate free speech on the Internet, she does not state that "unpopular stances" are necessarily associated with the group she is representing, consumers.

2) CORRECT ANSWER: C

See above for the explanation of the correct answer. A indicates an important historical moment, B criticizes providers of digital services, and D indicates that Clyburn supports free expression on the Internet. Only D describes a group that Clyburn presents herself as an advocate for, yet the line reference does not align directly with an answer to the previous question; D should not be taken as justification for Question 1 D, since Clyburn's quotation does not confine itself to "unpopular stances".

3) CORRECT ANSWER: B

While the foreign governments are "blocking access to websites" (line 20), the providers have "blocked applications on mobile devices" (lines 31-32), so that both groups are limiting electronic media access. B is the best answer. The "Framers" are past figures whom the Internet would have surprised, yet John Lewis is a contemporary politician who envisions specific uses for the Internet (eliminating A). The "loved one" uses the Internet to keep in contact with distant acquaintances, yet the "teachers" use the Internet to assign homework to students (eliminating C). And the "university" values fast Internet service, while the "commenters" value free expression" (eliminating D). Though similar in tone, the items for each of the other pairings do not occupy the same CONTEXT or have the same USES for the Internet.

4) CORRECT ANSWER: B
The word "routine" refers to a situation in countries where the government determines "the type of websites and content that can be accessed by its citizens" (lines 22-23). This is a practice that would happen on a widespread and daily basis in these countries, or would be customary. B is the best answer, while A and D both focus on the wrong issue (repetition as opposed to prevalence) and C, in context, would wrongly indicate that Clyburn is not interested in one of her main topics, Internet access restrictions.

5) CORRECT ANSWER: A
The questions involve the type of Internet service and content that should be available; ultimately, Clyburn argues that "the consumer" (line 49) should decide the issues she raises. In other words, the responses simply depend on the will of the consumers, not any more complicated factor: A is the best answer, while C and D would wrongly indicate that the questions (which involve communication and society at large) are insignificant. B is problematic in the context of the passage: while Clyburn believes that consumers should have power, her opinion is not shared by some governments and companies.

6) CORRECT ANSWER: D
The word "fixed" refers to a kind of "device" (line 43) that is directly contrasted with a "mobile device" (lines 42-43): something that is not fixed, in this context, would be unmoving or stationary. D is the best answer, while A wrongly indicates that the device has been broken and B and C both involve personality traits, not the simple issue of movement.

7) CORRECT ANSWER: B
Clyburn argues that open Internet access supports "a functioning free market" (line 18), and later goes on to explain that blocking such options "restricts competition and innovation" (line 33). Thus, restrictions on communications and the Internet can be economically counterproductive, making B the best answer and eliminating positives C and D. A is a trap answer: though this choice is negative, Clyburn most directly criticizes Internet-based discrimination that is based on OPINION, not based on RACE.

8) CORRECT ANSWER: D
In lines 65-68, Clyburn speaks positively of "more than four million commenters" who engage in "civic, and sometimes not so civil, discourse": she thus defends even impolite and provocative uses of Internet-based expression, so that D is the best answer. A misrepresents the discussion at the end of the passage, which indicates that the Internet COULD have helped to combat prejudice decades ago. B creates a false linkage between the topic of controversy and the earlier topic of teachers, while C returns to another topic from the passage (nations beyond America) but offers a recommendation (American involvement) that Clyburn never makes.

9) CORRECT ANSWER: C
See above for the explanation of the correct answer. A criticizes countries that attempt to control Internet usage, B indicates that teachers should be allowed to use the Internet as an effective learning tool, and D indicates that the Internet would have been valuable during the civil rights movement. Make sure not to falsely align A with Question 8 C, B with Question 8 B, or D with Question 8 A.

10) CORRECT ANSWER: B

While the second paragraph indicates that "the Framers [of the Constitution] would be pleased to see" (line 6) the Internet express America's founding principles, the final paragraph presents a speculation from John Lewis, a civil rights hero, about what might have been done "If we had the Internet during the movement" (lines 72-73). These hypothetical scenarios support B. Only the final paragraph involves testimony from a political leader (eliminating A), a policy recommendation (eliminating C), or a call for unity (eliminating D): the second paragraph praises diversity, but does not urge citizens to seek greater consensus.

5.04 | Bernie Sanders and Marco Rubio

1) CORRECT ANSWER: D

The author of Passage 1 believes that "some of the wealthiest and most powerful people in this country" (lines 3-4) have acted in ways that undermine and harm the middle class; in contrast, the author of Passage 2 criticizes different groups, claiming that "every single one of our institutions in this country" (line 67) has failed to adapt to a new century. D thus offers an effective comparison, while A in fact REVERSES the groups blamed by the two passages. Passage 2 defends everyday Americans against failed institutions (eliminating B), while Passage 1 blames wealthy people such as billionaires for the ONGOING problems that are arising in America (eliminating C).

2) CORRECT ANSWER: D

The author of Passage 1 compares the inequality in America to a state of "war" (lines 3 and 24) and states that "many of the Nation's billionaires are on the warpath" (lines 7-8). This consistent, extended analogy justifies D. A and B are both out of context: while a student new to or perhaps hostile to the ideas in the passage may find the writing exaggerated or humorous, there is no indication that the author (who is serious about his subject) wants it to be received as such. C is inaccurate: the only indication of a question occurs in line 17, and is used for dramatic effect (not to get the reader to think about an "open-ended" issue).

3) CORRECT ANSWER: C

In lines 33-37, the author of Passage 2 presents himself as a representative case in an America where "I could go as far as my talent and my work will take me" and where someone who does not start off with advantages could have the same future "as the son of a president, the son of a millionaire." This information supports C. B mistakes Rubio's emphasis on determination and hard work for an emphasis on HOW money is spent, while D neglects the idea that academics are a FORM of hard work. A is a trap answer: while Rubio is skeptical of many government institutions, he does not attack the role of communities, making "individualism" an overstatement of his position.

4) CORRECT ANSWER: A

See above for the explanation of the correct answer. B describes two college graduates who cannot locate job opportunities, C explains that the people described do not have gigantic dreams of wealth or power, and D criticizes the role of institutions in American life. Only C directly discusses the idea of opportunity in a general sense, but does not align with an answer to the previous question.

5) CORRECT ANSWER: C
In lines 38-40, the author of Passage 2 argues that some Americans question today's ideals of progress and mentions "four separate groups of Americans" (line 40): the individuals depicted as the passage progresses are representatives of these groups, so that C is the best answer. These individuals are related to the author's ideas, NOT to the author himself (eliminating A and B), while the fact that they are in fact working makes the idea of "paralysis" an extreme and inaccurate description (eliminating D).

6) CORRECT ANSWER: B
The word "runs" refers to a "small business" (line 55) that has faced difficulties, and that one of Rubio's individuals owned or operated during a difficult period. B is thus the best answer, while A and C both refer to physical movement (not to involvement), as does D, which would also wrongly indicate that the business has been ABANDONED.

7) CORRECT ANSWER: C
In lines 19-22, the author of Passage 1 describes a problematic situation in which "the middle class of this country collapses and the rich become much richer". However, the author of Passage 2 primary criticizes "institutions" (line 67) in lines 66-72, and does not target wealth distribution or even a group defined by wealth (such as the rich) for criticism. C is the best answer, while D must be eliminated because "wealthy businessmen" are not in fact analyzed in Passage 2. A introduces the topic of foreign affairs (which is not the main consideration of Passage 1), while B is contradicted by the fact that Passage 2 does define failed institutions as America's main problem.

8) CORRECT ANSWER: D
See above for the explanation of the correct answer. A mentions actual wars along with the figurative war involving wealth inequality, B explains that billionaires are aggressively pursuing wealth, and C explains that the wealthy have earned increasingly large amounts of money. None of these answers relates to the topic of struggling everyday Americans that Passage 1 and Passage 2 have in common: B and C mainly describe wealthy individuals WITHOUT describing the misfortune of the less wealthy.

9) CORRECT ANSWER: C
The word "exotic" refers to the kind of "dreams" (line 61) that everyday Americans do not have: exotic dreams, in this context, would be desires such as "looking to be billionaires" (line 62). Such a dream would be extreme or outlandish compared to more everyday ambitions: C is the best answer, while A and B are positives and are incorrect because Rubio PRAISES the ideas of everyday people. D normally refers to transportable objects, not to ideals or dreams, and must be eliminated.

10) CORRECT ANSWER: D
The author of Passage 2 describes two young Americans who "did go to college and graduated" (line 49); later, he explains that "higher education" (line 68) is one of America's failing institutions. Because Passage 1 focuses almost exclusively on issues of wealth and inequality, but never mentions education, D is the best answer. The author of Passage 1 argues that Americans have lost "their jobs, [and] their homes" in lines 16-17 (eliminating A and B) and does briefly refer to military conflicts in lines 1-2 (eliminating C).

5.05 | Kamal Khashoggi

1) CORRECT ANSWER: C
In the early paragraphs, Khashoggi uses the examples of Descartes, Aristotle, and other philosophers to discuss "the potency of abstract thought at its most incarnate" (line 18). Later, he explains that people in day-to-day life "have been condemned to philosophize from the beginning" (lines 47-48) and presents philosophical questions that occur on an everyday basis. This information supports C and can be used to eliminate D, which assumes that philosophy is now IRRELEVANT to society. A wrongly indicates "origins" (when in fact Khashoggi only explains HOW a viewpoint is significant, not WHERE exactly it first became popular), while B assumes that Khashoggi is advocating a partisan ideology (not EXPLAINING the strengths and weaknesses of an approach).

2) CORRECT ANSWER: A
The word "careful" refers to a "student of history" (line 17) who "knows the potency of abstract thought at its most incarnate" (line 18); such a student would take into account the examples that Khashoggi later offers, and would thus be aware or conscientious regarding history. A is the best answer, while B refers to avoiding danger, C refers to avoiding disagreement, and D (though tempting) is out of scope. Being "clever" or resourceful is not the same as simply being aware of important information, or being "conscientious".

3) CORRECT ANSWER: C
In one form of "bad philosophy", people "speculate on matters totally outside of their expertise" (line 53): for a person to address an economic issue, but lack the expertise to do so knowledgeably, would be a concrete example of this such bad philosophy. C is the best answer, while B mistakes the issue of expertise for the issue of DIRECT EXPERIENCE. (Because of his or her high level of knowledge, a general can be considered a military expert even with limited field presence.) A (bias) and D (failure) describe problems that are not directly related to the idea of judging what one does not really comprehend.

4) CORRECT ANSWER: A
Khashoggi explains that there is a "clash of ideas occurring both at the global and individual level" (lines 40-41): having parents from two nations and cultures gives him a direct, "ideological" (line 44) position in this clash. This information supports A. Although the individuals Khashoggi is addressing are part of this same globalized society, they do not necessary have similar cultural backgrounds (eliminating B). Note also that Khashoggi does not relate his parents explicitly to his background in philosophy: C and D must thus be eliminated as creating faulty linkages.

5) CORRECT ANSWER: A
In lines 21-24, Khashoggi argues that various forms of historical transformation have been motivated by "one if not a series of great philosophers and their ideas". This information supports A, while C and D both simplify Khashoggi's argument: philosophy is socially influential, but whether it DEFENDS or CHALLENGES norms is never fully explained. (In fact, because philosophers have both worked alongside powerful figures and given rise to radical changes, philosophy most likely can both defend norms AND overturn them.) B is a trap answer: while the ideas of philosophers from the past are still STUDIED, it is never argued that the specific theories of philosophers such as Aristotle or

Marx continue to guide practical policies or other social measures.

6) CORRECT ANSWER: B
See above for the explanation of the correct answer. A clarifies Khashoggi's philosophical topic, C indicates that institutions have often provided society with certainty, and D indicates that philosophical thinking is widespread in today's world. Note that none of these directly discusses philosophers from the past in the manner of B, so that all other choices must be eliminated.

7) CORRECT ANSWER: B
In lines 16-17, Khashoggi argues that "some don't see the power" in the violent mode of philosophical thought that is one of his main topics. B is the best answer, while philosophical violence itself is seen as in some ways productive (eliminating C) and as extremely important in its social impact (eliminating D). A is a trap answer: while important in past centuries, violence directed at thought is STILL important today. Khashoggi never directly establishes when such thought was MOST important.

8) CORRECT ANSWER: B
See above for the explanation of the correct answer. A indicates that meaningful thought is difficult to achieve, C indicates that Marx had a significant social impact, and D indicates that philosophers have had a meaningful impact on the sciences. Make sure not to wrongly take C or D, which both describe philosophers from past centuries, as a justification for Question 7 A.

9) CORRECT ANSWER: C
The word "grand" is used to describe "philosophical and social problems" (lines 60-61) that are contrasted with more personal responsibilities: scientific "problems" would thus be large in scope, important, and consequential, since they involve the large workings of society. C is the best answer, while B introduces a faulty negative. A and D both refer to questions of personality or mannerism, not to the SIGNIFICANCE of particular problems, and should be eliminated as out of context.

10) CORRECT ANSWER: D
The fourth paragraph begins with the idea that the world is not "empty of philosophy" (line 46) and moves on to consider the poor philosophizing of "anchors and pundits on CNN or Fox News" (line 52). In a similar movement from broad idea to specific recent events, the fifth paragraph begins by considering ways of approaching "the absence of ready-made answers and right philosophy" (line 55-56) and considers the significance of the current "refugee crisis in Europe" (line 68). This information supports D and can be used to eliminate B (since the paragraphs focus on significant political happenings) and C (since the author presents a few of his own arguments that are negative in tone, not the arguments of a different side or COUNTER-ARGUMENTS). A is a trap answer: while readers may not know how to practically respond to bad philosophy, these paragraphs never argue that readers may not know how to DEFINE concepts such as bad philosophy.

Made in the USA
Las Vegas, NV
19 July 2021